EXAM PRO
Evidence — Essay

What is *Exam Pro-Essay*?

Exam Pro-Essay is a study aid that helps law students prepare to take their Evidence exam. Answering the sample essay exams and the specific subject matter essay questions, followed by review of the corresponding answers and analysis, provides students with a more thorough comprehension of the Federal Rules of Evidence and a better understanding of how to take exams.

What *Exam Pro-Essay* offers *you*:

Exam Pro-Essay contains a total of 107 specific subject matter essay questions along with detailed and thorough suggested correct answers each containing clear, concise, to the point support as to why each answer is correct.

Exam Pro-Essay provides 7 complete sample essay examinations each containing four to six questions totaling 120 grading points to be completed in two hours.

Exam Pro-Essay provides answers to each of the 7 complete sample essay examinations stating the number of points allocated to a particular segment of each and every question.

Exam Pro-Essay contains questions raising confrontation clause issues as interpreted in *Crawford* and *Davis*. A textual exploration of *Crawford/Davis* is presented in Appendix C.

Why *Exam Pro-Essay* will work for *you:*

- ***Exam Pro-Essay*** Evidence answers provide detailed analysis applying the Federal Rules of Evidence to help you recognize similar issues on your exam and provide complete and accurate responses.

- ***Exam Pro-Essay*** contains essay questions with answers covering all of the specific subject matter areas comprising the law of evidence as codified in the Federal Rules of Evidence.

- ***Exam Pro-Essay*** expands your scope of learning and understanding beyond the sample questions by providing references in the Answers where useful to the appropriate Federal Rules of Evidence contained in Appendix B and by providing a textual discussion of the definition of hearsay in Appendix A.

- *Exam Pro-Essay* was written by Michael H. Graham, a respected and experienced law professor at University of Miami School of Law. Professor Graham has taught Evidence for over 30 years and has published numerous books and articles in the Evidence area.

Complimentary Study Aid

Students should also consider acquiring ***Evidence, Exam Pro-Objective*** also written by Professor Graham which contains sample objective examination questions arranged by subject matter in accordance with the Federal Rules of Evidence as well as eleven comprehensive true-false or multiple choice examinations. ***Evidence, Exam Pro-Objective*** contains 1,160 objective questions with answers in total

Derivation of *Exam Pro-Essay*

Exam Pro-Essay contains essay questions and answers some but by no means all of which also appear in GRAHAM, EVIDENCE: AN INTRODUCTORY PROBLEM APPROACH (West Second Edition 2007), a textbook designed for use in a law school evidence class.

Exam Pro-Essay
from Thomson West

EVIDENCE

By

Michael H. Graham
Professor of Law
University of Miami School of Law

Exam Pro

THOMSON
WEST

Mat #40602716

Thomson/West have created this publication to provide you with accurate and authoritative information concerning the subject matter covered. However, this publication was not necessarily prepared by persons licensed to practice law in a particular jurisdiction. Thomson/West are not engaged in rendering legal or other professional advice, and this publication is not a substitute for the advice of an attorney. If you require legal or other expert advice, you should seek the services of a competent attorney or other professional.

610 Opperman Drive
St. Paul, MN 55123
1–800–313–9378

Printed in the United States of America

ISBN: 978–0–314–18066–7

TEXT IS PRINTED ON 10% POST
CONSUMER RECYCLED PAPER

Table of Contents

Specific Subject Matter Essay Questions

Art.

Evidence Final Essay Examinations

Appendices

Table of Cases

SPECIFIC SUBJECT MATTER ESSAY QUESTIONS

ARTICLE I
GENERAL PROVISIONS

Preliminary Questions of Admissibility

Question: Manny, a 350 lb. ex-football player, is attempting to load a 150 lb. bag of metal parts onto the top of his Ford Expedition. Manny steps on the running board. To get the bag where he wants it positioned within the luggage rack on the roof, he steps on the running board with one foot. He lifts the bag over his head and lurches upward and forward. The bag lands where intended on the roof of the Expedition. However, the running board bends downward causing Manny to fall off. Manny breaks his arm and suffers other injuries as well. The Ford Expedition in fact is sold with many different style running boards. The one on Manny's Expedition was a flat running board with indentations near both doors. The expert hired by Manny's lawyer is an automotive engineer. He worked ten years on the Chevy Impala design and 10 other years in other car divisions of Chevrolet. He never worked on a SUV designed with a running board. Manny's expert is prepared to testify that if the Ford Expedition had a tubular running board, which is already a standard running board offered on some Ford Expeditions, then the accident would not have happened.

Ford intends to challenge Manny's expert witness on several grounds:

a) lack of qualification
b) lack of an adequate factual basis, Rule 702(1)
c) *Daubert/Kumho*/Rule 702(2) and in particular
d) the absence of testing.

Discuss the application of Rule 104 in this context, i.e., which, if any, determinations involve a matter of conditional relevancy, Rule 104(b), and which determinations, if any, are solely for the court, Rule 104(a).

Question: Lori, age 4, was playing at school during recess when an accident occurs involving Mary who was on foot and a car driven by Bob. Lori is prepared to testify that as she was swinging real high on the big kids' swing in the playground at school she saw a lady walk into the crosswalk when the sign across the street from her was green. Lori says she could see this only when she was at the top of her swinging, high off the ground. Lori also says she saw the car hit Mary as she was in the crosswalk when the sign was green. The school crossing guard is prepared to testify that Lori was in fact on the swing when the accident happened and that Lori told her the same story in a calm voice ten minutes after the accident. Discuss the application of Rule 104(a) and Rule 104(b) to the determination of whether Lori is a competent witness possessing personal knowledge as required by Rule 602.

Motions in Limine

Question: Counsel for Robert has caused his expert on high tension electric wire safety and a computer animation professional to prepare a computer animation illustrating counsel's theory of how the accident happened. Opposing counsel is as of now unaware of the existence of the computer animation. It is likely that Robert's counsel will have to disclose its existence at the next pre-trial conference where the judge is expected to require a list of proposed exhibits. Robert's counsel wants your advice as to whether he should make a motion in limine prior to trial seeking an order holding the computer animation admissible at trial. How would you advise Robert's counsel? If Robert's counsel's motion is denied, what must Robert's counsel do at trial, if anything, to preserve error for appeal?

Door Opening

Question: Butch is on trial for armed robbery of a gas station. On his direct examination, when asked by his counsel, "Butch, did you walk in to the XYS Shell station, point a gun at the clerk, and demand that he give you all his money?" Butch says, "Absolutely not. It wasn't me. I didn't rob nobody. I don't own a gun. I never ever even held a gun in my hands in my life." Counsel for the prosecution does not object to Butch's testimony. However, on cross-examination the prosecution asks, "Butch, isn't it a fact you were illegally in possession of a firearm in Oakland, California in 1998?" The prosecution is prepared to call the police officer who arrested Butch at that time to testify to the foregoing event if Butch denies the gun possession in answering the question prepondered on cross-examination. Defense counsel objects, "Your Honor, I object to that question as improper impeachment introducing inadmissible evidence of character." You are the trial judge. How do you rule and why?

Curative, Cautionary and Limiting Instructions

Question: George and Ringo are arrested for armed robbery of a liquor store. Officer Smith testifies that Ringo gave an oral confession to the police in which he said he stayed in the car while George stuck up the liquor store. Ringo does not testify at their joint trial. The clerk behind the counter testifies that she thinks it was George who robbed her but she is not 100% sure. Mary is called by the prosecution. On direct examination she says she saw a man run out of the liquor store. She heard a person scream at the same time, "Stop. Thief! I've been robbed." The man fleeing the liquor store jumped through the passenger side window of a late model Ford Explorer, black. When asked to further describe the person fleeing the liquor store, Mary says, "All I recall is a guy. Not old, not young. White. Average everything." When asked whether he had anything unusual such as tattoos, scars, a ponytail, etc., she said, "I don't recall noticing anything like that." The prosecution then impeaches Mary by means of an alleged prior inconsistent statement in which she stated that the man fleeing the liquor store had a long red ponytail and that he had a scull and cross-bones tattoo on his right arm. Mary says that she recalls talking to the police but does not recall saying anything like that. George has a long red ponytail and a scull and cross-bones tattoo on his right arm.

a) George's counsel at no time objects to the introduction of Ringo's confession that implicates George nor does he request a cautionary or limiting instruction. None is given by the trial court sua sponte. Discuss.

b) George's counsel at no time objects to any of the questions or answers given by Mary nor does he at any time request a cautionary or limiting instruction with respect to the prior inconsistent statement. None is given. Discuss.

Admissibility of Related Writings, Recordings and Oral Statements

Question: Matthew sends an e-mail to Mary breaking off their engagement. In the e-mail he agrees that Mary should keep the engagement ring on condition that the diamond brooch that was his grandmother's that she received from his parents at the engagement party is returned. Mary replies by e-mail many things including that the brooch was given to her by Matthew well before they were engaged and she intends to keep it as well. Matthew calls Mary and gives her the what for. In the conversation Matthew tells Mary that she knows that when he gave her the brooch, he said it was his grandmother's and that it was a pre-marriage gift which he would have to have back if things didn't work out. Matthew said she acknowledged having agreed to return the brooch and that at the time she agreed saying, "Sure, I'm not concerned. I know we will be happy forever." Mary's version of the telephone conversation with Matthew following the e-mails and his version of the circumstances and conversation that accompanied her receiving the brooch differs from Matthew's. Big surprise.

Mary sues Matthew to keep both the engagement ring and the broach. Mary testifies first at trial. Her counsel offers into evidence that portion of Matthew's e-mail agreeing that the engagement ring is to remain with Mary. Matthew's attorney moves to require that Mary's counsel also introduce at the same time the remainder of Matthew's e-mail.

The trial judge notices that lunch is in order and recesses the trial. The trial judge desires that you advise him as to how he should rule under Rule 106 when trial recommences after lunch. The trial judge is also concerned as to how he should proceed with Mary's e-mail and the oral communications if either counsel in addition moves that such evidence should be admitted under Rule 106 on Mary's direct examination at the same time as well.

ARTICLE II
JUDICIAL NOTICE

Adjudicative Facts

Question: At the conclusion of the government case in a prosecution for car theft, the trial judge states that the government failed to introduce evidence that the Mercedes 500 SL convertible purchased new three months ago was valued in excess of $10,000. The trial judge states that he has priced Mercedes cars before and knows them to cost much more than $10,000. The trial judge at the conclusion of the case instructs the jury that they are to accept as conclusive the fact that the car allegedly stolen, a three month old Mercedes 500 SL, was worth over $10,000 at the time of theft. Discuss the application of Rule 201 to the foregoing.

ARTICLE III
PRESUMPTIONS IN CIVIL ACTIONS AND PROCEEDINGS

Presumption in Civil Cases

Question: You are a law clerk to a judge new to the bench. The judge wants to be educated concerning the operation of presumptions in a civil case. Although the judge sits in a federal court, she has requested a full briefing as to the various approaches to presumptions that exist at common law. The particular problem at hand involves the receipt of a notice. The contract in question provides that if party X wants to extend the contract for two additional years, it must provide written notice of such to a given address. The contract states that notice is effective upon receipt. X says it mailed the notice. Y, the other party, denies receipt. The trial judge is aware of a presumption dealing with the mailing of a letter and wants its operation pursuant to all common law approaches fully explained. The trial judge advises that Y would lose a considerable amount of money if Y has to perform under the contract for an additional two years. Advise the trial judge as requested.

Presumptions in Criminal Cases

Question: Harry is on trial for receipt of stolen property, i.e., television sets. The trial judge is concerned that the jury may not realize on its own that it may infer knowledge that the televisions were stolen from the mere fact of possession of recently stolen property. She wants to employ a "criminal presumption" in this context. Explain how this "criminal presumption" would operate and how the jury would be instructed, if they should be instructed, as to its operation.

ARTICLE IV
RELEVANCY AND ITS LIMITS

Relevancy

Question: State whether the following evidence is:

(a) relevant or irrelevant
(b) direct or circumstantial

1. Testimony that a person accused of rape had a criminal attorney's business card in his wallet when arrested.

2. Testimony that a person accused of rape had a ticket stub to an adult movie in his wallet when arrested.

3. Evidence that an eleven year old girl did tricks as a prostitute in action for sexual battery of a minor.

4. Evidence of drunkenness at the time of an operation by a surgeon in a trial claiming improper diagnosis.

5. A man robs a store wearing a New York Yankee jacket. When the defendant is arrested a similar New York Yankee jacket is found in his closet. The manufacturer of the jacket reports that 200,000 of such jackets have been sold in the United States within the last three years.

Exclusion of Relevant Evidence

Question: The prosecution wishes to introduce three color photographs of a victim of a homicide depicting his location in a field near railroad tracks. The photographs also show that his testicles were removed and shoved in his mouth. The defendant asserts an alibi defense and offers to stipulate to the cause of death and to the dismemberment. Discuss.

Question:

(a) Discuss relevancy under Rule 401, including whether the evidence is direct or circumstantial, and admissibility under Rule 403 and any other pertinent Federal Rule of Evidence with respect to each of the following:

John, age 9, was hit at an intersection by a car driven by Mr. Smith. John claims he was walking his BMX bicycle in the crosswalk when he was hit. Mr. Smith asserts that John did a wheelie off the curb about ten feet down the road from the crosswalk right in front of his car.

1. Testimony that John did a series of wheelies on the sidewalk as he approached the intersection.

2. Testimony that John was walking his bicycle in the crosswalk when struck.

3. Testimony that John won a wheelie contest five months ago at his school.

4. Testimony that John's bicycle did not have a rear reflector.

5. Testimony that Mr. Smith was going 60 mph in a 30 mph zone one mile before the intersection.

6. Testimony that Mr. Smith did not have his glasses on while he was driving.

7. Testimony that Mr. Smith is married and has two children, ages 7 and 8.

8. Testimony that Mr. Smith's two children were hitting each other in the back seat at the time of the accident.

9. Testimony that John has red hair.

10. Testimony that Mr. Smith had a $1,000,000 liability automobile insurance policy.

(b) When Mr. Smith's car involved in the accident presented in the previous set of questions came to a halt it was itself hit by a truck driven by Mr. Brown. Is the evidence admissible over a Rule 403 and any other appropriate objection?

1. The accident occurred at 3:30 p.m. At 1:00 p.m. Mr. Brown had three beers at lunch.

2. Mr. Brown was arrested for DUI in 2003.

3. Mr. Brown was late for an appointment with his secretary at a nearby motel scheduled for 3:00 p.m.

4. Mr. Brown was convicted of burglary in 2006.

5. Three color photographs are offered showing John lying on the ground next to the car. Two color photographs are offered depicting John's damaged bicycle. One photograph is offered showing John in traction in the hospital. The defendants object to the introduction of all the photographs. They agree to stipulate that John was struck by the truck and that his left leg was broken.

Real and Demonstrative Evidence, Experiments and Views

Question: Cheryl is involved in an automobile accident. She is thrown from her car after being hit broadside. A local newspaper reporter happens by. She takes several pictures. One is of Cheryl lying on the asphalt road. She is awake, holding her nose. Blood is pouring out covering everything. It turns out that Cheryl had a broken nose, which was handled easily in the emergency room. However Cheryl's leg was extremely injured. She required the insertion of metal pins in her leg. She needed to wear a device around her leg that has metal pieces inserted in her leg in numerous places to support the bones during the healing period. Several pictures were taken of Cheryl in the device along with a videotape of her activities during a typical day.

Cheryl's car came to rest in the intersection. It was moved backward ten feet by some bystander to permit traffic to pass. Two of the pictures taken of Cheryl at the scene show the car in its readjusted position. Various pictures were taken of

Cheryl's car after it was towed to a repair shop showing the damage to the passenger side caused by the accident.

The defendant asserts that he didn't see the stop sign in time because it was covered by a bus station shelter which has posters on the glass blocking his view. In addition, the defendant says that numerous people apparently waiting for the bus had congregated between the bus shelter and the stop sign blocking his view as he moved nearer to the corner.

The plaintiff wishes to introduce each and every picture referred to above. The defendant wants to employ a scale model of the intersection showing the bus shelter with posters, people, the stop sign and both cars. He also wants to have a computer animation made showing his view as he approached the intersection. The defendant finally has several pictures taken three months after the accident showing the bus shelter and the stop sign.

Discuss the admissibility of the foregoing items.

Habit and Routine Practice

Question: Mary is hurt crossing the street when she is hit by a car. Mary asserts she was crossing on the crosswalk heading south on the west side of Grant when a car proceeding east on 7th Street failed to stop on time. On the other ha nd, the driver of the car asserts Mary walked right off the curb on the south side of 7th Street about 10 feet short of the crosswalk. Mary takes the bus to work. It leaves her on the Southwest corner of 7th Street and Grant. Her office is south two blocks on Grant. Mary testifies that everyday she exits the bus at 7th Street at Grant and proceeds to cross 7th Street north to the northwest corner to get coffee and a roll at Starbucks. She eats in. The store clerk at Starbucks is prepared to say that Mary is a regular customer. Mary testifies she always uses the crosswalk to cross 7th Street in both directions. Mary's friend, Alice, who about 40% of the time catches the same bus as Mary, will testify that every time during the last 4 months that she traveled with Mary, Mary went to Starbucks. Alice will testify that most of the time she went with Mary but not always. Finally, Alice will testify that Mary always crossed 7th Street at the crosswalk in both directions. Discuss the admissibility of the foregoing testimony.

Question: Dr. Jones is accused of failing to advise his patient that the prescription drug he was giving her should not be used with any antihistamines as it could cause extremely low blood pressure. The patient, Edith, in fact combined the two and wound up in the emergency room. Can Dr. Jones testify that it is his routine practice to advise patients when giving them a prescription for this particular drug not to combine it with an antihistamine? Can his nurse testify to having heard him give this advice invariably to other patients over the years?

Evidence of Character

Question: Harold and John are involved in a bar fight on July 4, 2006. After Harold said something to John's date Sally, an altercation ensued. Harold told the police John hit him with a beer bottle as he was turning to walk away from the bar for no reason at all. John told the police that Harold was drunk. He commented disrespectfully concerning Sally's anatomy, i.e., the size of her butt. John says when he told Harold to get out of here before he won't be able to, Harold went crazy and started punching. After a couple of blows landed, John says he picked up a beer bottle and hit John on the head. John is arrested for battery. Harold also brings a civil suit for battery. John asserts self-defense.

The trial judge assigned to both cases is new to the bench having been a domestic relations attorney before being appointed to fill a vacancy. The criminal trial is set for February 28, 2007 with the civil trial to follow shortly thereafter.

Two weeks before the criminal trial is set to begin John makes a motion in limine for an order permitting his minister to testify as a character witness. The proffer is that Minister Jones will testify to having known John through various church related activities for the last eight years. The Minister, if permitted, will testify that in his opinion John's character for peacefulness is excellent. He also will testify if permitted that John has been an assistant coach to the youth girls soccer team from 2000 through 2001 and that the Minister has observed several occasions in which John has calmed down tensions sometimes resulting in physical confrontation amongst his girls and with girls on other teams. John also desires to call fifteen young ladies who used to be on his soccer team to testify to his reputation for peacefulness and to the foregoing and other specific instances where John was the peacemaker. Each of these young ladies played on his soccer team in 2000 and 2001.

The prosecution counters with its own motion in limine asserting that if the minister or any of the young ladies is permitted to testify, then the prosecution seeks an order permitting the prosecution to call (a) Sam, a coach of another girls youth soccer team, to testify that John's reputation to peacefulness amongst the coaches was bad and as to two incidents of conduct, the first in which John encouraged one of his girls to kick an opposing player who had fallen down and another where John got in a shoving match with a parent of one of his own players over playing time and (b) Alfred to testify that Harold's reputation at his job at the auto plant thirty miles away where he has worked for the last five years for peacefulness is good. The prosecution also desires an order permitting it to cross-examine any reputation witnesses testifying positively as to John's character for peacefulness as to the two instances of conduct involving unpeacefulness of John witnessed by Sam as set forth above. The prosecution also wants to cross-examine the minister if he is permitted to testify as to John's arrest for misappropriating dues associated with the youth soccer program.

The trial judge asks you to advise as to what if anything of the foregoing is admissible in the criminal trial and in the civil trial scheduled for next month.

Other Crimes, Wrongs, or Acts

Question: Dennis is on trial for auto theft. The forensic evidence indicates that the car stolen and found stripped was opened through the use of a special shimmy bar inserted through the opening between the front window and the outer door panel. The shimmy bar is designed to grab on to the connecting bar from the door handle to the door lock to permit it to be raised thus opening the car door. The government plans to call Tim to testify that he sold Dennis a shimmy bar two days before the car theft. The government also wishes to introduce a prior felony conviction of Dennis three years ago for car theft. The police officer who investigated the prior case will testify that Dennis admitted employing a shimmy bar to open the stolen car.

Discuss the admissibility of Tim's testimony, the prior conviction, and the police officer's testimony.

When Dennis was arrested a search of the car he was driving revealed the presence of a small quantity of crack cocaine under the passenger seat. He has been charged with possession of a controlled substance. Mary, Dennis's girlfriend, was in the passenger seat when the car was stopped. Dennis claims not to know how the crack got in his car. He says several of his friends have been in his car over the last week and that maybe one of them or Mary put it there. Dennis has an arrest for possession of crack cocaine with intent to sell and a separate misdemeanor conviction for possession of methamphetamine. Finally a witness is prepared to testify that Dennis once showed him marijuana plants growing in the basement of a house Dennis was renting. Dennis offered to sell him marijuana at that time.

Discuss the admissibility of the foregoing other crimes, wrongs, or acts.

Similar Acts and Crimes in Sexual Assault and Child Molestation Cases

Question: Wilson is on trial for sodomy of 80 year old Sally Haight after breaking into her apartment. The attack occurred at night. The victim didn't have her glasses on. Mrs. Haight is unable to identify her attacker. Nimia Oppenheimer will testify that she is 75 years old and that she is pretty sure that Wilson is the man who broke into her apartment one week after the attack on the 80 year old lady. She will testify further that the man said he was going to give it to her "_ _ _" but that he left through a window after pushing her down on the floor when the door bell rang. Ten years ago Wilson was convicted of rape of his then wife. Two years ago he was arrested for aggressively fondling the breasts of a co-worker on the auto assembly floor. Unis, now twenty, is prepared to testify that she had consensual sex with Wilson when she was 12 which included sodomy. Finally, two male co-workers will testify that Wilson exposed himself to them in the bathroom last year at work. Both men will testify that Wilson grabbed the hand of one of them and tried to place it on his penis.

Discuss the admissibility of the foregoing evidence.

Victim's Past Sexual Behavior or Sexual Disposition

Question: A woman in her late twenties visits Miami on business. She arrives on a Friday to enjoy the weekend prior to her meetings the next week. On Friday night she goes to a restaurant/bar on Key Biscayne called Sundays on the Bay. She meets a man and invites him back to her hotel room at the Sheraton Royal Biscayne Hotel where they engage in consensual sex. On Saturday evening she again visits Sundays on the Bay, this time returning home alone. She maintains that during the early morning a man entered her room on the ground floor through a sliding window and raped her. The assailant is not the man she slept with on Friday. At the trial the defendant's attorney would like to cross-examine the alleged victim and/or proffer extrinsic evidence concerning: (1) the fact she had consensual sex on Friday with an almost perfect stranger, (2) the fact she is unmarried yet on birth control pills, (3) that she previously had an abortion and (4) has a reputation for first date sex in Lincoln, Nebraska, where she is from. Prepare to advise the trial judge how to rule on whether the defense attorney may employ the foregoing to impeach.

The evidence shows that the alleged victim displays vaginal bruises. Defendant is prepared to call witnesses who will testify that the alleged victim prefers "rough sex" arguing that her injuries could have come from her Friday night escapade. Such witnesses do not include her sex partner on Friday who is unidentified and thus can't be located. Defense counsel also wants to cross-examine as to the foregoing.

Advise the trial judge as to whether the cross-examination and/or defendant's proffered evidence should be permitted.

Subsequent Remedial Measures

Question: A woman wearing high heels trips when her heel gets caught in the flooring at the threshold entrance to a store located in an enclosed shopping mall. Following the accident, the store itself puts in a new threshold at the entrance. The store denies it was negligent. It also claims that the mall owner is the owner of and solely responsible for maintaining the threshold in a safe condition. The mall owner asserts a shared responsibility for the threshold with the store owner. Following the accident the mall installed a "Be Careful–Step" sign near the threshold. The store and the mall each call witnesses to opine the threshold did not create an unreasonable risk of injury. The mall's witness is head of its maintenance department. The store's expert is a nationally known expert in mall safety.

a. Is evidence of replacement of the threshold admissible against the store to prove negligence?

b. Is evidence of the warning sign admissible against the mall to prove negligence?

c. Can the store expert be impeached by threshold replacement and the mall expert by the warning sign if they testify that the threshold prior to the accident was in a reasonably safe condition?

d. Is either evidence of replacement of the threshold or the warning sign admissible for a purpose other than proving negligence or for impeachment?

Compromise and Offers to Compromise

Question: Harry and Sally are involved in an automobile accident when Harry's car veers to the right causing Sally's car traveling alongside on a multilane freeway to swerve into a ditch. Harry stopped his car. As he approached Sally who had exited her car Harry said, "It's my fault. I will pay whatever your insurance doesn't cover to get your car fixed." Sally said nothing. Later Sally developed pain in her right shoulder. She brings a personal injury action to collect damages arising from her injury as well as the damage to her car. Harry and Sally's lawyers meet to see if they can settle the lawsuit. Harry's lawyer presents a report to Sally's attorney from an expert explaining how the accident, in his opinion, occurred. The lawyer states that Harry contends that both he and Sally were going about 75 m.p.h. in a 55 m.p.h. zone when the accident occurred. The expert states that as they were traveling side by side a tie rod broke on Harry's two-month old car. The expert opines this caused Harry to swerve. The expert's report provided to Sally's attorney contains a copy of a laboratory examination report conducted on the tie rod. A settlement is not reached.

At trial Sally's attorney wishes to introduce Harry's statement at the accident scene that the accident was his fault and his statement that he will pay for the damages to Sally's car not covered by insurance. Sally's attorney also wishes to introduce Harry's statement presented by his lawyer during the settlement conference that Harry was going 75 m.p.h. at the time of the accident. Discuss the admissibility of each of these statements as substantive evidence.

Discuss the admissibility of the later statement for the purpose of impeachment if Harry at trial testifies to driving at 55 m.p.h. when the accident occurred.

Counsel for Sally wants to employ the laboratory examination report on the tie rod obtained at the settlement conference in cross-examining Harry's expert at trial and as substantive evidence. May she do so? If not, what action, if any, should Sally's counsel take to fulfill her desire of being able to cross-examine Harry's expert from the report and introduce the report as substantive evidence?

Payment of Medical and Similar Expenses

Question: A delivery man is hurt on his way to an office located on the factory floor. As he is lying on the hard concrete awaiting an ambulance, the manager of the plant says to him, "Don't worry. We will pay all your hospital bills. I told my maintenance man to clean up that grease spill twice this morning." Discuss the admissibility of the manager's statement.

Inadmissibility of Pleas, Plea Discussions, and Related Statements

Question: Mitzi is involved in an automobile accident. She is charged with reckless driving. She is also sued by the driver and passengers of the car she hit. In the criminal proceeding, Mitzi's lawyer calls the prosecution and asks to talk about a deal. Mitzi, the attorney says, would plead guilty to speeding, and running a red light, and agree to a 6 month license suspension. The prosecution agrees to recommend the plea to the court. At the plea hearing the trial judge asks Mitzi whether she in fact was speeding and ran the red light. Mitzi said "Yes." The trial judge then asked the prosecution what else if anything happened. The prosecution said that a woman stopped at a subsequent light was hit in the rear by Mitzi's car going about 60 m.p.h. The driver and her two children in car seats in the rear were all severely hurt. The trial judge refuses to accept the plea agreement. Discuss the admissibility of Mitzi's lawyer's statements to the prosecution and Mitzi's statement at the plea hearing in the subsequent criminal prosecution and the civil suit.

Liability Insurance

Question: A company that sells automatic garage door openers asserts that the men who do the installations are independent contractors. As such, the company contends that it is not responsible for an automobile accident that occurred as the installer was proceeding from one job to another. Plaintiff wants to introduce evidence that the company's automobile liability coverage specifically included the car driven by the installer at the time of the accident. Discuss the admissibility for whatever purpose relevant of the existence of the insurance policy.

ARTICLE V
PRIVILEGES

Lawyer-Client

Question: Harry, age 13, is involved in an accident when he is hit while on his scooter on a sidewalk by a car backing out of a driveway. Harry and his mom consult Jim, attorney, concerning bringing a personal injury accident. In the room is Sally, introduced as an attorney although she was in fact disbarred, and Sam a law student clerking in the office. Later Harry is sent by Jim to see Bob, a mechanical engineer hired to inspect the scooter, and tell him how the accident happened. Bob was retained to testify at trial. Prior to the taking of Harry's deposition, Jim visits Harry's home to prepare him. The deposition preparation occurs in the dining room. Present are Jim, Harry, Harry's father, and Harry's 9 year old brother who listens attentively. The following morning Harry at show and tell in class describes in detail what happened during the prior evening at the deposition preparation meeting. Discuss as to each of the foregoing whether the communication from Harry to Jim or Bob and vice versa are protected by the attorney client privilege.

When the car came to a halt after hitting Harry, John, who was rollerblading on the same sidewalk, tried but was unable to avoid the car then blocking the sidewalk. As part of preparation for trial, John and his attorney meet with Harry and his attorney to discuss the upcoming trial. Discuss whether these statements made at the meeting are protected by the attorney client privilege when sought by the defendant or if offered by either Harry or John against each other.

Husband and Wife Privileges

Question: Mary and John were married on July 4, 1990. On August 9, 1999 Mary observes John burying a 7–Eleven bag under a flagstone in the back yard. Later that evening, Mary asks John what he was doing outside. John says that he is into loan sharks big time and robbed a 7–Eleven earlier that evening to get some money to hold them off. It turns out that a store clerk was beaten up in the robbery. Three weeks later John is arrested. A civil suit for damages is filed a few months thereafter. On March 30, 2000 John's criminal trial begins. The prosecution subpoena's Mary to testify. By this point she had had it with John. She has thrown him out of the house and seen a lawyer about filing for divorce. She is anxious to testify about what she knows. Mary's divorce becomes final on December 1, 2000. In May 2001, the civil lawsuit against John is tried. Mary is subpoenaed to testify for the plaintiff store clerk. She is still very anxious to tell what she knows. Discuss whether John can prevent Mary from testifying in whole or in part in either or both proceedings.

ARTICLE VI
WITNESSES

Competency of Lay Witnesses

Question: Tim Brown was working at the Texaco station when he observed an accident involving John, age 9, and his bicycle with the car driven by Mr. Smith. Discuss Tim Brown's competency as a witness:

1. Tim Brown, who needs glasses for driving, did not have his glasses on when he says he observed the accident.

2. Tim Brown was lying back on the dolly on his back and claims to have leaned to observe the accident upside down.

3. Tim Brown three years before the accident suffered from chronic alcoholism requiring hospitalization for six months. He was not drinking either at the time of the accident or when called to testify.

4. Tim Brown has had problems recalling events since his hospitalization.

5. Tim Brown has a perjury conviction stemming from investigation of his income tax returns for 1999.

6. Tim Brown refuses to say anything other than "I am a truthful man and will thus tell the truth," when asked to take an oath or affirmation.

7. Tim Brown says that he was talking to a customer while also lying under a car working but thinks, although he is not positive, that John got off his bicycle at the corner and was walking it in the crosswalk when hit.

8. John when asked on voir dire examination as to competency by the judge what happens when you tell a lie says "my mother hits me with a ruler". John promises to tell the truth when testifying.

9. Tim Brown gave an oral statement to Mr. Smith's lawyer stating that he didn't see the accident but only heard the crash. Will Mr. Smith's trial lawyer be permitted to testify as to Tim Brown's inconsistent statement?

10. A juror wishes to testify on behalf of plaintiff's challenge to the jury verdict. The juror has advised John's attorney that the jury employed a quotient verdict. Will the juror be permitted to do so?

Direct Examination; Generally

Questions:

1. Dr. Astin, a treating physician at the hospital where plaintiff was taken following the accident, is advised by the attorney for the plaintiff to refer to his "protocol" whenever he wishes in giving his testimony. Is this proper?

2. When Dr. Astin fails to recall the result of a test conducted by an independent laboratory, examining counsel asks him to read a document and put it down. Obviously, the document was not prepared by the witness. Can counsel now ask Dr. Astin once again to state the findings of the laboratory?

3. The defendant's attorney on cross-examination wishes to introduce the laboratory report into evidence. Can she do so? For what purpose?

4. Plaintiff brings a personal injury action against the driver of a truck and the company that employed the driver. Plaintiff's counsel calls to the stand a fellow worker of the defendant driver who was also a passenger in the truck involved in the accident. Can plaintiff's counsel employ leading questions as a matter of right?

5. Plaintiff's counsel calls an eight year old boy who witnessed the foregoing accident. Is the question, "Do you live with your mother and father on Elm Street?" objectionable as leading?

6. The mother of the plaintiff, who is fifteen, witnessed the foregoing accident from her home. Will she be excluded from the courtroom upon invocation of "The Rule".

7. The defendant trucking company's sole owner also happened to be a passenger in the truck when it had an accident. Will the owner of the trucking company be excluded from the courtroom upon invocation of "The Rule"?

8. Can a witness for the prosecution to a bar fight after stating that she can't recall how the fight started be asked "Didn't the defendant walk up to Mr. Battle and hit him with a beer bottle on the head for no reason?"

9. Is the question "Was the floor of the bank slippery or was it otherwise?" leading?

10. Every party has the right to require a person testifying to the content of a conversation to include in that testimony at the time presented the entire substance of the conversation. Yes or No? Explain.

Leading Questions

Question: John, age 9, while on his bicycle was involved in an accident with a car driven by Mr. Smith. John is called to testify. He is asked by his attorney on direct examination "Isn't it a fact you were walking your bicycle across the street in the crosswalk when you were hit by the car?" Is this question objectionable as leading?

At trial the attorney for Mr. Smith calls as his first witness, Barbara Green, John's mother. She asks her "Tell us whether or not your son John loves to do wheelies off curbs?" Is this question objectionable as leading?

Refreshing Recollection

Question: John testifying in the foregoing automobile accident case when asked how many lanes of traffic were there on Main Street in each direction where he crossed with his bicycle at Maple Avenue answers "1". His counsel then asks, "Isn't Main Street a four lane road, two in each direction at Maple Avenue where the accident happened?" When asked "Where was the car driven by Mr. Smith when you first saw it?", John says "I don't recall." Counsel next asks "John, wasn't the first time you saw the car driven by Mr. Smith when it made a left turn on a red light and hit you while you were crossing Main Street walking your bicycle in the crosswalk?" John said he still didn't recall. Counsel now approaches the witness and hands him a document. Counsel inquires. "In the police report you have in front of you doesn't it say that you told Officer Jones that you saw a car make a turn on a red light while you were walking your bicycle across the street at the corner." Discuss whether any of the questions asked by John's counsel are objectionable.

Cross Examination

Question: A train hits and injures three people in a car at an intersection. The car is thrown diagonally across the intersection destroying the light and bell signal that controlled traffic going in the opposite direction. The railroad is the sole defendant in an action for personal injuries. The attorney for the three occupants at trial calls the train engineer to authenticate an automatic speed recorder indicating that the train was doing 64 M.P.H. at the time of the accident and that the authorized speed was only 35 M.P.H. After eliciting said testimony plaintiff's attorney turns the witness over to the attorney for the railroad. Is the defendant's railroads examination of the trainmen at the juncture of the trial direct or cross-examination? May defense counsel employ leading questions? Can defense counsel inquire of the train engineer as to the speed and location of the car driven by the occupants and the presence of crossing signals?

Impeachment; Generally

Question: Plaintiff in a train accident litigation described in the foregoing problem calls an occurrence witness Mary to the witness stand. She testifies that the railroad crossing light and bell signal she observed didn't light or ring when the train approached. She states that she was 60 feet away facing the car as it approached the railroad track from the opposite side on a bright sunny day wearing her sunglasses which matched her red dress. On cross-examination defense counsel wants to ask her (1) about her recent hospitalization for hallucinations, (2) whether she is an alcoholic based upon rumors at work to that effect, (3) whether in fact she couldn't have had her sunglasses on at the time she says she saw the accident because they were being repaired, (4) whether she saw one of the injured occupants who claims to be wheel chair bound playing tennis two weeks before trial, (5) whether she had been let go from her job at the railroad last year for alleged incompetence, (6) whether she falsified her time card at her current job by having a fellow employee punch out for her, and (7) whether she said in an oral statement to a defense investigator made over the telephone two days after the accident that she was 100 feet away, the weather was overcast and she was wearing jeans and a blue sweater, and that she doesn't recall noticing whether the light and bell signal where operating at the time of the accident. Counsel also wants to introduce extrinsic evidence establishing each and every fact asserted to be true in the foregoing questions if Mary fails to acknowledge same when asked. Discuss whether each question should be permitted or not by the trial court over objection and whether extrinsic evidence is admissible over objection if Mary fails to acknowledge the truth of what is being asserted in the questions propounded to her.

Prior Inconsistent Statements

Question: Mildred is a witness to an armed robbery of a convenience store. A trial she testifies she was standing on the corner waiting for a friend, that a man around 35–40 years old, 5'10" roughly 140 pounds, white, wearing a red ski cap, blue jacket, and jeans came running out of the convenience store. Mildred stated the man had a knife in one hand and a plastic bag bearing the logo of the convenience store in the other. She testifies further that as he ran about 80 feet past her she saw him throw a knife into a dumpster and get on a bus taking on passengers. Mildred could not identify the defendant at a line up.

An investigator for defense counsel calls upon Mildred. Mildred agrees to speak with him. The investigator will testify if called that Mildred told him that as she was walking home after work she saw a man running out of the convenience store. He was no more than 30 years old, white and that she was not sure what he was wearing. She said the man was between 60 to 100 feet from her when he threw a knife down the sewer before boarding a waiting bus. When asked if there was anything else that she noticed, she said no. The investigator wrote out the foregoing. The statement was signed by Mildred.

Prior to defense counsel commencing cross-examination, the prosecution requests that Mildred be shown her written statement prior to any questions being asked. Should the request be granted? Following a court ruling, defense counsel begins to cross-examine Mildred concerning her prior statement to the investigator. As to each assertion or lack thereof in the statement allegedly made to the investigator, prepare to discuss whether defense counsel should be permitted to cross-examine and whether extrinsic evidence may or must be introduced if the witness does not admit making the statement. Assume counsel on cross-examination asks Mildred, "Did you ever tell anyone that the knife was thrown somewhere other than the dumpster?" on cross-examination to which she replies, "Not that I can recall." Can the cross-examiner introduce on the defense case in chief the written statement as extrinsic evidence to establish she said "sewer"?

Contradiction by Other Evidence

Question: Allen testifies for the plaintiff that as he was exiting McDonald's after going through the drive through and picking up his order of an Egg McMuffin, he observed a red car go through a stop sign hitting another car. Can Allen be questioned on cross-examination as to whether the red car in fact stopped at the stop sign and as to whether in fact Egg McMuffins were not available that morning at that particular McDonald's? Can Robert testify for the defendant that the red car involved did stop at the stop sign? Can Audrey testify that the particular McDonald's wasn't serving Egg McMuffins that morning because its delivery of Canadian bacon was delayed?

Untrustworthy Partiality

Question: Lori testifies for the prosecution that Harry hit Sam with a lamp at a restaurant bar. Harry is the lead research scientist at a laboratory that does AIDS research on monkeys. Harry's attorney desires to cross-examine Lori to establish untrustworthy partiality. She wishes to inquire (a) whether Lori is a member of an animal rights group, (b) whether she is having an affair with Sam who is married, (c) whether Lori is aware that an anonymous donor has promised to pay $25,000 to anyone who can stop the use of monkeys for research at the laboratory, and (d) whether Lori entered in a plea agreement arising out of her participation in the brawl that preceded Harry being hit. Are any of the foregoing questions objectionable? Can the defense without asking Lori on cross-examination about the subject call Sarah as a witness on its case in chief to testify that she handed Lori a flyer announcing the $25,000 award?

Conviction of a Crime

Question: Craig is on trial in June 2001 for armed robbery of a convenience store. Craig's defense is alibi. His alibi witness is Harold. The prosecution has disclosed an intention to impeach Craig and Harold with the following prior convictions:

a) Craig:

(1) A felony conviction in state court in Jackson, Mississippi, on July 1, 2007 for armed robbery of a convenience store for which he was sentenced to 2 years but was released after 11 months.

(2) A misdemeanor conviction for making false statements on a customs declaration in federal court in Jackson, Mississippi, in 2006 for which he was fined.

(3) A misdemeanor conviction for making false statements on a customs declaration in federal court in Jackson, Mississippi, in August 1994 for which he was fined.

(4) A state felony conviction for battery in Birmingham, Alabama, in 2004 for which he was sentenced to probation.

Craig pled guilty to the two customs form violations. He also asserts that the battery conviction arose out of a domestic dispute. He still maintains that he acted in self defense when he was attacked by a man who had accused him of insulting the man's girlfriend in a club.

b) Harold:

(1) A state felony conviction for battery in Birmingham, Alabama, in 2002 arising out of the same club fight.

(2) A misdemeanor conviction in state court in Athens, Georgia, for defacing public property in 2003.

(3) A juvenile conviction in state court in Athens, Georgia, for defacing public property in 1978.

Both of the defacing public property convictions arose out of protests against abortion clinics.

As Craig's attorney, oppose under Rule 609 the employment of each of the prior convictions to impeach Craig's and Harold's character for truthfulness. In addition, argue for whatever information you would like to have disclosed to the jury with respect to any prior conviction the trial judge permits to be employed to impeach.

Prior Acts of Misconduct

Question: Tucker testifies on his own behalf in a criminal case in which he is charged with car theft. On cross-examination, the prosecution attorney desires to ask the following questions:

(1) Isn't it true you were fired from your job two months ago for falsifying your time records?

(2) Isn't it a fact you were arrested for armed robbery four months ago?

(3) Didn't you fail to file tax returns for the last three years?

(4) Weren't you indicted for embezzling money from your Uncle John in 1986 in Orlando, Florida?

(5) Isn't it a fact that you beat up a Jets fan three years ago at a Miami Dolphins football game?

(6) Didn't you turn back an odometer before you sold your car in Butunga last year (not a criminal offense).

As defense counsel oppose the asking of the foregoing questions. If the trial court were to permit one or more of the foregoing questions to be asked, would extrinsic evidence be admissible if the witness denies the truth of the matter asserted therein?

Character of Witness for Untruthfulness and Truthfulness

Question: Tucker testifies on his own behalf in a criminal case in June 2007 in which he is charged with car theft. On cross-examination, he is cross-examined as to whether he failed to file tax returns for the last three years. In addition, Tucker is impeached with a prior conviction for bank robbery in the federal court in Mississippi in 2003. Finally the prosecution impeaches him with his original statement made upon arrest claiming to be in a location other than where he testified on direct he was at the time of the car theft. The prosecution's final question, withdrawn following objection as argumentative, was, "Were you lying to the police, lying on the direct examination or were you lying both times? Which is it?"

Tucker wants to call as a witness Dr. Jonas Pepper, a professor at a technical college Tucker attended and Tucker's semi-pro soccer coach for three years. Dr. Pepper would testify based on his contact with Tucker during his time at school and while on the soccer team that in his opinion Tucker is a truthful person and that he would believe him under oath. Tucker graduated in 2006. Dr. Pepper is prepared to testify that he has some contact with Tucker during the past year. May Tucker call Dr. Pepper to testify as to his character for truthfulness?

Assuming Dr. Pepper is permitted to testify, on cross-examination of Dr. Pepper prosecution counsel desires to inquire of the extent of contact with Tucker during school as well as the extent Dr. Pepper has been in contact with him thereafter. Prosecution counsel also desires to inquire of Dr. Pepper as to the prior conviction for bank robbery and as to each of the acts it wished to employ in cross-examining Tucker himself as set forth in the prior problem, i.e.:

(1) Do you know that Tucker was fired from his job two months ago for falsifying his time records?
(2) Do you know that Tucker was arrested for armed robbery four months ago?
(3) Do you know that Tucker failed to file tax returns for the last three years?
(4) Did you know that Tucker was indicted for embezzling money from his Uncle John in 1996 in Orlando?
(5) Do you know that Tucker beat up a Jets fan three years ago at a Miami Dolphins football game?
(6) Do you know that Tucker turned back the odometer on a car he sold in Butanga last year?

Prosecuting counsel also wishes to ask Dr. Pepper, "If you knew about these acts and that Tucker stole the car that is the subject of this trial, would it still be your opinion that Tucker has a good character for truthfulness?"

Discuss the propriety of the foregoing cross-examination. If Dr. Pepper denies knowledge of the events or that such events occurred, can the prosecution introduce extrinsic evidence of the acts presented in the questions and/or that Dr. Pepper had knowledge thereof?

Religious Beliefs or Opinions

Question: Harry testifies as an expert on reconstruction costs against an insurance company in a case arising out of a fire at a church rectory. Can counsel for the insurance company on cross-examination ask Harry whether he is a member of the same religion as the church that experienced the fire? Can Harry be asked whether he is an elder in the particular church that experienced the fire?

Impeachment of a Party's Own Witness

Question: Someone robs a liquor store at gunpoint. When the police arrive, Wes gives the officer a statement that he observed a tall man, at least 6'5", wearing a yellow jacket, exit the store carrying a bag in one hand and what could have been a gun in the other. The man got into the passenger seat of a red Pontiac firebird being driven by a young woman which left skid marks as it sped off.

Prior to trial Wes when contacted by the prosecution advises that he really doesn't want to get involved and that he can't remember much about the robbery at all. Wes confirms the day the trial begins to the prosecution that all he now recalls is that a red Pontiac firebird sped away leaving skid marks.

The prosecution calls Wes to testify. On direct examination Wes testifies to being across the street from the liquor store when a person came running out saying, "I've been robbed!" Wes testifies that a red Pontiac firebird squealed leaving tire marks a few seconds before he heard the clerk scream for help. When asked whether he saw anyone exit the liquor store prior to the car speeding away or whether he could identify the occupants of the car, Wes said he doesn't recall anything more than he already testified to.

The prosecution wants to impeach Wes with his statement he gave to the police. Wes will admit speaking to the police. He will testify if asked that he doesn't recall what it is he told them at the time.

Should the prosecution be permitted on direct examination of Wes to impeach him with his prior statement to the police?

Refutation

Question: On direct Harry testifies to being 40 feet from an intersection when he saw a truck run a red light. On cross-examination, Harry admits speaking with defendant's investigator two months after the accident but denies telling him he was 140 feet away from the intersection. On redirect examination can plaintiff's counsel ask "Harry, isn't it true you told the investigator you were 40 feet from the intersection when you observed the truck go through a red light?" and "Isn't it true you had an unobstructive view on a bright sun lit day?" On recross can defense counsel inquire "Didn't the investigator show you his notes of your conversation which indicated that you were 140 feet away and ask if you had any corrections to make before he left?"

Court Calling and Interrogation of Witnesses

Question: The defendant testifies in a criminal case asserting an alibi defense to an armed robbery of a convenience store. His fingerprints were found on the counter and the cash register located behind the counter. Well into the direct examination of the defendant the trial judge asks "Mr. Jones, are you really asking the jury to believe that the police planted your fingerprints on the counter and the cash register?" Discuss the propriety of the question and the appropriate response, if any, by defense counsel.

Exclusion and Separation of Witnesses

Question: At trial John's attorney calls John to testify. John is 9 years old. His mother, who will be a witness on damages only, remains in the courtroom at counsel table even though the rule on witness had been invoked. Prior to testifying John's mother read him a statement he had given to the police at the accident scene. John also spoke briefly before testifying with a witness to the accident who had just been excused as a witness about a few questions asked on cross-examination. Discuss the propriety of the foregoing under Rule 615.

ARTICLE VII
OPINIONS AND EXPERT TESTIMONY

Opinion Testimony of Law Witnesses

Question: Harry witnesses a bank robbery which involved the shooting of three people. He was outside the bank when the shooting began. Harry is called to testify. His testimony is as follows:

"I was standing around reading a newspaper I just bought when I heard three loud gunshots from a pistol. I looked toward the bank and saw a man about 5'10", 160 pounds, dark hair, brownish skin, probably Hispanic, run out of the bank brandishing a pistol. He ran full out to a truck waiting at the intersection and leaped into the bed. The truck spun rubber as it sped away. I think the truck was blue or green, probably a Ford, but I'm not positive. I then went into the bank. The scene was terrible. Real horrible. Blood everywhere. Three murdered people lie dead on the concrete floor. I felt sick to my stomach."

Discuss the admissibility of the foregoing testimony under Rule 701.

Qualifications of Experts

Question: Aldo is a tile layer. He learned his trade in Costa Rica as a child working with his father on the job. He has been in the United States working as a tile layer for 10 years in South Florida. His cousin was involved in an accident in a department store in Maine. She asserts she hurt herself when she tripped on a tiled threshold leading to the parking lot. At the time of the accident the tile threshold had been salted to melt snow and ice. The grout between the tile had risen in some places and was missing in others. Aldo's cousin can't recall if she tripped on the raised part or her heel got caught in an indentation.

Is Aldo qualified to testify that the threshold was not reasonably safe? Can Aldo testify that the tile was improperly installed and/or maintained? What additional information would you want to have if you were the trial judge before making these determinations?

Bases of Opinion Testimony by Experts

Question: An expert is called to testify by the plaintiff that the floor in a department store was not reasonably safe, i.e., it was too slippery. The department store is the sole defendant. The expert wishes to rely upon a statement made to him by a casual employee of an independent contractor who was present when the floors were waxed the night before the accident. The person told the expert that one of his coworkers had applied two coats of X2L the evening before the accident where plaintiff slipped. The employee does not testify at trial. He can't be found. The owner of the waxing company will testify if called that for the type of floor involved his employees are instructed to apply one coat of X2L wax only. The expert will opine that experts who review accidents alleged to have occurred because of a slippery floor customarily, regularly, and ordinarily rely upon statements from persons having personal knowledge of facts relevant to the accident.

May the expert testify in reliance upon the statement of the employee? Can the expert disclose the content of the statement to the jury? If so, for what purpose?

Disclosure on Direct Examination

Question: Ace Manufacturing consults an expert witness who is prepared to testify that its clothes iron is not defective and unreasonably dangerous. The expert sends the clothes iron to be tested by an independent testing laboratory. She also exams the product herself, reviews the product's technical design against alternatives available in the industry, reviews the literature and government regulations, and considers and tests herself an alternative design suggested by plaintiff's expert. Her sole testimony at trial is as follows:

"I am a mechanical engineer. I have fully examined the iron in question. In my opinion to a reasonable degree of engineering certainty, the iron is not defective and unreasonably dangerous. It is a safe product."

Discuss the admissibility of the expert's testimony.

Disclosure on Cross-Examination

Question: The expert in the litigation concerning the clothes iron is an employee of Ace Manufacturing. She previously worked for the Clothes Iron Maker Manufacturers Association. She has testified 30 times on behalf of manufacturers of irons. Her full time job involves the defense of product liability actions.

Plaintiff's expert test results for the suggested safety design differ from those obtained by the defense expert. In addition, plaintiff asserts that the facts employed by the independent laboratory as a basis for conducting the test of the iron on behalf of the defendant are inconsistent with the actual facts surrounding the accident and that several important facts were omitted entirely.

Assume whatever facts you feel appropriately reflect the above and prepare to cross-examine the defense expert.

Opinion on Ultimate Issue

Question: Mary is injured at work in a warehouse while operating a forklift. The forklift was being employed to lift and carry two empty pallets. As Mary was proceeding onto an incline where two buildings had been converted into one, as the front wheels of the forklift entered upon the incline the two pallets slid forward into the cab injuring Mary. Mary's attorney, Ellen, hired an industrial engineer, Bill, familiar with warehouse operations and forklift design and operations to testify at the trial. In preparation for trial, Bill modifies the forklift in question with a guard to prevent the empty pallets from falling into the cab. He tests the forklift as modified generally in the warehouse and specifically over the incline where the accident occurred. Bill is prepared to testify based upon his test results and other facts, data, and opinion, some admitted into evidence, others reasonably relied upon under Rule 703, supported in addition by several excerpts from learned treatises admitted into evidence and read to the jury pursuant to Rule 803(18), that the forklift employed at the warehouse that injured Mary was defective and unreasonably dangerous. The defendant forklift manufacturer objects that Bill's opinion is an opinion on an ultimate issue made inadmissible by Rule 704(a) and Rule 702 because the opinion is a legal conclusion. Should the manufacturer's Rule 702 and 704(a) objection be sustained or overruled?

Mental State or Condition

Question: An F.B.I. agent is called to testify against Alex in the cocaine possession with intent to distribute case. The agent's testimony details his surveillance of Alex and his coconspirators including their acquisition of the cocaine in question. The F.B.I. agent testifies that he was the lead agent in the raid of a warehouse where various implements and products used to cut and package cocaine were discovered along with guns, money and, of course, the cocaine itself. The F.B.I. agent testifies that Alex possessed the cocaine with intent to distribute. Is the testimony admissible under Rule 704(b)? If not, how would you restructure the government's expert witness testimony to facilitate admissibility?

"Gatekeeping" Under *Daubert* /*Kumho* /Rule 702: Determining Reliable"

Question: Antonio Benedi was admitted to the hospital in a coma and near death due to liver failure. Benedi, who regularly consumed three to four glasses of wine a night, had taken Extra–Strength Tylenol in normal over the counter doses for 5 days. Blood tests revealed therapeutic amounts of Tylenol still in his blood but no alcohol. Benedi received a liver transplant. Plaintiff's experts claim that a warning should have been placed on the Tylenol package of the possible danger of liver failure to heavy drinkers. Plaintiff's experts relied upon history, examination including microscopic appearance of Benedi's liver, lab and pathological data, and a study of peer reviewed literature.

No epidemiological studies were relied upon. Should plaintiff's expert be permitted to testify?

Subjects of Expert Testimony

Question: Alfred is accused of robbing a 7–Eleven. The police find a shoe print in the mud outside the store at a location where the robber can be placed. They also find hair on the ground nearby. A video camera in the store records the robbery. The perpetrator is wearing a ski mask. He is talking on a portable phone. The video camera picks up the conversation. The robber speaks in slang used by a particular gang in town. The method of the robbery is consistent with a gang initiation. The robber removed his ski mask as he ran out of the store. From about 60 feet away an elderly white women identifies him as a teenage black male. She picks him out of a lineup. The defendant, Alfred, wants to introduce an expert witness on eyewitness identification. The defendant, Alfred, also wants to take a polygraph. What expert witnesses can you expect each side to consider calling? As to each, discuss the admissibility of the expert's testimony.

Court Appointed Experts

Question: John brings a product liability case asserting that a prescription drug he took for erectile dysfunction resulted in a permanent erection which is both painful and embarrassing. John intends to call his own expert witnesses. John also wants the trial court to appoint an expert to evaluate John's assertion. John wants the court appointed expert to testify as a court appointed expert at trial, i.e., the court would disclose to the jury the fact the trial court appointed the expert witness. The manufacturer objects. The case is scheduled to be tried to a jury.

On behalf of John put forth the arguments in favor of court appointment. On behalf of the manufacturer put forth the arguments against court appointment. Discuss the question of whether the fact of court appointment should be disclosed to the jury.

ARTICLE VIII
HEARSAY

DEFINITION OF HEARSAY

Rules 801(a)-(d)

Questions:

1. Plaintiff offers testimony by a police officer that upon arriving at the accident scene he spoke with an occurrence witness, Mary Jane, who told him the truck went through a red light. Is the statement hearsay? Discuss.

2. Police officer then testifies that he went over to the plaintiff who was still in her damaged car and asked her how she was and that the plaintiff said, "My leg feels broken." Is the statement hearsay? Discuss.

3. Two weeks before the accident plaintiff notified her insurance company to cancel her uninsured motorist coverage. Is the notification hearsay? Discuss.

4. The police officer testifies that the sign on the truck said "Acme Electrical Services". Is this hearsay? Discuss.

5. The police officer testifies that he noticed that the speedometer in plaintiff's car still registered 48 mph. Is this hearsay? Discuss.

6. The police officer testifies that he measured the truck skid marks at 28 feet. Is this hearsay? Discuss.

7. Mary Jane gave a signed statement sworn to under oath before a notary to plaintiff's investigator that the truck went through a red light. Plaintiff's attorney offers the document into

evidence through the testimony of the investigator. Is the document hearsay? Discuss.

8. Defendant truck driver offers testimony by the police officer that plaintiff while still in her car offered the police officer $100 to ticket the truck for going through a red light. Is it hearsay? Discuss.

9. The truck driver leaves the scene of the accident. Is this hearsay? Discuss.

10. Plaintiff claims that the accident was caused by faulty brakes on a red Buick which resulted in the red Buick going through the yield sign into the intersection hitting plaintiff's car broadside. On the day before the accident, Roberta Jones the owner of the red Buick had her car serviced. The plaintiff calls Bill Knight, an employee in a garage owned and operated by Jim Harris. Bill Knight testifies as follows:

Roberta Jones brought her red Buick into the garage for service about one week before the accident. After examining the brakes, Jim Harris told me that the master cylinder had a leak. I overheard Jim talk to Mrs. Jones when she came to pick up the car. Jim said, "Ma'am, your master cylinder is bad. Do you want it fixed now?" Roberta said, "No, I am in a hurry. I will see to it later." As she was walking away I heard Roberta Jones say to her son, "I have to drive slowly on the way home. My brakes are bad."

Discuss the admissibility of the testimony of Bill Knight in relation to the rule against hearsay.

Prior Inconsistent Statements

Question: On behalf of Sam, Harry testifies at trial that Sue Ann drove her car through a red light causing an accident. On cross-examination Harry admits signing an affidavit and making a statement that was videotaped that the light facing Sue Ann was green. He also denies at trial that his earlier statements were true. Can Sue Ann's attorney have either or both of Harry's statements admitted as substantive evidence under Rule 801(d)(1)(A)? Are either or both statements admissible for purposes of impeachment? Are they hearsay for such a purpose?

What if Harry had adopted his prior statements as true at trial? Would the statements now be admissible as substantive evidence? If Harry had made his statement (1) at a deposition or (2) before the grand jury, would either statement be admissible under Rule 801(d)(1)(A) as substantive evidence?

Prior Consistent Statements

Question: Bob went home immediately following the accident and told his wife that he had observed Mary run a red light causing an accident with Ted. Two years later at trial Bob so testifies. Can Bob be asked on direct examination following his description of the accident what he told his wife? Can Bob's wife later testify to Bob's prior statement to the same effect? On cross-examination, Mary's counsel inquires whether Bob's son two weeks before trial became a business partner of Ted. Can Bob and/or his wife now testify to the prior consistent statement Bob made to his wife, i.e. that Mary ran a red light causing an accident?

Prior Identification of a Person After Perceiving Him

Question: Mary Sue has her purse stolen on the street near her home. It was a snatch and run. Mary Sue got a quick look at the perpetrator when she turned around after feeling her purse being ripped off her shoulder. Later that day Mary Sue picked out a picture of the defendant from a mug book as being the perpetrator. Three weeks later she identified the same person at a lineup. At the trial nine months later Mary Sue fails to identify the accused as the perpetrator saying only that it looks a little like him but she can't be sure. She added that if pressed for an answer she would say probably that he is not the same man. When asked if she viewed pictures to see if she could identify anyone as the perpetrator, she testifies to having done so but does not recall anything about whether she was or was not able to identify anyone at that time. Her answer with respect to the lineup is identical. May a police officer who was present when the mug shot identification took place and at the lineup testify that Mary Sue positively identified on both occasions the defendant as the person who stole her purse?

Statements of Party Made in Individual Capacity

Question: A limousine owned by the occupant is involved in an accident. The limousine has extremely heavily smoked windows totally surrounding the rear compartment. A man emerges from the rear of the limousine reeking of alcohol and smoking marijuana. He stumbles around eventually leaning on the trunk of the limousine. He then puts on his glasses. He says, "Sorry, it's my fault. My driver negligently ran a red light." Is this statement admissible as an admission of a party opponent?

Plea of Guilty

Question: Bobby Joe ran his car into the car in front of him causing personal injury. The police officer gives Bobby Joe a ticket for following too closely even though Bobby Joe told him the car in front stopped short in the roadway after it ran out of gas when the car could have easily pulled off the road onto an available shoulder. Bobby Joe appeared in court. When the police officer appeared, Bobby Joe being late for work entered a plea of guilty and paid a $50 fine. The ticket was not punishable with jail time. Is the plea of guilty to a traffic ordinance admissible as an admission of a party opponent against Bobby Joe in the personal injury action?

Statements of Party Made in Representative Capacity

Question: Tony, who was appointed as guardian over his mother who suffers from Alzheimer's, was having lunch with some friends. As part of casual conversation Tony says, "You know some old people can really be dangerous without knowing it. My mom often thinks she is a kid playing on a playground." Tony's mom two weeks later is accused of having pushed another old lady causing her to fall down. Is this statement admissible against Tony's mother?

Persons in Privity or Jointly Interested

Question: Bob owned some land located in the woods which had been in his family for some time. Once while out hunting on the land he told his neighbor in the presence of others that a particular gorge represented the far reaches of his land and that they were now entering public park property. Several years later after Bob had died leaving his land to his daughter Sally, a dispute arose with the parks department in which Sally asserts that her land extends about 500 yards north of the gorge. Is Bob's statement admissible against Sally as an admission of a party opponent?

Manifestation of Adoption or Belief in Truth of Statement

Question: Harry, Bob and John were having lunch at a fast food restaurant. Harry says "That jackass George will never figure out that the money he loaned us is secured by nothing but paper. The documents are too complicated for that idiot." Bob says "I wish I was as confident that Adam won't get it either." John says nothing. Are the statements made by Harry and Bob admissible as admissions of a party opponent in a lawsuit brought against Harry, Bob and John for fraud by George and Adam?

Vicarious Admissions

Question: A security alarm repairman is involved in an accident. His van hit a car from the rear stopped at a traffic light at 11:00 p.m. The security alarm repairman exits the van which bears the name of the security alarm company for which he works and says, "I am on my way home from an emergency call. I'm really tired. I just didn't see you stopped at the light in time." The security alarm company asserts that the security alarm man was using the van which is in his possession 24/7 on personal business at the time. It also asserts that all employees who have use of a van for business purposes sign a statement acknowledging that the scope of their employment does not extend to making statements concerning their driving. Is the security alarm repairman's statement admissible as an admission of a party-opponent against the security alarm company?

Statements by Coconspirator

Question: A is in a room with B, C and D. D is either an undercover DEA agent, an informant, or a co-conspirator who later enters into a plea agreement and testifies for the prosecution. At the meeting A says, "We need to get out to the drop spot in the Everglades on time. If we are late like we were for the last drop of cocaine, E will have all of us eliminated." B says "Yeah, I don't want E mad at me," C says nothing. Discuss the admissibility of A's and B's statements as an admission of a party-opponent against A, B, C and E.

HEARSAY EXCEPTIONS; AVAILABILITY OF DECLARANT IMMATERIAL

Present Sense Impression

Question: Margaret is driving while talking on her cell phone. She was leaving a message on an answering machine when she drives by a shopping mall. She leaves the following message, "Sally, you won't believe what I just saw. A huge man, close to seven feet, just came out of a liquor store carrying a gun. The owner came out after him but couldn't catch him. What is the world coming to?" Can the recorded message be admitted as a present sense impression? Is there a confrontation clause issue when offered in a criminal prosecution against the defendant?

Excited Utterance

Question: Mary contends that she was sexually assaulted by her date in lovers lane. She runs out of the car and heads home on foot. It takes her a good hour to get home. She passes several stores with telephones (she had money for a call) and her favorite Aunt's apartment. When she arrived home she went immediately upstairs. Her mother seeing her run upstairs follows her. Mom says, "Are you okay?" "What happened?" Mary tells her mother that her date raped her. Will Mary and/or her mother be permitted, over objection, to testify to the statement Mary made?

Then Existing Mental, Emotional, or Physical Condition; Intent as Proof of Doing Act Intended; Statement as Proof of Fact Remembered or Believed; Will Cases

Question: Bob and Ralph died when the company plane crashed in the ocean near Boston. A week before leaving on his flight from New York to Boston, Bob said to his wife at dinner, "I really miss you when I'm away. I love you so much. I wish I didn't have to go to Boston on business next week with my assistant Ralph Murphy." At trial of a lawsuit for wrongful death brought on behalf of both men's families, issues are raised with respect to the loss of consortium claim of Bob's wife as well as whether Bob and Ralph were traveling on company business at the time of their death. For what purposes are Bob's statements admissible?

Question: A man says to a woman he just met at three a.m. in a bar "I love you and will respect you in the morning if you come back to my place with me now." Is the man's statement admissible as a statement of existing mental, emotional, or physical condition under Rule 803(3)?

Question: In an extortion prosecution, the alleged victim said to his friend "I've got to get the protection money together for Mark. He already has broken the legs of two other store owners who didn't pay on time." Is the statement admissible under Rule 803(3) and, if so, for what purpose?

Statements for Purposes of Medical Diagnosis or Treatment

Question: Upon arrival by ambulance at the hospital a patient answered questions asked by a nurse who wrote down the patient's answers on an intake form. The patient, female, age 23, reports being hit while rollerblading on Lincoln Road by a car at an intersection. She said she went through the don't walk sign because she thought there were no cars coming as other people were crossing in front of her. She also related the car that hit her was a pizza delivery car—it had a Dominos sign on the windshield. Patient reported that she was in great pain and that her left ankle felt broken. She said she had sprained that ankle several times in the past and it never hurt this much. What portion, if any, of the patient's statements are admissible when testified to by the nurse under Rule 803(4) when offered by either the plaintiff or the defendant, Dominos?

Recorded Recollection

Question: The action is to collect on a homeowner's policy with respect to stolen property. The homeowners, husband and wife, prepared a list of items stolen for the police about 6 hours after returning home to their burglarized condo. His wife wrote down the items either of them noticed were missing as they together inspected the condo. They both reviewed this list for accuracy and completeness when they were done. At trial, three years later, the husband even after reviewing the foregoing list can recall only five of the 30 items listed therein as having been stolen. Is the list of stolen items admissible as a hearsay exception? Must the wife also be called as a witness? If the list of stolen items is admissible, how should it be published to the jury?

Records of Regularly Conducted Activity; Business Records

Question: An ambulance driver was called to the XYZ warehouse where a worker had been injured as a result of a forklift accident. When the ambulance driver arrived, the worker was seated on the ground leaning against the forklift clutching his left arm. The worker said "My left elbow really hurts. Something must have broken when the pallet slid off the forklift over the guard onto my arm. I was only lifting the empty pallet at a 20 degree level when it slid over the guard. That guard should have been higher. If it was I wouldn't have gotten hurt." The ambulance driver examines the elbow and takes the worker's vital statistics. He then escorts the worker to the ambulance. En route the ambulance driver calls the emergency room to advise that he was bringing in a patient with a severely damaged elbow. The hospital emergency room employee records the conversation. The ambulance driver fills out a report and submits it to the hospital containing all of the information set forth above. The ambulance driver is employed by Quick Ambulance Service which has a contract with the municipal government to provide local ambulance service to the city's hospitals. Upon arrival at the emergency room, in addition to various observations and test results all duly noted in the patient's chart, an MRI is taken of the worker's elbow. The damage is so severe the orthopedic surgeon decides to send the MRI on the medical internet to an orthopedic surgeon in another city for a consultation on how to proceed. A response is received shortly to the effect that the extent of the injury warrants consideration of an elbow replacement. Such a procedure is successfully completed several days later. All of the foregoing is reflected in the business records of the hospital. At trial two years later the plaintiff's lawyer representing the worker in a products liability action against the forklift manufacturer calls a records custodian at the hospital to authenticate the hospital records of the worker and otherwise lay the foundation for their admission at trial. The records custodian has been employed six months. She works in the administrative wing of the hospital and has no personal knowledge of the persons creating the business records nor the medical procedures regularly followed by either the ambulance driver or any of the hospital personnel. The first time she ever saw the hospital records being offered into evidence was the morning of the trial. Discuss the admissibility of each of the various components of the hospital record as a business record under Rule 803(6) when offered by the plaintiff.

When the worker reaches the emergency room, the worker is asked by an attending physician "What happened?" The hospital record contains an entry by the attending physician stating "Patient states that empty pallet slid off forklift over the guard onto his arm." He added that the accident was his fault because he had failed to secure the empty pallet to the forklift as was his normal practice. Defense counsel seeks to introduce the foregoing portions of the hospital record. Discuss.

Question: The warehouse human resources department pursuant to standard practice conducts an investigation into the forklift accident. In addition to speaking to the injured worker, the person conducting the inquiry speaks to two other workers who claim to have observed the accident. A third person experienced in handling the forklift in question who did not see the accident offered an opinion as to how the accident happened. All statements were incorporated into the investigative report as were physical observations of the forklift as well as results of tests conducted to try to duplicate the accident. The warehouse inquiry concludes that the worker elevated the forklift 30 degrees or more which caused the pallet to slide and hit him. No conclusion was reached as to the adequacy of the safety guard on the forklift. Is the report admissible under Rule 803(6) when offered into evidence by the warehouse and/or the forklift manufacturer through the appropriate witness from the warehouse?

Absence of Entry in Records of Regularly Conducted Activity

Question: The Acme Trucking Company is involved in litigation arising out of an accident. The plaintiff asserts that an Acme truck failed to stop in time as a result of faulty brakes. Acme contracts its brake work out to B & B Brake Service. In accordance with the service agreement all truck brakes are to be completely rebuilt at 50,000 miles. The Acme truck had 60,000 miles at the time of the accident. The business records of B & B Brake for the truck in question do not show any maintenance work done on the brakes of the truck other than a minor adjustment at 25,000 miles. Is the business record of B & B Brake Service admissible in evidence under Rule 803(7)?

Public Records and Reports

Question: A police officer arrives at the scene of a bank robbery and observes a person fleeing the bank. The individual enters a waiting car and speeds away. The police officer enters the description of the fleeing individual and the car in his official incident report. The police officer does not testify at trial. Can the prosecutor have a certified copy of the police report admitted under Rule 803(8)? Would the report be admissible if the police officer had testified?

Question: A forensic investigative team arrives at the scene. After discovering from witnesses that the bank robber was not wearing gloves, they dust for fingerprints on the counter where the bank robber demanded money. Four identifiable fingerprints were located. The forensic investigation, however, concluded that none of the prints matched the defendant. Can the defendant introduce the forensic examination report under Rule 803(8)?

Question: The bank robbery and trial both occur in the year 2025. Beginning in 2015 everyone who becomes a naturalized citizen is required to give a DNA sample. John became a naturalized citizen in 2020. The forensic examiner discovers a piece of hair on the bank teller's counter. Another forensic examiner conducts the DNA comparison test and writes a report concluding that the DNA matches, i.e., the DNA from the hair matches the DNA sample previously given by John. Between writing the report and trial, the forensic examiner who did the comparison leaves for Indonesia and can't be located. Is a certified copy of the DNA report admissible against John? Would the DNA report be admissible through the testimony of the missing forensic examiner's supervisor?

Records of Vital Statistics

Question: A doctor at a private hospital prepares a birth certificate for a newborn, Sally Money, and forwards it to the county clerk's office as required by law. The birth certificate lists Sam Smith as the father. Sam Smith dies 25 years later. Two years thereafter Sally Money brings a lawsuit against the estate of Sam Smith claiming to be his child. Is the birth certificate admissible to prove Sam Smith is her father?

Absence of Public Record or Entry

Question: The government wishes to introduce a certified copy of the public record of the state agency that issues gun permits which shows that no gun permit was issued to the criminal defendant for the gun found on his possession. Is the certified copy admissible?

Statements in Ancient Documents

Question: A person named Mary Flower is left a bequest of $100,000 in the will of Samantha Jones. A letter is offered by plaintiff who claims to be the Mary Flower. The plaintiff testifies that her mother gave her the letter along with an entire shoebox of correspondence prior to her death in 1991. The letter is dated July 4, 1972, addressed to Petunia Flower, plaintiff's mother. The letter signed by a Samantha Jones states that she will forever be thankful for what Petunia did for her husband as a nurse in Vietnam and that someday her kindness will be repaid. Is the letter admissible under Rule 803(16)?

Market Reports, Commercial Publications; Mortality Tables

Question: A plaintiff involved in an automobile accident calls the auto repairman who has agreed to repair the damaged car to testify as to the cost to repair the damage suffered by the car in the accident. The auto repairman states that the cost of repair would be $11,500 and that $6,430 of the cost would be for parts. To establish the cost of the parts that would be needed to fix the car the witness testifies to looking up each required part in one of several books provided by parts suppliers and using the purchase price shown as the cost. Is testimony of the repairman as to the cost of the parts as reflected in the supplier books admissible under Rule 803(17)?

Learned Treatises

Question: On cross-examination of defendant's expert medical witness, the orthopedic surgeon denies that the A.H. Wells Annual, a collection of articles reporting current medical research, is a reliable authority in the field. The surgeon then denies having ever heard of Dr. I.A. Prolific or her article entitled, "The Ins and Outs of Knee Surgery" contained in the 2006 A.H. Wells Annual. Counsel for the plaintiff at side bar then represents to the court that on rebuttal plaintiff's expert, who has already testified, will opine that the A.H. Wells Annual is recognized as a reliable authority in the field. Should the court permit the cross-examination to continue under Rule 803(18)? If so, can the contents be read to the witness on cross-examination and/or the article itself be introduced into evidence through the testimony of plaintiff's expert as an exhibit?

Judgment of Previous Conviction

Question: Alfred was convicted of a misdemeanor theft of a box of pocket knives. He was identified in court by a truck driver who saw Alfred remove the box from the back of his open truck as he was returning from making a delivery. When Alfred was arrested one week later, none of the pocket knives were recovered. Sam, Alfred's brother and roommate, is accused of armed robbery with a pocket knife. The pocket knife meets the description of the knives stolen from the truck. Can the prosecutor employ Rule 803(22) to admit Alfred's conviction in Sam's trial?

HEARSAY EXCEPTIONS, DECLARANT UNAVAILABLE

Definition of Unavailability

Question: Harry, age 11, is called to testify in a murder case. Harry witnessed his mother's boyfriend kill her by hitting her repeatedly with a baseball bat. When called to testify, Harry testifies to looking down the staircase and seeing his mother and her boyfriend yelling at each other. When asked what happened next, Harry says he doesn't remember. When showed a copy of his statement to the police and asked again what happened, Harry does not answer. He simply stares down at the floor. Is Harry unavailable?

Former Testimony

Question: Car A is hit by Car B. The driver of Car A is John, its owner is Mary. Mary is John's wife. Mary was not in the car at the time of the accident. Car B is owned and was operated by Mike. The first action involves Mary's claim for property damage in the amount of $2,500 against Mike. Mary calls Bob as an occurrence witness who was standing on the corner. Mike calls Harry who is also an occurrence witness who was also standing on the corner. The second action is by John for personal injuries in the amount of $250,000 against Mike. Bob and Harry engage in a duel between the first and second trial, both die. First, is Bob's testimony admissible against Mike when offered by John in the second action under Rule 804(b)(1)? Is the problem one of lack of mutuality or lack of a similar motive to develop the testimony given the small amount sought in the first action? Second, is Harry's testimony admissible against John in the second action? Is the problem now one of lack of mutuality, lack of being a predecessor in interest, lack of a similar motive to develop, or lack of an opportunity to develop Harry's testimony?

Statement Under Belief of Impending Death

Question: Marshall Swartz walks into the saloon. His ever faithful sidekick Irving Goldberg is with him. As they enter through the double swinging doors, they see Sam Levy lying on the floor. He is clutching his stomach. Blood is all over. Marshall Swartz says, "Who done it?" The man points to Harold Silverman who is standing near the bar. He says, "He murdered me. I'm sure happy I changed the beneficiary on my insurance policy from Harold to my mother. That S.O.B. will get nothing. Tell my mother I love her." Irving goes over to Sam and says, "He's gone Marshall." Discuss the admissibility of the statements of the deceased in a homicide prosecution or in a civil action by Harold to collect on the insurance policy.

Statement Against Interest

Question: The police obtain a warrant to search the apartment of Tim and Alfie for drugs. Upon arrival, Tim lets the police in. Before the police even begin to search, Tim says, "The marijuana is mine but the crack is Alfie's." The marijuana is a small quantity equal to only possession while the quantity of crack cocaine rises to the level of possession with intent to distribute. Tim is released on bail. A bartender is prepared to testify that Tim came into his bar that afternoon and said, "Last time you'll see me for awhile. The stuff in the apartment the cops found was all mine, the marijuana and the crack. I told Alfie I would get even." At Alfie's trial, Tim can't be located by either the prosecution or the defense following a good faith effort. Discuss the admissibility of Tim's statements.

Statement of Personal or Family History

Question: Mary, Marilyn's mother, told her on numerous occasions that Mary's grandmother's father, Tony, was once a priest in a small town outside Bari, Italy. Mary is now dead. May Marilyn testify to some or all of Mary's statement under Rule 804(b)(4)?

Forfeiture by Wrongdoing

Question: Ace is on trial for robbing a 7–Eleven. The only witness is the store clerk, Pete. While on bail Ace tells several friends including Sam that the store clerk will not testify against him. When called to testify at Ace's trial, the store clerk says that he has blanked out everything about the robbery completely and right now in the witness stand doesn't even recall that there was a robbery. Is a statement by Pete the store clerk to the police at the scene stating that he recognized the man who robbed him at gun point at the 7–Eleven as Ace admissible under Rule 804(b)(6)?

Hearsay Within Hearsay

Question: On viewing a report of an airline crash on television Beatrice screams out, "Oh my God, my sister Lucy told me yesterday she was flying Cheapo Airlines to Chicago this morning with her husband. They're both dead. Oh, my God.!" Beatrice suffers a heart attack and dies. The plane exploded over Lake Michigan. The authorities have no way of telling if all bodies were recovered. Some partial remains can't be identified. Cheapo Airlines passenger manifest does not list Lucy and her husband as passengers. Cheapo Airlines is notorious for having inaccurate passenger manifests. Lucy's children wish to collect on their mother's and father's insurance policy. To do so they are required to establish that their parents are dead. Discuss the admissibility of Beatrice's statement upon hearing the news on television under Rule 805.

Attacking and Supporting Credibility of Declarant

Question: Harry witnessed an automobile accident. At the time of his deposition, counsel for the plaintiff was aware that although Harry maintained at the deposition that the light for the plaintiff had turned red, that Harry had told a friend of his that he never saw the color of the traffic light, only the crash. Plaintiff's lawyer did not inquire of the alleged inconsistent statement at the deposition. Following the deposition, plaintiff's counsel learned that Harry is red green color blind and that he had been recently fired from his job at a small company operated by plaintiff's brother in which plaintiff has a small financial interest. By the time of trial Harry had moved outside the jurisdiction of the trial court. Reasonable efforts failed to secure Harry's appearance. Is the deposition testimony admissible? In what manner can the credibility of Harry be attacked by plaintiff's attorney if the deposition testimony is in fact admitted at trial?

Residual Exception

Question: Janice, age 5, starts crying when her mother tells her at 7:00 A.M. on a Tuesday morning to get ready to go to her day care center. Janice who previously loved to go to the day car center, says in a shouting voice, "I don't want to go there anymore, Mr. Larry hurts me where I pee pee." An examination by a doctor of Janice's vaginal area revealed bruising and soreness.

Discuss the admissibility of Janice's statement in a civil suit.

The Confrontation Clause

Question: Mabel tells her girlfriend Sally that she will be leaving town for a while. When asked why, Mabel says, "My husband Tony and I got a real good haul from robbing the Big

K–Mart yesterday. Time to get out while the getting's good." Sally calls the police who pick up Mabel and Tony at the airport. Following her arrest, Mabel enters into a plea agreement with the prosecutor. In accordance therewith she testifies at the grand jury that she went inside, pointed a gun at the clerk, grabbed the money and ran into a waiting van driven by Tony. At Tony's trial, Mabel in breach of her plea agreement asserts her Fifth Amendment privilege against self-incrimination. Discuss the admissibility of Mabel's statement to Sally and her grand jury testimony in state and federal court.

ARTICLE IX
AUTHENTICATION AND IDENTIFICATION

ILLUSTRATIVE TESTIMONIAL FOUNDATIONS

Testimony of Witness With Knowledge

Question: Harold is hurt when a blender blows up sending flying glass throughout the kitchen. His hand is cut severely. Harold calls for help. His wife bandages his hand and takes him to the hospital. His daughter upon returning from work cleans up the kitchen. She places all the pieces of the blender she can find including those gathered by sweeping the floor and the blender stand in a brown shopping bag. She rolls up the top of the bag and puts it in a closet. In addition to Harold, his wife and his daughter, and a maid also resides in the house. The maid was off the day of the accident. The bag remains in the closet at home for two months before being given to an investigator working for the attorney Harold hired. The investigator delivers the brown bag unopened to an expert hired to testify in the products liability action against the blender manufacturer. Authenticate the exhibit. Which witnesses do you intend to call?

Nonexpert Opinion on Handwriting

Question: Mark is on trial for shoplifting. The store detective testifies that following his detection Mark made a statement admitting the shoplifting. The store detective continues by stating that he gave Mark a yellow pad and told him to write down what he did. The prosecution shows the store detective a sheet of yellow paper marked State's Exhibit A. The store detective testifies that State Exhibit A was written by the defendant in his presence. Is this sufficient evidence of authentication?

Assume instead that the prosecution called Bruce to the witness stand. Bruce and Mark were together ten years ago in boy scout summer camp. Bruce testifies that he read at that time several letters Mark wrote before Mark mailed them to his parents. Bruce testifies that he is pretty sure that the handwriting on State's Exhibit A is Mark's. Is this sufficient evidence of authentication?

Comparison by Trier or Expert Witness

Question: Bob is on trial for homicide for shooting his wife Mary. A bullet was removed from Mary during the autopsy. A gun of the same caliber as the removed bullet was found in Bob's car when he was arrested. Discuss which witnesses are necessary to call to testify at trial to authenticate the removed bullet, to authenticate an exemplar consisting of a bullet fired from the gun found in Bob's car, and to conduct a ballistics comparison.

Distinctive Characteristics and the Like

Question: Jeannette receives a letter bearing the name Toyota and the Toyota symbol stating that as a current Toyota owner of a Tundra, vehicle identification number XXX41X41XX, if she takes the enclosed key to her local Toyota dealer and tries it on the ignition of a designated Camry, she will receive the car if it starts and a $25 consolation prize if it doesn't. Jeannette goes to her local dealer who advised that Toyota has no such promotion at this time. Jeannette sues Toyota for $25 plus other damages.

Discuss the different ways available for Jeannette to authenticate the letter she received.

Voice Identification

Question: Claudia's purse is stolen in a snatch and grab. Claudia never saw the person who yanked her purse off her shoulder. She did hear him say, "Don't turn around or I'll kill you." When

Tom is arrested for a different purse snatching, Claudia is brought to a line up to see if she can identify Tom as her assailant. Five men are asked to repeat what the assailant said. Tom does so and is later identified by Claudia as the culprit. Can Claudia testify to her voice identification of Tom at his trial for purse theft?

Question: Melvin is an undercover police officer. He arranges to purchase drugs from Tom and Jamal. The meeting to deliver the drugs occurs in a park. The police arrange to have a directional microphone aimed where the three are talking.

(1) Assume that the entire conversation is tape recorded. Melvin is available to testify at the trial of Tom and Jamal for illegal sale of drugs. Prepare to authenticate the tape recording.

(2) Assume that at the conclusion of the transaction, Barry a coconspirator arrives. He recognizes Melvin as a police officer. Melvin is killed. Two other police officers operating the directional microphone begin by listening to the conversation at the same time it is being recorded. Assume that neither of two police officers monitoring the tape recording had ever met either Tom or Jamal prior to the incident. Both know Barry very well.

(a) Assume that one of the police officers continues to listen to the conversation as it's being recorded while the other runs to attempt to warn Melvin of Barry's appearance. Authenticate the tape recording at a trial of Tom, Jamal and Barry for murder and for the illegal sale of drugs.

(b) Assume that both police officers monitoring the conversation leave to help Melvin. The tape continues to record in their absence. Authenticate the tape recording at trial of Tom, Jamal and Barry for murder and for the illegal sale of drugs.

Telephone Conversations

Question: A person calling Toots at home asserts that he is calling on behalf of the Ace Ventura Dog Training Academy ("AVDTA"). Toots agrees to have her dog enter an obedience course and mails $500 to AVDTA at a post office box. After not hearing from AVDTA for several weeks, she calls the number in the telephone book listed for AVDTA. The person answering the telephone states that while they do offer obedience training courses for dogs for $500, they do not do telephone solicitations. Toots wants her money back. Can Toots present sufficient evidence to identify the person she spoke with on one or both telephone calls as a representative of AVDTA?

Public Records and Reports

Question: A question arises in an action to collect on an insurance policy resulting from a fire whether the business's sprinkler system was in proper working order at the time of the fire as required by the policy. An inspection report prepared by an independent inspection company, possessing a license from the city to prepare such reports, was filed with the building department as required by law. The owner of the business subpoenas the record of inspection. A clerk from the building department appears in court possessing the original report filed with the building department by the authorized independent inspector indicating that the sprinklers were in good working order. Can the clerk properly authenticate the report? Is it otherwise admissible in evidence?

Ancient Documents or Data Compilation

Question: Dennis and Steve enter into a bet legal in the jurisdiction as to the date upon which Joe DiMaggio's 56 game hitting streak ended. How would you go about introducing evidence to establish the date?

SELF-AUTHENTICATION

Question: Carla is suing for injuries arising from an accident involving a gas hot water heater in her home. The pilot light went out. When she went to re-light the pilot the gas hot water heater burst in flames. The gas hot water heater bears a tag (1) stating it was manufactured by XXX Gas Hot Water Heater

Company of Oakville, Ohio. When Carla was in the hospital her sister brought her a newspaper (2) from Cleveland containing a story of an extremely similar gas hot water heater accident. Carla can't now locate the newspaper article. Upon returning home, Carla located in the library a book (3) published by the Occupational Health and Safety Department of the State of Ohio containing diagnosis of proper pilot light safety devices and diagrams showing how pilot lights are sometimes defectively designed. Carla has a maintenance agreement that covers her home appliances including the gas hot water heater. She has copies of service orders (4) dealing with prior problems associated with the pilot on the gas hot water heater. Finally, when Carla did some remodeling work last year, the gas hot water heater had to be relocated. An inspection report of the gas hot water heater (5) was prepared by the city inspector as part of the permitting process evaluating the condition of the gas hot water heater. The report contains statements from Carla of prior failure of the pilot light although the inspector found nothing wrong with the gas hot water heater at that time.

As Carla's lawyer, discuss the extent to which Rule 902 may be employed to introduce each of the 5 items referred to above.

ARTICLE X
CONTENTS OF WRITINGS, RECORDINGS AND PHOTOGRAPHS

Nature of An Original

Question: A man enters a general store in a small town in North Dakota. He hands the store clerk a credit card. The clerk places the credit card in a machine in which he has also placed a credit card form. Sliding the top of the machine across the credit card places an imprint of the credit card on the form. The form consists of a top sheet and two carbon imprinted copies. The top sheet is labeled merchant and the second and third bank and customer respectively. The man signs the form. The clerk hands the man the "customer" copy. How many "originals" are there?

Assume the man purchased equipment for his business. He takes his "customer" form and hands it to an employee. In the regular course of business two copies of the "customer" form are made and incorporated into the business' records. The information on the form is also entered into the company's computer system and processed in the ordinary course of business.

Discuss the concept of an "original" with respect to each of the many different ways the man has to prove payment for the equipment in an action by the general store to collect on an account stated.

Requirement of An Original

Question: Bobby Hampster is allegedly beaten by three police officers. The police officers claim Mr. Hampster was resisting arrest and that they were just using reasonable force to restrain him. A passerby happened to have a video camera and taped the entire incident. In a civil action for battery, the plaintiff wishes to testify as to what happened. Does the presence of the videotape preclude such testimony? The plaintiff wants to call the passerby to testify as to what she observed on the video camera screen as the videotape was being recorded. May she do so over objection?

The plaintiff now wants to offer the videotape itself. Is the videotape properly admitted under the Original Writing Rule? What if it was a copy of the original videotape? Can the passerby's husband testify that his wife played the videotape for him when she returned home and describe what the videotape showed? Would he be able to do so if the videotape was "eaten" by the videotape machine and subsequently thrown away?

Admissibility of Duplicates

Question: Petunia wishes to introduce a xerox copy she made of a contract entered into with XYZ Corporation for the purchase of a dining room table. Petunia is claiming that the contract calls for delivery on 04/01/2001 while XYZ Corporation contends that the actual written contract calls for delivery on 09/01/2001. Is the duplicate admissible to the same extent as an original?

Admissibility of Other Evidence of Contents

Question: Irwin enters into a single contract with A, B & C for the purchase of a new van. Pursuant to the contract A was to deliver a new BQZ van to B who was to remove the roof and install a camping top. C was then to outfit the BQZ van as specified. Irwin is unhappy with the conversion camping van as delivered. He sues A, B & C. Before trial Irwin discovers that he has lost his original contract. He is able to locate a copy he had made and given to a friend who had expressed interest in obtaining a similar conversion camping van. During discovery Irwin requests A, B, & C to produce their copy of the contract. C never does. C's attorney withdraws from the case advising that C has apparently disbanded his business. C's attorney also advises he is unable to locate C to collect his attorney's fees. A testifies at a deposition that there never was a written contract on the van conversion. B testifies at a deposition that he can't recall whether any written contract was executed and that all his paperwork on the van conversion was lost in a fire that destroyed most of his factory three months ago. As Irwin's attorney, discuss how you would introduce into evidence the copy of the contract Irwin obtained from his friend.

Public Records

Question: Melvin needs to establish that he was born on a certain date to be old enough to collect social security. Melvin takes a trip to Poland to visit relatives. He goes to the local hall of records and locates his original birth certificate. Melvin discovers that no one in the hall of records possesses the authority to provide a certified copy and moreover the copying machine is broken. Melvin hand copies the birth certificate. Is the hand copy admissible under Rule 1005 in place of the original?

Summaries

Question: Sam's curtain manufacturing plant experienced a fire. In addition to fire insurance, Sam has business interruption insurance. The insurance company disputes the damage claim submitted by Sam for lost inventory, damage repair, and business interruption. Sam hired the accounting and consulting firm of AAA Bentley to help prepare the claim and to provide an expert witness for trial if necessary.

Discuss how the expert witness testimony of the AAA Bentley consultant as well as pretrial discovery is impacted by the availability of Rule 1006.

Functions of Court and Jury

Question: Joanne entered the hospital for a scheduled intestine surgery. While the operation was successful, Joanne nevertheless became a vegetable as a result possibly of improper application of anesthesia. Joanne's relatives assert that the anesthesia she received was incorrect for a person who ate 1 hour before arriving at the hospital. The hospital asserts that she ate 9 hours before arrival, not 1. In support of the hospital's position, the hospital produces what it asserts is the original admitting form signed by Joanne on the morning of her surgery. Question 3 asks "When did you last eat?" The answer "9" appears before the printed word hour(s). Joanne's relatives locate a nurse who is prepared to testify that after Joanne became a vegetable, she went down to the records room at the hospital to review Joanne's file. She is prepared to testify that the admitting form executed the morning of the surgery said "1" before the word hour(s) in response to Question 3. The nurse also will testify she made a xerox copy of the admitting form which she has in her possession.

Discuss the admissibility under Rule 1008 of what the hospital claims to be the original of the admitting form as well as the nurse's testimony that it said "1" when she observed the admitting form, along finally with the xerox copy allegedly made by the nurse.

EVIDENCE FINAL ESSAY EXAMINATIONS

EXAM 1—QUESTIONS

Question 1: (40 points) An accident occurs at an intersection between a car driven by Sam and a truck driven by Bernie. At the time of the collision, John was working at a gas station fixing a broken water hose. His fellow worker Ed was under the car. John observed the crash. After finishing tightening the water hose, he said to Ed in a calm voice "Another accident. That stupid truck driver ran the red light. I told you earlier that the light was stuck on red since this morning." Alice also observed the accident. She called her mom on her cell phone. "Oh my God, the truck just ran the red light that's been stuck all day long on red and hit the car. The car flipped over. I hope everyone is okay. Bye." An unidentified person runs up to Alice after she hangs up and says in a mad voice, "Damn, the truck never slowed down. It must have been going 60 mph through the intersection." John leaves town prior to trial. The plaintiffs call Ed and Alice to testify to the various statements made at the scene of the accident. Which statements are hearsay? Which statements are admissible under which hearsay exception?

Question 2: (40 points) Dennis enters a Wal-Mart. He brings a television set to the checkout counter. When the clerk scans the television a $285 price appears. Dennis hands the clerk fifteen $20 bills. The clerk, having received training in spotting counterfeit money, after inspecting a $20 bill presses a silent alarm system. Wal-Mart security detains Dennis and turns him over to the police. Subsequent inspection of the fifteen $20 bills reveals that ten are counterfeit and five are genuine. Dennis asserts lack of knowledge, i.e., I had no idea the bills were counterfeit. The prosecution has the following evidence it wishes to offer at Dennis' trial.

a) Testimony by a clerk in a dry cleaning store that two weeks before Dennis paid for his cleaning with three twenty dollar bills and that inspection of her till following closing revealed three counterfeit twenties identical to the ten counterfeit twenties for which he is on trial.

b) Testimony by another clerk in a clothing store that on the same day Dennis was arrested, he had given her a twenty dollar bill which she determined to be counterfeit. When she mentioned it to Dennis he said he had no idea whether it was or wasn't counterfeit but that he would give her another $20 bill in any event. The clerk agreed and Dennis left the store.

c) The police upon searching a garage belonging to Dennis discover a very sophisticated copying machine capable of producing the counterfeit bills passed by Dennis. Dennis says he borrowed the copying machine from a friend to do a school project.

d) Dennis had been convicted three years ago for manufacturing and distributing counterfeit bills, a crime punishable by imprisonment in excess of one year.

Discuss the admissibility of the foregoing evidence under Rule 404(b).

Question 3: (20 points) Margaret is suing a fellow high school teacher for defamation. The lawsuit revolves around a high school publication prepared solely by Mary containing a picture of Margaret with a caption which together she asserts holds her up to ridicule and contempt. The publication was created by incorporating a digital photograph into the text of the publication on a computer and printing out a single copy. This copy was then placed in a xerox machine. The 500 copies thus produced were then distributed to the students.

a. Is the original writing rule applicable?
b. If so, what constitutes an original?

Question 4: (20 points) A police officer arrives at the scene of a bar fight. She is told by the bartender that X hit Y over the head with a beer bottle. The bartender says that she picked up the bottle from the bar counter where X put it following the fight. She hands a beer bottle to the police officer.

a. What should the police officer do at this point?

b. If she in fact did what you advise, can the beer bottle be authenticated at trial without employing a chain of custody?

c. Which witness or witnesses would the prosecutor need to call?

d. What questions would the prosecutor ask each such witness?

EXAM 2—QUESTIONS

Question 1: (20 points) Ace Forklift Company produces a forklift for factory warehouse use that does not have a mesh guard in the front protecting the driver from items sliding down the forks into the cab. Such events are extremely rare. They are only likely to happen when the operator is moving more than one empty pallet. Drivers do not like the mesh guards as they feel confined. They also assert that the mesh guard is annoying to look through when looking down and that the mesh guard also impedes their line of sight. Mary is hurt while operating an Ace warehouse forklift when the top pallet slid off another pallet into the cab. Ace decides to conduct some tests itself to determine whether a mesh guard in front of the cab should be mandatory on all warehouse forklifts. The report indicates significant risk of injury when several empty pallets are moved with the forklift. Ace decides that all new warehouse forklifts will have a mesh guard and that a warning against removal of the mesh guard would be placed on the forklift itself. At trial an expert called by Ace will testify that for warehouse use a forklift is not defective and unreasonably dangerous by virtue of not having a mesh guard and that a mesh guard would impede the driver's line of sight. As Mary's attorney, what if any of the foregoing will you be able to introduce at trial and under what conditions and for what purpose(s) will you be able to do so?

Question 2: (20 points) A seventy year old man suffering from a mild stroke and occasional memory loss is called to testify that the defendant was the person who robbed him at gun point outside the food store. The alleged victim has very poor sight even with his glasses on, which they were not. It was 11:00 p.m. on a moonless night in a poorly lighted parking lot. The victim was convicted of Medicare fraud two years ago. The victim takes medication for an ulcer which makes him irritable and nervous. The victim agrees to state that he promises to tell the truth but will not swear an oath to God. Although the robbery only took 15 seconds, the victim is prepared to identify the defendant as the perpetrator in court. Is the victim a competent witness?

Question 3: (20 points) A police officer offers testimony on behalf of the plaintiff that upon arrival at an accident scene, a lady trapped in her car following an accident said, "I can't believe what happened. The truck ran a red light and smashed right into my car. My chest really, really hurts bad. Tell my husband I love him. I'm still alive." The lady dies on her way to the hospital.

The next witness for the plaintiff testifies that she was standing at the intersection talking to her friend. She further states, "The truck just ran the red light. It smashed hard into the side of the lady's car." Later in her testimony when asked what happened next, she testifies, "I told my husband later that night that I saw a horrific accident when a truck ran a red light."

In the personal injury action, with respect to the foregoing for what purpose(s) is the testimony/statement relevant in the lawsuit when offered by the estate of the deceased lady. Is it hearsay when offered for such a purpose hearsay and if so is it nevertheless admissible.

Question 4: (20 points) At a criminal trial, the prosecution offers the testimony of a police officer that during his investigation several weeks after an armed robbery shooting that Mary Smith told him that she had witnessed the armed robbery shooting and that the man who did the shooting had a big flower tattoo on his upper right arm. Defense counsel did not object.

The police officer then authenticates several pictures of the victim of the shooting in pools of blood on the convenience store floor. Defense council blurts out, "I object." The objection is denied.

Is the testimony of the police officer stating what Mary Smith told him admissible?

Discuss fully and apply the applicable standards of review on appeal with respect to the *two matters* testified to by the police officer.

Question 5: (20 points) Officer Jones arrests Sam for possession with intent to distribute. A search incident to arrest discovers 10 bags of a white powder substance. Officer Jones places the items in an evidence pouch which he seals. He writes certain identifying information on the evidence pouch on the side that he just sealed and then gives the sealed pouch to Officer Smith. Officer Smith gives the evidence pouch to Officer Brown who hands it to Officer Green at the police station evidence locker desk. Officer Green asks Ms. Gray to put the evidence pouch in the safe and log it in. Several days later, C.S.I. Blue removes the evidence pouch from the safe, opens the pouch on the end opposite that employed by Officer Jones, tests one of the bags, determines the substance to be cocaine, places the ten bags back in the evidence pouch, reseals the evidence pouch, writes certain identifying material on the evidence pouch near the end that he opened and resealed and hands it to Ms. Stevens to be replaced in the evidence locker. On the morning of trial, Ms. Stevens asks Ms. Gray to get the evidence pouch which she does. Ms. Stevens hands it to C.S.I. Blue who brings the evidence pouch to court. As the prosecutor, which witnesses will you need to lay a sufficient chain of custody for the evidence pouch. Did everyone involved do what they were supposed to do?

Question 6: (20 points) Robert was shot in the back of the head in a playground near his home. He was 17 years old. Robert was a member of the Fly By Shooting Gang. Mary, a female member of the same gang, saw what happened. She is prepared to testify that two boys, outfitted in the colors of the Over My Dead Body Gang, walked up to Robert, threw him onto the ground, stomped on him, yelled "Never, Never, Never," and murdered Robert, execution style. Officer Evans has 25 years police experience with the gang unit. He is prepared to testify that placing of a gun behind the left ear is the revenge modus operandi of the Over My Dead Body Gang. He is also prepared to testify that "Never, Never, Never" in Over My Dead Body speech means that no one can come into their territory and do harm without suffering the ultimate penalty, death.

Discuss the admissibility of the testimony of Mary and Officer Evans.

EXAM 3—QUESTIONS

Question 1: (40 points) Harry is on trial in 2007 for robbing a liquor store in a ski mask, combat boots, smoking a cigar and carrying a shotgun. He told the clerk to put the money in a backpack he was wearing. Harry was previously convicted in 2001 for armed robbery of a liquor store. On that occasion he was dressed and acted exactly as he is accused of acting with respect to the current criminal charge. Harry was also convicted of perjury in 1999 in connection with a welfare fraud scheme.

At Harry's trial discuss *all* the ways it might be possible for either or both of Harry's prior convictions to find their way before the jury. Be sure to state in detail any additional evidence that might be needed for the conviction to be employed.

Question 2: (20 points) The defendant moves in limine in advance of trial to exclude the testimony of one of plaintiff's expert witnesses in a toxic tort case. The trial judge, based on documents reviewed including the expert's deposition states:

I am going to exclude the expert from testifying. I find that her proposed testimony is simply not relevant to any issue in the case.

At trial the plaintiff fails to call the expert the judge had previously excused as a witness.

Discuss whether the plaintiff has preserved error for appeal. If not, how could the alleged error have been preserved.

Question 3: (40 points) An armed robbery occurs at a convenience store. The clerk is told by the robber to put all the money in the till in a plastic bag. The robber was wearing a ski mask and carrying a pistol. Mary was a customer in the store. Mabel was outside walking to the store from the parking lot. As the robber leaves he runs right past Mary. She notices a big snake tattoo on his right forearm. Mabel sees the robber tear off his ski mask as he exits the store, get into a blue Expedition and drive away.

Mabel calls 911. She screams, "Just saw an armed robbery, Hispanic looking man, around 20 years old, about 5 ft.

9 ins., 160 pounds, just took off in a blue Expedition at corner of Main and First." Mabel does not wait for the police to arrive. She is never located.

Mary does wait for the police. She tells the Police Officer Jones, in a calm voice, that the man who robbed the convenience store was about 5 ft. 10 in., 150 pounds with a big snake tattoo on his right forearm. The police employ the information concerning the tattoo to arrest Juan. Mary identifies Juan at a lineup by his tattoo. Police Officer Jones was present at the lineup for identification. He is available to testify for the prosecution.

Prior to trial Mary tells the prosecuting attorney that everything is now hazy in her memory. Mary tells the prosecuting attorney that, if called as a witness, she will testify that while she recalls the robbery she no longer can identify the tattoo on Juan's arm as being identical or even similar to the tattoo she saw on the robber when he fled the convenience store.

The prosecuting attorney desires a memo *fully* exploring the admissibility of each of the foregoing items of evidence for *any purpose* at trial as testified to by Mary, Police Officer Jones, and the custodian of the 911 tape recording.

Question 4: (20 points) Bob over the years sold many widgets to Harry. Harry would call to order the widgets. Bob would then mail a contract to Henry for the sale of the widgets. Harry would sign the contract and mail a copy back to Bob. Bob asserts that when he shipped widgets in late October 2000 pursuant to a contract dated September 14, 2000 which he says was executed by Harry, Harry refused to accept the widgets saying he never ordered them. Bob and Harry have never met in person. May Bob lay a sufficient foundation at trial that Harry called him to order the widgets and that the contract dated September 14, 2000 bears Harry's signature?

EXAM 4—QUESTIONS

Question 1: (20 points) Counsel for John, a 9 year old plaintiff, offers a certified copy of a police report. The police officer states in her report that she arrived at the accident scene only seconds later and was approached by a person who said in an excited voice, "Officer! Officer! the car ran right into that little boy as he was walking his bicycle across the street!" Defense counsel for Mr. Smith, the driver of the car, requests that the court requires John's counsel to read another portion of the police report which states that the same occurrence witness told the police officer after she calmed down that she had observed John doing wheelies on the sidewalk as he approached the intersection. In addition Mr. Smith's counsel requests that the court also order John's counsel to introduce an ambulance report that indicated that John appears to have suffered only a minor scrape near his left knee and an oral statement by John to a bystander to the effect that he felt fine. How should the court rule?

Question 2: (40 points) Robert is on trial for assault and battery arising from an incident in a local club. He is 35 years old, married with two children. He was in the club entertaining out of town customers. Robert is very friendly with State Representative Mary Powell. They went to high school together and have remained close over the years.

Robert's lawyer is not sure whether it is best for Robert to testify at trial. Robert is a very strong looking man who looks like a marine officer which he once was. In addition Robert has a five year old conviction for assault and battery which arose from an incident at a little league baseball game.

Robert's lawyer wants to be advised about how, under what circumstances, can he call Powell as a character witness. He also wants to be advised as to the nature of her permitted testimony. Finally, Robert's lawyer is concerned about the cross-examination of Powell as to Robert's prior conviction for assault and battery if she testifies as a character witness as to one or more pertinent traits of character.

Question 3: (20 points) The government is prosecuting John Gary for possession of cocaine with the intent to distribute. One of the elements of one of the charges is that the cocaine possessed be valued at excess of $10,000. The government fails in its case in chief to elicit such testimony from any witness, although it did put in evidence the weight and purity of the cocaine seized.

Council for defendant moves for a directed verdict of acquittal.

You are the prosecuting attorney. What are your options? Discuss fully.

Question 4: (20 points) Allen sues X, Y, and Z for injuries he suffers when an automatic metal pressing machine ejects hot metal out on to his leg. Allen settles with Z, the installer of the machine prior to trial. Z's representative testifies that Y, the maker of the machine, produced a metal press that was defective and unreasonably dangerous. Prior to trial, X, Allen's employer, enters into settlement discussions with Allen. X's attorney produces X's company records indicating earlier similar accidents occurring with identical automatic metal pressing machines bought from Y and installed by Z and copies of letters of complaint sent by X to Y and Z demanding machine modification. X also prepared a document detailing all measures X had taken prior to Allen's accident to address the problem, including a log of letters sent to Y and Z, changes in operational procedures to reduce the risk of injury, etc. Allen's settlement discussion with X breaks down prior to trial. As Allen's attorney, what if any of the foregoing is admissible at trial and under what conditions and for what purpose(s) is it admissible? Is there anything you could do as Allen's attorney to make admissible something that is not admissible under the circumstances in which you acquired it?

Question 5: (20 points) The estate of Greedy Evans sues Marvin Niceguy claiming that Greedy had loaned Marvin $2,000 on July 4, 1966 to start a business and that with interest accrued the unpaid debt now amounts to $100,000. Marvin maintains that in 1976 Greedy forgave the debt. He produces an affidavit sworn to before a notary, dated July 4, 1976, purportedly signed by

Greedy, stating that because of Marvin's exceptional contribution to the community and in honor of the bicentennial celebration, all amounts due and owing on a loan made of July 4, 1966 are hereby waived and forgiven. As Marvin's attorney discuss as many ways as you can think of to authenticate the affidavit as having been executed by Greedy Evans.

EXAM 5—QUESTIONS

Question 1: (40 points) A truck runs a stop sign killing the driver of a car which had the right of way. A police officer arrives about 30 minutes after the accident. The police officer files a report detailing his physical findings at the accident scene. The report also contains pictures of the scene as well as the stop sign. The police report details the police officer's discussion with various witnesses to the accident. Each of the four witnesses interviewed told the police officer the defendant's truck simply ran the stop sign. The report also indicates that the driver of the truck said to the police officer, "It was my bad. Never saw the stop sign."

Both a civil action and a criminal prosecution are brought.

The police officer is unavailable to testify at trial.

Discuss the admissibility pursuant to the Federal Rules of Evidence *only* of the police report in the civil action and the criminal prosecution.

Question 2: (20 points) You are a law clerk to a federal district judge. She asks you to comment upon a request by the prosecution for a jury instruction stating: "I instruct you that if you find beyond a reasonable doubt that the defendant Mary Jones was present in a car in which illegal weapons were located, that you must find that Mary Jones possessed the illegal weapons?" The judge in addition wishes to be advised as to whether it would matter if the instruction read, "you may but are not required to find" in place of "you must find."

Question 3: (40 points) Jamal Jones is a police officer with five years experience. He has spent the last six months assigned to the gang unit of the local police force. Officer Jones was one of several police officers who raided an apartment occupied by Harold Smith. Found in the apartment were 10 cellophane packages containing crack cocaine, material suitable for cutting crack, cellophane bags, 3 guns and $22,000 in small bills. On the walls of the apartment in yellow paint was painted "Yellow Rangers" accompanied by big sunflower designs. The police know that the "Yellow Rangers" are a mega gang in town and the sunflower is their symbol. Harold Smith's defense is that the cocaine is not his. Several other people live in the apartment as well. The apartment is rented to a corporation with alleged ties to the "Yellow Rangers".

In answering the following questions discuss whether it matters whether Officer Jones is testifying as a lay witness or expert witness:

1) The cocaine belonged to Harold Smith;

2) Harold Smith possessed the cocaine with an intent to distribute;

3) The "Yellow Rangers" are a gang that is heavily involved with drugs;

4) Harold Smith is lying when he says the drugs were not his.

Question 4: (20 points) Harold, age 3, is asked by the police if he knows where there are television sets. The police suspect his parents of having stolen 30 television sets from a warehouse three days ago. Harold says "Sure, mom and dad have lots of TVs." The police ask "Can you take us there?" Harold says "Sure." Harold walks from the front of his home two blocks to a public storage facility. Harold then points at a garage store unit and says "In there." The police obtain a warrant and discover 30 television sets, the serial numbers of which match the televisions that were stolen from the warehouse. At a civil trial of his parents for theft, Harold is found incompetent to testify. Discuss the admissibility of Harold's statements under the rule against hearsay.

EXAM 6—QUESTIONS

Question 1: (20 points) Samantha, age 19, asserts that John, also age 19, raped her as she was returning home from jogging through town late one evening. She says John, with whom she had attended high school, was standing outside his house when she jogged by, that he ran after her, threw her down and raped her. John's story is different. He asserts that as he got out of his car in front of his house he saw Samantha leave through the side door of Bill's house. Bill, a neighbor of John's, is a married man. John says he said to Samantha as she walked by "Looks like Bill got lucky tonight." Samantha replied, "F_ _ _ _ _ _." and kept walking. Samantha lives at home with her parents. Her father is a preacher at a fundamentalist church. Samantha had previously reported a sexual battery six months ago, which she retracted when the accused presented three unbiased alibi witnesses. It is also heavily rumored in town that Samantha engaged in sex with several members of the football team after getting drunk following the state championship game. Her reputation for chastity within the small town is not good.

As John's attorney, set forth which of the foregoing evidence you desire to introduce at trial pursuant to Rule 412. Discuss fully why you believe such evidence is admissible. If any evidence has been left off the list, explain fully why such evidence has not been included on the list.

Question 2: (30 points) An accident occurs at an intersection between a car driven by Sam and a truck driven by Bernie. At the time of the collision, John was working at a gas station fixing a broken water hose. His fellow worker Ed was under the car. John observed the crash. After finishing tightening the water hose, he said to Ed in a calm voice "Another accident. That stupid truck driver ran the red light. I told you earlier that the light was stuck on red since this morning." Alice also observed the accident. She called her mom on her cell phone. "Oh my God, the truck just ran the red light that's been stuck all day long on red and hit the car. The car flipped over. I hope everyone is okay. Bye." An unidentified person runs up to Alice after she hangs up and says in a mad voice, "Damn, the truck never slowed down. It must have been going 60 mph through the intersection." John leaves town prior to trial. The plaintiffs call Ed and Alice to testify to the various statements made at the scene of the accident. Which statements are hearsay? Which statements are admissible under which hearsay exceptions?

Question 3: (20 points) The bank robbery and trial both occur in the year 2025. Beginning in 2015 everyone who becomes a naturalized citizen is required to give a DNA sample. John became a naturalized citizen in 2020. The forensic examiner discovers a piece of hair on the bank teller's counter. Another forensic examiner conducts the DNA comparison test and writes a report concluding that the DNA matches, i.e., the DNA from the hair matches the DNA sample previously given by John. Between writing the report and trial, the forensic examiner who did the comparison leaves for Indonesia and can't be located.

Is a certified copy of the DNA report admissible against John under Rule 803(8)? (10)

Is the certified copy of the DNA report admissible against John under the confrontation clause? (10)

Question 4: (30 points) Sam claims to have accepted an offer to sell to John industrial cleaners by signing and mailing back to John one of two copies of a purchase order previously signed by John. The second copy was retained by Sam for his files. John claims to never have received the document. The offer to purchase itself provides that the contract is complete upon receipt by the offerer of an executed copy of the offer. Sam also made a copy of the fully executed contract prior to mailing it back to John.

a. How many originals are there, if any?

b. How many duplicates are there, if any?

c. May Sam introduce the duplicate in place of the original under Rule 1003?

d. Are all the originals unavailable?

e. Can or must Sam establish that he mailed a fully executed contract through his testimony in court?

f. Can or must Sam establish the existence of a fully executed contract by introducing the copy he claims he made prior to mailing?

Question 5: (20 points) Irwin Stuckey is arrested and charged in a drug importation conspiracy. When the police search Irwin's apartment, they find a document bearing the letterhead Budget Rent A Car, Bogota, Colombia, the dates March 4–7, 2001, and the printed name Irwin Stuckey as the lessee of the car. Only what appears to be the first page of the rental agreement is found, i.e., the document does not bear a signature. As the prosecutor, how would you go about authenticating the document? Consider all possibilities.

EXAM 7—QUESTIONS

Question 1: (40 points) Harry is charged with robbery and sexual assault of Brenda. He is alleged to have followed Brenda home to her apartment and pushed her inside when she opened the door. At the time he was wearing a plain blue ski mask. After pushing her inside, he pushed her down into a chair and tied her up with rope he found in the kitchen. He gags her with a handkerchief he found in the bedroom. After burglarizing the house, he reached over her shoulder and fondled her breasts through her clothing before exiting the apartment through the front door. As he is exiting the apartment he removes his ski mask. Brenda at a line-up identifies Harry telling the police she saw his face through a mirror at the end of the room near the door. Another woman, Sybil, had earlier reported a robbery and sexual assault as well. She says that she noticed a man following her from the mall and can identify that man as Harry. As she entered her apartment, a man she assumes is Harry, wearing a green ski mask, pushes her into her apartment. He drags her into the bedroom and ties her with the bed sheets and pillowcases. He does not gag her. He then robs the apartment. Prior to leaving he pulls down her pants off from the bottom. He does not touch her. Harry has a conviction for exposing himself in public and an arrest for fondling the penis of a 4 year old boy.

Discuss the admissibility under Rule 404(b) and Rules 413 and 414 of the other crimes, wrongs, or acts evidence as set forth above.

Question 2: (20 points) Prior to trial defense counsel makes a motion in limine asserting that the rifle found in the defendant's apartment along with a handgun which was similar to the handgun a witness testified was employed in a purse snatching not be admitted at trial. The trial court in denying the motion filed an order stating, "Motion denied." At trial, the rifle is admitted into evidence. Defense counsel does not object.

a) Discuss fully all of the grounds for the motion in limine that support exclusion of the rifle.

b) Discuss whether defense council has preserved error for appeal with respect to the admissibility of the rifle.

Question 3: (40 points) Betty was in her college history class when a man runs into the room. He grabs the teacher's purse from her shoulder as she enters the classroom and flees. The man was wearing a stocking over his face. He appeared to be about 5'10", 160 lbs., mid-twenties in age. Betty says that she saw him pull the stocking cap off once he ran out of the room. She says he had long black hair in a ponytail. None of the other students were able to observe the perpetrator when he left the room because of where they were seated in relation to the door.

The police arrest Harry for the purse theft. He has two arrests but no convictions for purse snatching. In each of the instances, he was alleged to have come up from behind a woman, grabbed her purse off her shoulder, and run away. The two prior victims each said the man was wearing a stocking mask and that he pulled it off as he ran away revealing a ponytail.

a) Betty will testify that while seats are not assigned in her history class she always sat in the front row near the windows opposite the door to the classroom. Is her testimony admissible? Is Sally's testimony that Betty always occupies the foregoing seat admissible? Betty is Sally's history classmate.

b) Are the two arrest reports admissible as other crimes, wrongs, or acts evidence against Harry under Rule 404(b)? If so, for what purpose(s) other than to prove character for conformity? Is the testimony of the two prior victims admissible against Harry? If so, for what purpose(s) other than to prove character for conformity?

Question 4: (20 points) Jim calls 911 on the telephone and says, "Dennis is after me with a knife. Send help!!!" When the police arrive Dennis is found stabbed to death. Is the 911 tape admissible as an excited utterance under Rule 803(2)? If not, why not? Is the 911 tape admissible under the confrontation clause? If not, why not?

SPECIFIC SUBJECT MATTTER ESSAY ANSWERS

ARTICLE I
GENERAL PROVISIONS

Preliminary Questions of Admissibility

Answer:

(a) The question of qualifications of an expert is a matter to be decided solely by the court pursuant to Rule 104(a). Since the weight to be assigned by the jury to the expert's testimony is in part dependent upon the jury's assessment of the witness' qualifications, the process of qualification of the expert witness and voir dire, if any, directed solely to qualification by opposing counsel, is ordinarily conducted in the presence of the jury.

(b) An expert witness' opinion is speculative and conjectural if the expert's testimony is not based upon sufficient facts, data, or opinions, Rule 702(1), admitted into evidence or reasonably relied upon by experts in the particular field, Rule 703. The trial judge, Rule 104(a), decides whether a sufficient basis for the expert's particular opinion exists.

(c) Under *Daubert/Kumho/*Rule 702(2), the trial judge, Rule 104(a), must decide whether sufficient assurances of correctness are present with respect to the particular explanative theory being espoused by the expert to warrant jury acceptance, i.e., the expert's testimony is the product of reliable principles and methods, Rule 702(2).

(d) The absence of testing is a component of determining whether the expert's testimony is the product of reliable principles and methods, Rule 702(2), and is thus a Rule 104(a) determination to be made solely by the trial court.

The ultimate weight, if any, to be given to an expert's opinion is a jury decision.

Answer: In determining whether Lori is competent to testify, the proponent of her testimony must introduce evidence sufficient to support a finding that the witness has personal knowledge of the matter related, i.e., the lady was in the crosswalk facing a green crosswalk sign when struck by the car, Rule 602. Rule 602 is a specific application of Rule 104(b). Lori may testify if a reasonable jury viewing all the evidence in support most favorably to Lori can find that it is more probably true than not true that Lori was on the big kid's swing in the school playground at the time of the accident, that from the top of her swing she had an opportunity to observe the accident, that Lori did observe the accident, that she recorded such observation in her mind, that she recalls the event observed accurately at the time of trial, and that Lori is communicating such observation in a manner that the jury is capable of understanding. In support of this finding is Lori's testimony itself. Rule 602 states that evidence to prove personal knowledge may, but need not, consist of the witness' own testimony. In addition the school crossing guard will testify that Lori was in fact on the swing when the accident happened. In addition, there will be other evidence offered at trial describing the intersection where the accident occurred and its relationship to the swing in the playground. Together the foregoing satisfies Rule 602. Lori's prior consistent statement is inadmissible in the first instance under Rule 801(d)(1)(B). Since only admissible evidence may be considered in making a Rule 602 (Rule 104(b)) determination, it may not be considered by the court in deciding whether sufficient evidence of personal knowledge has been offered to permit Lori to testify. Whether Lori's prior consistent statement becomes admissible later in the trial is dependent upon the cross-examination of Lori's by Bob's attorney, i.e., whether an express or implied charge of recent fabrication or improper influence or motive is made.

Motions in Limine

Answer: Robert's counsel should bring a motion in limine seeking an order declaring that the computer animation will be admitted at trial upon the foundation presented at the motion in limine being presented at trial. Robert's counsel is going to have to disclose the existence of the computer animation shortly in any event. While the making of a permissive motion of limine is unlikely to be successful in light of the substantial nature of the foundation required for its admissibility, thus in reality, requiring that plaintiff's case in chief at trial be virtually presented twice, the motion in limine will serve a very useful purpose in educating the trial judge about the computer animation as well as plaintiff's theory of the case. While the motion in limine will similarly educate opposing counsel, presentation of the computer animation during discovery will do likewise. Finally, if the computer animation is persuasive, the process of moving in limine for admission of the computer animation at trial may foster settlement. If, as is to be expected, the trial judge declines to rule on the motion in advance of trial, i.e., a "definitive ruling" is not made, Robert's counsel must of course offer the computer animation, as Robert's counsel most certainly will, at trial to preserve error for appeal, Rule 103(a).

Door Opening

Answer: Overrule the objection. The "door" has been opened both to cross-examination and the introduction of extrinsic evidence as to Butch previously possessing a gun. A statement by the criminal defendant as to never having done something is clearly the most common door opening event. The accused is bolstering his character, in the case of Butch his character for peacefulness, by asserting that he has never handled a gun. While an objection on the basis that Butch's declaration is inadmissible evidence of character would be sustained, the jury will have heard his protestation—an instruction to the jury to disregard will itself be disregarded. Once the accused sets the boundaries by overstepping and making a "never" statement, the trial court after considering the trial concerns denominated in Rule 403 against the probative value of cross-examination and extrinsic evidence to impeach the accused's "never" statement, will almost invariably permit the prosecution to cross-examine and introduce extrinsic evidence. Thus, here one would expect the trial judge to permit Butch to be asked on cross-examination about the illegal possession of a gun in Oakland, California, in 1998 and to permit extrinsic evidence if Butch denies the truth of the matters asserted in the cross-examiner's questions. While the question should not include the word "illegally", such niceties are frequently not observed when the cross-examiner is permitted to enter through the door opened by the accused. On the other hand, if Butch were to deny possession of the gun, the police officer to make his testimony understandable to the jury should be permitted to disclose that he arrested Butch for illegal possession of a firearm.

Curative, Cautionary and Limiting Instructions

Answer:

(a) Introduction of Ringo's confession made to the police following his arrest stating that George stuck up the liquor store while he, Ringo, stayed in the car is error under *Bruton* and its progeny, *Williamson* and *Lilly* and plain error under *Young*. Under the facts of the problem, neither a motion to strike accompanied by an instruction to disregard (curative instruction), nor a cautionary and/or limiting instruction, would have been effective to undue the harm. A mistrial should be declared.

(b) Since Mary gave relevant testimony describing generally the events of the robbery and more importantly specifically describing the getaway car, Mary was not called by the prosecution for the "primary purpose" as a "mere subterfuge" to place her prior inconsistent statements before the jury. Accordingly under Rule 607 Mary may be impeached with her prior inconsistent statement to the police. Since the prior inconsistent statement is hearsay not falling with any not hearsay definition, Rules 801(d)(1) and (2), and not meeting the requirements of any hearsay exception, Rules 803, 804, and 807, the prior inconsistent statement is admissible solely to impeach. Under such circumstances, the trial court, pursuant to Rule 105, upon request, must give the jury a cautionary and/or limiting instruction restricting the evidence to its proper scope. Failure on the part of the trial curt on its own to give a cautionary or limiting instruction to the jury with respect to a prior inconsistent statement admissible solely to impeach is plain error, where, such as in the problem at hand, the government's case is weak and the statement extremely damaging if considered by the jury as substantive evidence. [Note: Is there any significance in the fact that Mary testifies on direct examination to not recalling a tattoo or a ponytail? The fact Mary doesn't recall something as obvious as a red ponytail or a tattoo may be interpreted by the trier of fact as evidence that the perpetrator of the crime did not possess said characteristics. Under the totality of the circumstances, impeachment by means of a prior inconsistent statement seems proper.]

Admissibility of Related Writings, Recordings and Oral Statements

Answer: When Mary's counsel offers that portion of Matthew's e-mail in which he states that Mary may keep the engagement ring, Matthew's attorney may invoke Rule 106 to make Mary's counsel introduce at that time the remaining part of the same writing conditioning his agreement with respect to the engagement ring on Mary returning his grandmother's broach. Clearly the remaining part of the e-mail "ought in fairness be considered contemporaneously with" the portion offered by Mary's counsel, Rule 106. Once Matthew's counsel has caused Mary's counsel to offer that part of the original e-mail that conditioned the concession on the engagement ring upon return of the broach, Mary's counsel should be permitted to introduce Mary's e-mail in response under Rule 106 to the extent it deals with the broach in that that portion of her e-mail is another writing which ought in fairness be considered contemporaneously. That's it. Oral statements are not encompassed within Rule 106. Thus both parties may proceed to introduce their version of the oral communication that followed the initial exchange of e-mails as each sees fit, in accordance with the rules of evidence.

ARTICLE II
JUDICIAL NOTICE

Adjudicative Facts

Answer: Rule 201 governing the judicial notice of adjudicative facts provides that for an adjudicative fact to be judicially noticed it must be one not subject to reasonable dispute in that it is either (1) generally known within the territorial jurisdiction of the trial court or (2) capable of accurate and ready determination by resort to sources whose accuracy cannot reasonably be questioned. The fact that a three month old Mercedes 500 SL convertible is worth over $10,000 is both generally known in many if not all territorial jurisdictions and is certainly capable of accurate and ready determination by resort to sources whose accuracy cannot reasonably be questioned. Here the trial judge simply stated that he personally knows that the car is worth much more than $10,000. The trial judge's personal knowledge, however, is not a permitted basis upon which judicial notice may be taken. Moreover, the trial judge improperly instructed to jury in a criminal case to accept as conclusive the fact judicially noticed, i.e., that the 500 SL Mercedes convertible was valued in excess of $10,000. Consistent with the concept that a directed verdict may not be entered against the accused and its functional equivalent, an instruction by the trial court to the jury to accept a given fact as having been conclusively established, may not be given against the accused, Rule 201(g) provides that in a criminal case, the court shall instruct the jury that it may, but is not required to, accept as conclusive any fact judicially noticed.

ARTICLE III
PRESUMPTIONS IN CIVIL ACTIONS AND PROCEEDINGS

Presumptions in Civil Cases

Answer: A presumption may be defined as a rule of law which requires that the existence of a fact (presumed fact) be taken as established when another fact or other facts (basic facts) are established, unless and until a certain specified condition is fulfilled. Two basic approaches to defining unless and until are in contention. The first approach, known as the Thayer "bursting bubble" theory of presumptions, provides that when the basic facts (A) are established, the presumed fact (B) must be taken as established unless and until the opponent introduces evidence sufficient to support a finding by a reasonable trier of fact of the nonexistence of the presumed fact. The burden of production is shifted to the opposing party. Upon introduction of such evidence the presumption is overcome and disappears, without regard to whether the evidence is actually believed. The second approach in contention, known as the Morgan shifting burden of persuasion theory of presumptions, provides that if the basic facts (A) are established, the jury is instructed that it must find the presumed fact (B) unless and until the opponent persuades the trier of fact that the nonexistence of fact (B) is more probably true than not true. Pursuant to the Morgan approach, application of a presumption shifts both the burden of production and the burden of persuasion to the opposing party. Backers of the Morgan approach assert that the Thayer "bursting bubble" approach affords too slight an effect on presumptions. They stress that presumptions rest upon the same considerations of caution, convenience, policy, fairness, and probability which govern the allocation of the elements of the case originally and are an aspect of allocation working within the larger framework of the elements of the case.

A presumption operates with respect to the mailing of a letter that if the basic facts are established, i.e., documents in properly addressed envelope with proper postage placed in proper mail depository possessing proper return address is not returned, it is presumed that the letter was received unless and until the party to whom the letter was mailed rebuts the presumption. Under the Rule 301 Thayer theory, the burden of producing evidence is shifted to Y if the trier of fact finds that the letter was mailed, etc. Y must satisfy the burden of production to avoid a directed verdict. Y thus must produce evidence which when viewed most favorably to Y is sufficient to support a finding by a reasonable trier of fact that the nonexistence of the presumed fact is more probably true than not true, i.e., evidence demonstrating that he did not receive the letter. Upon production of such evidence (for example, testimony by Y to that effect), the procedural effect of the presumption is completely extinguished, "the bubble has burst." Any natural inference from mailing to receipt remains to be considered by the trier of fact.

The Morgan theory not only places the burden of production but also the burden of persuasion upon Y. Not only would establishing mailing of the letter, etc., require Y to produce evidence sufficient to support a finding by a reasonable trier of fact of the nonexistence of the presumed fact, i.e., receipt of the letter, but it would also require Y to persuade the trier of fact that it is more probably true than not that Y didn't receive the letter. Thus the procedural effect of the presumption does not "burst" upon the introduction of the contrary evidence sufficient to support a finding. The procedural effect of the presumption continues and places the burden of persuasion upon Y.

Presumptions in Criminal Cases

Answer: A presumption in a criminal case operates merely as an instructed inference advising the jury that they may but are not required to draw a certain inference. Here the jury would be instructed that if they find beyond a reasonable doubt that the television sets were stolen, that they may but are not required to infer that the television sets were possessed by the accused with knowledge that they were stolen. The jury would be instructed in addition that if they draw such an inference, then they are to consider that inference with all the other evidence in the case in deciding whether the government has convinced them beyond a reasonable doubt that the accused possessed the television sets with knowledge that they were stolen.

ARTICLE IV
RELEVANCY AND ITS LIMITS

Relevance

Answer:

1. Relevant circumstantial evidence. Possession of a criminal attorney's business card is evidence of consciousness of guilt.

2. Relevant circumstantial evidence. At a minimum the adult movie ticket stub (assuming the movie house does not cater to a gay clientele) tends to establish that the possessor is interested in heterosexual sex outside of a monogamous relationship.

3. Irrelevant circumstantial evidence. Although the evidence does tend to establish consent by the eleven year old to sexual activity, the law states that consent is not a defense, i.e., consent is not an ultimate fact constituting a material proposition that is an element of the criminal offense. Thus, the evidence does not have any tendency to establish a fact of consequences.

4. Irrelevant circumstantial evidence. If the complaint had alleged negligent performance of the surgery, the evidence of drunkenness would have been relevant circumstantial evidence. However, drunkenness at the time of surgery does not tend to establish that earlier in time an improper diagnosis was made. Once again, the evidence does not tend to establish an ultimate fact, material proposition, and thus does not tend to establish a fact of consequence.

5. Relevant circumstantial. The fact that the defendant possessed a New York Yankees jacket similar to the one worn by the man robbing the store is clearly relevant. Evidence of possession of the jacket satisfies the requirement of "any tendency" to establish a fact of consequence.

Exclusion of Relevant Evidence

Answer: Despite their gruesomeness and potential unfair prejudicial effect on the jury, Rule 403, relevant photographs will almost always be found admissible where they, for example, tend to prove the manner and cause of death, the nature, number, extent, and location of the wounds, the manner in which they were inflicted, the amount of force used, the position, condition, and location of the body, the willfulness of the act in question, to corroborate a defendant's confession, or to aid in understanding and to corroborate the testimony of a pathologist or other witness.

Notice that the gruesomeness was caused by the perpetrator of the crime. If the gruesomeness was caused by an autopsy procedure itself, it is more likely that the photograph will be excluded in light of its relatively slight probative value.

The defendant will argue that the jury will be shocked, horrified, disgusted, etc., by the photographs of the amputated testicles of the victim stuffed in his mouth and will want to punish someone. The only person available to punish is the defendant. The prosecution will argue that the photographs are relevant and that the jury is capable of employing the photographs solely for such purposes. Moreover, the prosecution will argue that even if the jury might react emotionally to the gruesomeness of the photographs, the jury fully understands that the photographs themselves are not relevant in determining whether it was the defendant who committed the dastardly acts. In short, the jury can compartmentalize any emotional reaction and thus separate out any emotional reaction from the question of who committed the offense, i.e., they will not take it out upon the accused.

Applying the approach suggested by Weinstein's Evidence, i.e., giving the evidence its maximum reasonable force and the minimum reasonable prejudicial value, gruesome photographs are universally admitted. Any other constriction would mean that the more gruesome the crime, the greater the difficulty the prosecution would have in proving its case.

With respect to the defendant's offer to stipulate to the cause of death and to the dismemberment, even assuming that the stipulation covers all purposes for which the photographic evidence is relevant, following *Old Chief* it is extremely unlikely that the trial court will exclude the evidence in response to the defendant's argument of reduced incremental probative value. The traditional arguments against reduced incremental probative value resulting from a willingness to stipulate, i.e., "right to prove one's own case" and "moral weight of the evidence" have been reinforced by *Old Chief*:

> In sum, the accepted rule that the prosecution is entitled to prove its case free from any defendant's option to stipulate the evidence away rests on good sense. A syllogism is not a story, and a naked proposition in a courtroom may be no match for the robust evidence that would be used to prove it. People who hear a story interrupted by gaps of abstraction may be puzzled at the missing chapters, and jurors asked to rest a momentous decision on the story's truth can feel put upon at being asked to take responsibility know that more could be said than they have heard. A convincing tale can be told with economy, but when economy becomes a break in the natural sequence of narrative evidence, an assurance that the missing link is really there is never more than second best.

Answers:

(a)

1. Relevant circumstantial evidence, admissible. Tends to establish capacity, proficiency, inclination, and proximity. Would not be excluded under Rule 403 as does not raise danger of unfair prejudice or any other Rule 403 concern.

2. Relevant direct evidence, admissible. Walking bicycle in crosswalk is ultimate fact establishing material proposition, i.e., fact of consequence, that John was not negligent. There is no real Rule 403 issue.

3. Relevant circumstantial evidence, admissible. Shows capacity, proficiency, and inclination. There is no real Rule 403 issue.

4. Relevant circumstantial evidence, inadmissible. Shows a character for being uncareful which is barred by Rule 404(a).

Given the way the accident occurred, absence of a "rear" reflector is not relevant for any other purpose.

5. Relevant circumstantial evidence, admissible. Has tendency to establish that Mr. Smith may have been speeding at the time of accident. If offered to show character for carelessness, the specific instance of conduct, i.e., speeding, would be barred by Rules 404(a) and 404(b). There is no real Rule 403 issue.

6. Relevant circumstantial evidence, admissible. Failure to wear glasses is relevant by bringing into question Mr. Smith's capacity to acquire the personal knowledge, Rule 602, testified to on the witness stand. There is no real Rule 403 issue.

7. Relevant circumstantial evidence, admissible. Permissible introductory background evidence offered as an aid to understanding. There is no real Rule 403 issue.

8. Relevant circumstantial evidence, admissible. The fact the children were fighting tends to establish that Mr. Smith may have been distracted at the moment of the accident bringing into question the weight to be given to his testimony. There is no real Rule 403 issue.

9. Irrelevant circumstantial evidence, inadmissible. The fact John has red hair does not make it more or less probable he did a wheelie off the curb in front of an oncoming car. The law will not recognize an argument that red headed people are more fiery and emotional and thus more likely to act negligently.

10. Relevant circumstantial evidence, inadmissible. The evidence is relevant even though the inference cuts both ways. A person with insurance is arguably more prudent and thus a more careful driver. On the other hand, a person with insurance has less to lose and is thus less likely to be careful. The evidence would be excluded under Rule 403 on the grounds of unfair prejudice and must be excluded in any event under Rule 411.

(b)

1. Exclude on objection of unfair prejudice and misleading. The evidence of three beers two and one half hours earlier standing alone lacks sufficient probative value when considered in light of the possibility of the jury concluding that he was intoxicated at the time of the accident. Moreover, certain people just do not like people who drink much less people who drink and drive. Not all courts would, however, reach the same conclusion, i.e., it is a decision within the discretion of the trial court.

2. Exclude on objection of unfair prejudice and misleading. This evidence possesses incredibly slight probative value in tending to establish that Mr. Brown was driving while impaired by alcohol at the time of the accident. The danger of the jury overvaluing the evidence is significant as is the risk of unfair prejudice in the sense of a negative emotional reaction to a drunk driver. Evidence of the arrest is an inadmissible opinion in any event. Evidence would have to be offered on personal knowledge that Mr. Brown drove while under the influence of alcohol in 2003. Moreover, when offered to show character for intemperance, the evidence is character evidence inadmissible under Rule 404(a) and Rule 404(b).

3. Admit over objection of unfair prejudice. While a member of the jury could hold it against Mr. Brown that he fools around with his secretary, the evidence tends to establish that Mr. Brown was in a hurry and thus possibly speeding and/or that he was inattentive or unprepared having his mind, his hand, and/or his eyes on Mary Jackson.

4. Exclude on objection of unfair prejudice. A prior conviction less than ten years old not involving dishonesty or false statement is admissible to impeach a witness other than the criminal defendant under Rule 609(a) upon application of the Rule 403 standard. It is suggested that the preferred ruling is to exclude. The probative value of a prior conviction in 2006 for burglary in assessing credibility of a witness in a civil case on the basis that violation of a serious law of society makes it more likely that with such a conviction the witness will lie on the

witness stand, is substantially outweighed by the danger of unfair prejudice, i.e., Mr. Brown is a criminal who deserves further punishment. Most but not all trial courts would agree.

5. Admit one picture of each set only over objection of unfair prejudice and the needless presentation of cumulative evidence.

The stipulation is "grudging." The fact that John was struck by the truck does not establish the degree of force involved. The degree of force can be inferred from the picture of the bicycle. The stipulation also does not establish the degree of discomfort experienced by John when in traction. The photograph of John in traction clearly would assist the jury in reaching this determination. The stipulation does not address at all the location of John while lying on the ground after the accident or the pain and suffering experienced at that time. Moreover there is something to be said for letting the jury feel the "moral force" of the evidence and permitting each party to prove his own case. See also quotation from *Old Chief* in the answer to the *Problem* directly supra.

The argument of unfair prejudice fails. The photographs have significant incremental probative value. The danger of unfair prejudice is great only if the court decides that the jury's emotional reaction to the severity of the injuries will result in a desire to make the defendants before them pay and thus in reality alter the burden of proof as to liability. Courts do not find such an argument persuasive.

The arguments of unfair prejudice and needless presentation of cumulative evidence are, however, likely to result in less than all three pictures of John at the accident scene being admitted. The same is true as to the two pictures of the bicycle. Unless each picture depicts something the others do not, it is likely that only one of each will be admitted.

Real and Demonstrative Evidence, Experiments and Views

Answer: With respect to the pictures taken by the local newspaper reporter at the scene, the pictures of Cheryl showing her location and condition are relevant on the issue of fault as well of course on the issue of damages. Pictures of Cheryl, authenticated by the testimony of any person with personal knowledge of the matter depicted (the photographer is not required) that the photographs fairly and accurately represent the scene of the accident at the relevant time, i.e., when all the items involved have come to rest, are admissible subject to Rule 403. If evidence is admitted that the photographs although taken a few minutes after the accident fairly and accurately represent the accident scene except for the fact that Cheryl's car had been moved backward ten feet, since the jury will not likely be misled once this change is explained, the photograph showing the general scene including Cheryl's car will be admitted over a Rule 403 objection. Rule 403 will not serve to exclude any pictures of Cheryl's leg even if her leg appears obviously broken. Gruesome if otherwise relevant photographs of personal injuries resulting from an accident will be admitted over a Rule 403 unfair prejudice objection—jury will be horrified by what they see and hold it against the defendant in determining liability in spite of instruction not to do so. The only real issue with respect to the photograph taken at the scene of the accident that might lead to exclusion of one or more of the photographs is the presence of blood everywhere. Although the presence of blood may be explained as coming from a broken nose, for which Cheryl is also seeking compensation, the injury turned out to be minor. Whether the presence of so much blood is likely to mislead or unfairly prejudice the jury to the point where exclusion of the photographs is warranted upon application of Rule 403 rests in the discretion of the trial court. Whether Cheryl thought she had a broken nose or something else is relevant in assessing emotional distress damages and thus whether to admit or exclude under Rule 403.

The pictures of Cheryl showing her in a leg device are relevant and admissible over a Rule 403 objection on the question of damages as is, in the court's discretion, the videotape of Cheryl's activities wearing the leg device on a typical day, known as a day in the life film. In determining whether the day in the life film should be admitted not only must the trial curt evaluate its probative value on the issue of damages versus the risk of unfair prejudice, the trial court must assure herself that the film is not in fact assertive conduct by the plaintiff, i.e., voluntary responses, thus making the film hearsay and inadmissible.

The pictures taken of the passenger side of Cheryl's car after it was towed to the repair shop are admissible if an adequate foundation is presented that the condition of the car at the time the pictures were taken fairly and accurately represent the condition of the car when it came to rest at the accident scene—nothing in the process of towing or storage altered the condition of the car depicted in the photographs.

The defendant should be permitted to employ a scale model of the intersection showing the bus shelter with posters, people, the stop sign and both cars provided the defendant introduces evidence sufficient to support a finding as to the actual existence at the scene of the accident of such matters and that their depiction on the scale model fairly and accurately represents such matters. Given the use the defendant intends to make of the scale model, i.e., to illustrate his defense that he could not see the stop sign, the defendant will be required to establish that the scale model extremely accurately represents the scene including being to scale. To help establish the foundation for the scale model (and also the computer animation) the defendant will offer several photographs of the bus shelter and sign taken three months later. These photographs are admissible upon a foundation that they fairly and accurately represent the bus shelter and the stop sign at the relevant time, i.e., the moment of the accident. Anyone with personal knowledge of the bus shelter and the stop sign at the time of the accident may testify; the photographer is not required. Finally, if an adequate foundation as to the bus shelter with posters, people, the stop sign and both cars at the relevant time, a computer animation would be of assistance in determining the defendant's line of sight as he approached the intersection eventually driving through the stop sign and hitting plaintiff's car. The defendant's expert must lay a foundation establishing that the computer animation fairly and accurately depicts the line of sight of the defendant based upon the facts, data, and opinions describing the scene of the accident that the defendant has been able to introduce into evidence. Given what appears to be the scientific, technical, or other specialized knowledge that needs to be brought into play to produce a computer animation allegedly illustrating the defendant's line of sight as he approached the accident, Rule 702 must be complied with. The expert or experts employed by the defendant to produce the computer animation must establish to the satisfaction of the trial court, Rule 104(a), pursuant to Rule 702 the presence of sufficient assurance of correctness, i.e., their testimony is the product of reliable principles and methods, Rule 702(2), reliably applied to the facts of the case, Rule 702(3), to permit the jury to view the computer animation, i.e., that which is displayed fairly and accurately represents what the defendant saw assuming that the facts, data, or opinions presented by the defendant in support, Rule 702(1), are in fact true, accurate, and correct.

Habit and Routine Practice

Answer: Mary's conduct constitutes a habit of an individual admissible to prove that the conduct of Mary was in conformity with such habit on the particular occasion, Rule 406. Habit describes one's regular response to a repeated specific situation to the extent that doing the habitual response becomes semi-automatic and extremely regular. Habit testimony is admissible regardless of whether or not corroborated and regardless of the presence of eyewitnesses, Rule 406. Habit may be established by testimony in the form of an opinion or by specific instance of conduct sufficient in number to warrant a finding that the habit existed. Mary, Alice, and the store clerk at Starbucks may testify to Mary's habit, with the store clerk's testimony being limited to Mary being a regular customer.

Answer: Dr. Jones' conduct constitutes routine practice evidence admissible under Rule 406 to prove that Dr. Jones in fact warned his patient not to combine the prescription drug with any antihistamines. There is sufficient evidence through Dr. Jones and his nurse of an extremely regular semi-automatic response to a repeated specific situation. Testimony in the form of an opinion is admissible to establish routine practice.

Evidence of Character

Answer: Minister Jones may testify in the criminal prosecution as a character witness for John as to the pertinent character trait of peacefulness, Rule 404(a)(1). Minister Jones is sufficiently aware of and may testify as to John's character for peacefulness at the relevant time, here July 4, 2006—the date of the bar fight—in the form of opinion testimony, Rule 405(a). Minister Jones may not testify as to John's character for peacefulness in the civil suit for damages; evidence of character is excluded in civil cases under Rule 404(a) on the basis if an overall assessment of its probative value measured against the trial concerns outlined in Rule 403. In neither the civil or criminal case may Minister Jones testify as to John's conduct as assistant coach of the youth girl's soccer team. Nor may any of the fifteen girls so testify. Rule 405(a) provides that in all cases in which evidence of a trait of character of a person is admissible (which excludes totally civil cases), proof may be by testimony as to reputation or by testimony in the form of an opinion only; specific instances of conduct are not permitted.

If Minister Jones testifies in the criminal case as to John's reputation as to the pertinent character trait of peacefulness at the relevant time of the bar fight, the prosecution is then permitted under Rule 404(a)(1) to introduce reputation or opinion character evidence as to the same pertinent character trait of John to rebut. Thus Sam may be called by the prosecution to testify that John's reputation for peacefulness amongst the coaches was bad if that reputation relates to the relevant time. When reputation testimony is offered, the reputation may be that possessed in the neighborhood in which the person resides or among any group of his associates (church with respect to Minster Jones and youth soccer coaches for Sam). The requirement that the reputation relate to the relevant time, here the date of the bar fight, makes Sam's testimony problematic at best. Sam, if permitted to testify, would be relating John's reputation for peacefulness in 2000 and 2001. Since the bar fight took place in July 2006, a trial court should not permit Sam to testify. What is unquestionable is that Sam may not testify as to specific instances of conduct of John associated with his youth soccer coaching activities. Rule 405(a) provides that in all cases in which evidence of a pertinent trait of character is admissible, proof may be solely by testimony as to reputation or by testimony in the form of an opinion.

At this juncture, it has been determined that John may call Minister Jones to testify as to John's reputation for peacefulness. John has not offered character evidence in the form of reputation or opinion as to the alleged victim, Harold. Thus in the criminal case (in civil cases character evidence to prove conduct in conformity is not admissible) since the accused has not offered evidence of the pertinent trait of character of the alleged victim, the prosecution may not offer character evidence in the form of reputation or opinion testimony of the alleged victim. Rule 404(a)(2) provides that the prosecution may offer evidence as to the pertinent trait of character of the alleged victim solely to rebut such evidence offered by the accused. Thus Alfred may not testify as to Harold's good reputation for peacefulness at the relevant time.

With respect to the prosecution's motion in limine for an order permitting cross-examination of Minister Jones, the only witness who will be permitted to testify as a character witness, Rule 405(a) provides that on cross-examination inquiry is allowable into relevant specific instances of conduct, i.e., relevant to the pertinent character trait of peacefulness. Cross-examination as to whether Minister Jones heard that John was arrested for misappropriating dues associated with the youth soccer program, even assuming a good faith basis as to the underlying act—misappropriation of dues, is not permissible as misappropriation of dues involves dishonesty and not the pertinent trait of peacefulness. Minister Jones may, however, be cross-examined as to the two instances of conduct involving unpeacefulness allegedly witnessed by Sam. Sam, who claims to have personal knowledge of both instances of conduct, provides the prosecution with a good faith basis for inquiry. Whether Minister Jones has heard about John encouraging one of his girls to kick an opposing player and/or has heard about John getting into a shoving match with a parent of one of his players over playing time, may properly be inquired of on cross-examination. Lack of familiarity with such matters or rumors or reports thereof is relevant to an assessment of the basis of the character witness' testimony. Familiarity with such matters or rumors or reports thereof explores the character witness' standard of "goodness" and "badness." Neither instance of conduct is too remote to be inquired about.

Other Crimes, Wrongs or Acts

Answer: Rule 404(b) provides that while evidence of other crimes, wrongs, or acts is not admissible to prove the character of a person in order to show action in conformity therewith, it may, however, be admissible for other purposes, such as proof of motive, opportunity, intent, preparation, plan, knowledge, identity, or absence of mistake or accident. Evidence in the form of testimony by Tim on personal knowledge, i.e., evidence sufficient to support a finding viewed most favorably that the matter is what the proponent claims, Rule 104(b), that he sold Dennis a shimmy bar two days before the car theft is admissible to show plan and preparation from which to infer identity, i.e., Dennis used the shimmy bar to commit the auto theft for which he is on trial. The prior felony conviction for auto theft is not admissible under Rule 404(b) because it is not relevant for a purpose other than the prohibited purpose of being relevant to prove the character of Dennis in order to show action in conformity therewith. Similarly, the testimony on personal knowledge of the police officer that Dennis admitted employing a shimmy bar to open and then steal the car that resulted in the aforementioned prior conviction is not admissible under Rule 404(b). Stealing a car using a shimmy bar is a very common occurrence. It does not come close to being so unusual and distinctive as to be like a signature thus ear marking the two crimes as the handwork of the same person, i.e., evidence of modus operandi to prove identity. Since the prior car theft employing a shimmy is not relevant for a purpose other than proof of character for conformity, the evidence of the prior conviction as well as the police officer's testimony is inadmissible under Rule 404(b).

The prosecution will be permitted to introduce as relevant to knowledge of the presence of the small quantity of crack cocaine and as relevant to intent to possess the small quantity of cocaine in its case in chief evidence of Dennis' prior possession of crack cocaine testified to by a witness with personal knowledge of his possession (evidence of his arrest is inadmissible) and as well as evidence from a witness with personal knowledge of his prior possession of methamphetamine (the prior conviction is hearsay not admissible under the hearsay exception provided in Rule 803(22) for a judgment of previous conviction because the conviction was for a misdemeanor). Similarly the testimony of the witness to the effect that Dennis once showed him marijuana plants growing in the basement of a house Dennis was renting and offered to sell him marijuana at that time will be admitted by the court once again to establish knowledge and intent. Overall, generally speaking evidence of either prior possession of any drug or of prior possession of any drug with intent to distribute will be admitted in a subsequent trial of the same person for possession alone or possession with intent to distribute of the same or any other drug. Where federal courts may fairly be said to show any disagreement is where prior drug possession of let's say a small quantity of marijuana is offered as relevant to knowledge and intent with respect to possession of let's say crack cocaine with an intent to distribute. Even more questionable would be the admissibility of a possession of a small quantity of marijuana in a subsequent prosecution for the manufacturing of a complicated drug with intent to distribute.

Similar Acts and Crimes in Sexual Assault and Child Molestation Cases

Answer: Rule 413 provides that in a criminal case in which the defendant is accused of an offense of sexual assault, evidence of the defendant's commission of another offense or offenses of sexual assault is admissible, and may be considered for its bearing on any matter to which it is relevant. The matter to which such other acts of sexual assault is relevant is to establish a character of the accused for depraved sexual conduct, sometimes called lustful disposition, to show action in conformity therewith. Rule 403 is applicable. Since use to establish character is permitted, the risk of unfair prejudice from the jury employing the evidence of prior instances of sexual assault conduct for an impermissible purpose of drawing the bad man inference, i.e., did it once, did it again, is not present. However the risk of unfair prejudice arising from the jury being horrified by evidence of the accused's prior specific instances of sexual abuse leading to a willingness to convict upon the current charge in partial reliance on another aspect of the bad man inference, i.e., committed other crimes for which he has not been punished, is present. In fact, it has been asserted that unfair prejudice as it operates under Rule 403 as applied to specific instances of conduct otherwise admissible under Rules 413-415 alters the ordinary pattern in that the similarity of the prior specific instance of conduct and the crime currently charged creates less of a risk of unfair prejudice rather than more. In terms of applying Rule 403 to the specific instances of conduct stated in the problem, the defendant's alleged conduct with Unis, i.e., consensual sex including sodomy, constitutes an act of child molestation and is thus not admissible in a prosecution for an offense of sexual assault; Rule 413(a) applies only to another offense of sexual assault. Application of Rule 403 will not result in exclusion of Nina Oppenheimer's testimony as to a similar sexual assault, nor will it likely result in exclusion of the alleged rape by Wilson of his wife ten years ago. The specific instances of conduct involving exposure with an attempt to force one of the two men to perform an act of nonconsensual sexual contact is more problematic particularly if, as expected, two other prior specific instances of sexual assault are determined by the trial court to be admissible. The alleged attempt by Wilson to have a man grab his penis illustrates the problem in applying Rule 403 to Rules 413-415 evidence. If the purpose is, as stated, to admit evidence of sexual depravity and lustful disposition, where if at all should the line be drawn with respect to non similar sexual assaults or offenses of child molestation? Is the touching of the vaginal area of a 12 year old female admissible in a prosecution for sodomy of a 4 year old boy?

Victim's Past Sexual Behavior or Sexual Disposition

Answer: The trial judge should decide that pursuant to Rule 412 the defendant may not inquire as to any of the four items on cross-examination nor offer extrinsic evidence establishing any of the four items. Rule 412(a)(1) bars introduction in any civil or criminal proceeding involving alleged sexual misconduct, subject to stated exceptions that are not applicable, evidence offered to prove any alleged victim engaged in other sexual behavior. Items (1), (2) and (3) are thus inadmissible. Rule 412(a)(2) bars introduction in any civil or criminal proceeding involving alleged sexual misconduct, subject to stated exceptions that are not applicable, evidence offered to prove any alleged victim's sexual predisposition. Item (4) is thus inadmissible.

With respect to evidence of vaginal bruising, Rule 412(b)(1)(A) provides an exception permitting admissibility in a criminal case of evidence of specific instances of sexual behavior of the alleged victim's offered to prove that a person other than the accused was the source of the alleged victim's injury. Thus, if the criminal defendant had been able to locate her sex partner on Friday who was prepared to testify that their consensual sex was rough enough to have caused the bruises later observed, cross-examination and extrinsic evidence of the rough consensual sex on Friday would have been admissible. However, the alleged victim's sex partner on Friday is unidentified and thus not available as a witness. The evidence the defendant is actually capable of introducing is not evidence of a specific instance of conduct that could account for the vaginal bruises but rather evidence of rough sex that could not have caused the vaginal bruises observed offered to show sexual disposition of the alleged victim for the inference that she acted in conformity therewith on Friday night resulting in the vaginal bruises. Such evidence fall outside the Rule 412(b)(1)(A) exception and is thus inadmissible; inquiry on cross-examination and extrinsic evidence are both precluded.

Subsequent Remedial Measures

Answer: Rule 407 provides that when after an injury or harm allegedly caused by an event, measures are taken that, if taken previously, would have made the injury or harm less likely to occur, evidence of the subsequent measures is not admissible to prove negligence, culpable conduct, a defect in a product, a defect in a product's design, or a need for a warning or instruction. Rule 407 does not require the exclusion of evidence of subsequent measures when offered for another purpose, such as proving ownership, control, or feasibility of precautionary measures, if controverted, or impeachment.

a. Replacement of the threshold by the store after the event causing personal injury is a subsequent remedial measure that is not admissible against the store to prove negligence.

b. Installation of the "Be Careful—Step" sign by the mall after the event causing personal injury is a subsequent remedial measure that is not admissible against the mall to prove negligence.

c. Impeachment of store and mall expert witness by reference to the threshold and sign should not be allowed even though Rule 407 states that it does not require exclusion of evidence of subsequent remedial measures when offered for impeachment. Most decisions correctly prohibit impeachment when the evidence introduced by a defendant, here through the two expert witnesses, goes no further than to maintain that nothing improper occurred. This is to prevent the impeachment exception effectively destroying the rule excluding evidence of subsequent remedial measures designed to encourage such measures to be taken. On the other hand, if the evidence offered by the defendant, whether through lay or expert witness testimony or otherwise, goes beyond what is necessary, here not create an unreasonable risk of injury, and asserts that a party's conduct was the "safest", "most reasonable", "best alternative", etc., then impeachment by means of the subsequent remedial measure is in order.

d. Evidence of replacement of the threshold is admissible against the store for the purpose of proving ownership and control under Rule 407 because the store is controverting that it is responsible for maintaining the threshold in a safe condition claiming that responsibility rests solely upon the mall.

Compromise and Offers to Compromise

Answer: Rule 408 provides that evidence of (1) furnishing or offering or promising to furnish, or (2) accepting or offering or promising to accept, a valuable consideration in compromising or attempting to compromise a claim which was disputed as to either validity or amount, is not admissible to prove liability for or invalidity of the claim or its amount. Evidence of conduct or statements made in compromise negotiations is likewise not admissible. Rule 408 does not require the exclusion of any evidence otherwise discoverable merely because it is presented in the course of compromise negotiations. Rule 408 also does not require exclusion when the evidence is offered for another purpose, such as proving bias or prejudice of a witness, negativing a contention of undue delay, or proving an effort to obstruct a criminal investigation or prosecution.

When Harry made his statement that the accident was his fault and that he will pay for damages to Sally's car not covered by insurance he was not disputing either the validity of Sally's claim or the amount of the claim. Thus Rule 408 does not preclude introduction of his statement to prove liability for plaintiff's claim.

Harry's statement presented by his lawyer during the settlement conference that Harry was going 75 m.p.h. at the time of the accident is barred by Rule 408 which provides in sentence two that evidence of statements made in compromise negotiations is not admissible to prove liability for a claim.

With respect to the admissibility of Harry's statement to impeach, Rule 408 precludes admissibility of evidence of a statement made in compromise negotiations when the evidence is offered to impeach through a prior inconsistent statement or contradiction.

As stated Rule 408 would not permit Sally to employ the copy of the laboratory report on the tie rod received by her during compromise negotiations to impeach Harry's expert on cross-examination. The laboratory report having been presented during compromise negotiations is also not admissible as substantive evidence to prove liability for the claim. However, Rule 408 does not require exclusion of any evidence otherwise discoverable merely because it was presented in the course of compromise negotiations. The laboratory report, because it was reviewed prior to trial by an expert witness called to testify by Harry, is discoverable. If the laboratory report is obtained by Sally during discovery, Sally may offer the laboratory report as substantive evidence assuming it is otherwise admissible. It is important to distinguish the situation of a report or other document prepared solely for the purpose of settlement negotiations. Such a report is not otherwise discoverable.

Payment of Medical and Similar Expenses

Answer: Rule 409 provides that evidence of furnishing or offering or promising to pay medical, hospital, or similar expenses occasioned by an injury, is not admissible to prove liability for the injury. No requirement is imposed that there be an actual dispute as to liability or amount at the time of the furnishing or when an offer or promise to pay medical, hospital, or similar expense is made. Statements or conduct not a part of the offer, promise or payment itself are *not* precluded from being introduced into evidence by the provisions of Rule 409. Accordingly, the portion of the manager's statement that promised to pay all the delivery man's hospital bills is inadmissible while that portion of the manager's statement where he stated that he had told the maintenance man twice that morning to clean up the grease spill is admissible.

Inadmissibility of Pleas, Plea Discussions, and Related Statements

Answer: Rule 410 provides that in any civil or criminal proceeding evidence of any statement made in the course of any proceeding under Rule 11 of the Federal Rules of Criminal Procedure controlling the acceptance by the trial court of an accused's plea of guilty, Rule 410(3), and any statement made in the course of plea discussions with an attorney for the prosecuting authority which do not result in a plea of guilty or which result in a plea of guilty later withdrawn, Rule 410(4), are not admissible against the criminal defendants as either substantive evidence or for the purpose of impeachment. Rule 410 applies to statements made by defense counsel on behalf of the accused as well as the accused's own statement. Plea discussions clearly were commenced between the defense attorney on behalf of the accused and an attorney for the prosecuting authority—the defense attorney called and asked to "talk about a deal." The accused thus exhibited an actual subjective expectation to negotiate a plea at the time of the discussion and the accused's expectation that he was entering into plea negotiations was clearly reasonable given the totality of the objective circumstances. Accordingly, neither Mitzi's lawyer's statements to the prosecutor nor Mitzi's statement at the plea hearing are admissible against Mitzi as either substantive evidence or for impeachment in either the subsequent criminal or subsequent civil suit.

Liability Insurance

Answer: Rule 411 provides that evidence that a person was or was not insured against liability is not admissible upon the issue whether the person acted negligently or otherwise wrongfully. Rule 411 does not require the exclusion of evidence of insurance against liability when offered for another purpose, such as proof of agency, ownership, or control, or bias or prejudice of a witness. Evidence that the company included the installer's automobile on the company's liability insurance policy is not admissible upon the issue of whether the installer acted negligently with respect to the automobile accident but is admissible on the issues of agency, ownership, and control with respect to the installer himself.

ARTICLE V
PRIVILEGES

Lawyer-Client

Answer: Harry is age 13. His mom is Harry's representative. Her presence does not destroy confidentiality, Standard 503(b)(4). Sally and Sam are the lawyer's representatives—are employed to assist the lawyer in the rendition of legal services, Standard 503(a)(3). The fact that Sally has been disbarred does not negate the presence of the lawyer-client privilege as Standard 503(a)(2) provides that a lawyer includes anyone reasonably believed by the client to be authorized to practice law. Bob, the expert, is also a representative of the lawyer. However, since Bob is an expert hired to testify, statements made to him are not intended to be confidential—a testifying expert may always be asked to state what he or she was told by the client about the matter at hand. Preparation of Harry for his deposition in the dining room of Harry's home does not fall within the lawyer-client privilege. Harry's father is a representative of Harry. His presence does not defeat confidentiality. If Harry's father was present alone with Jim and Harry, all of Harry's communication would have been protected by the lawyer-client privilege, along with Jim's statements that constitute legal advice or tend to directly or indirectly reveal the substance of his client's confidence at a minimum. However, the presence of Harry's 9 year old brother, known to everyone, indicates a lack of intent that the communications be confidential and thus the lawyer-client privilege does not apply. Even if the lawyer-client privilege had attachment, Harry waived the privilege by his disclosure of the evening's events at show and tell. Standard 511 provides:

> A person upon whom these rules confer a privilege against disclosure of the confidential matter or communication waives the privilege if he or his predecessor while holder of the privilege voluntarily discloses or consents to disclosure of any significant part of the matter or communication. This rule does not apply if the disclosure is itself a privileged communication.

The meeting between Harry and his attorney and John and his attorney as to a matter of common interest, Standard 503(b)(3), also called "joint defense" or "pooled information", results in the statements being made at such a meeting being protected by the lawyer-client privilege not only when sought by third parties but also when desired to be disclosed by any other person participating in the meeting. Thus neither John nor his attorney may testify over objection to any statement made at that meeting by Harry or his attorney and vice versa.

Husband and Wife Privileges

Answer: When Mary observes her husband burying the 7-Eleven bag under the flagstone in the back yard she was married to John. On March 30, when John's criminal trial begins Mary is prepared to testify as to the matters she observed. Since the testimonial husband-wife privilege belongs solely to the testifying spouse in a criminal case, she may testify if she wants to. John may not stop her. Moreover, since her marriage is a sham at that point, Mary could not assert the testimonial husband-wife privilege even if she wanted to. As to the matters told to her by John concerning the loan sharks and the actual robbery of the 7-Eleven, these communications were intended to be confidential and thus are protected by the husband-wife confidential communication privilege. The husband-wife privilege applies in both civil and criminal cases. Both spouses are holders of the privilege. The husband-wife privilege survives the marriage becoming sham or a divorce. Thus John may assert the husband-wife confidential communication privilege to keep Mary from testifying in both the civil and criminal proceedings as to what he told her in confidence. As previously mentioned, the testimonial husband-wife privilege does not apply in a civil case.

ARTICLE VI
WITNESSES

Competency of Lay Witnesses

Answers:

1. Competent. He possesses minimum credibility. His failure to wear his glasses is of course admissible to impeach his credibility and thereby to affect the weight to be assigned by the jury to his testimony.

2. Competent. He possesses minimum credibility. His unusual position claimed to have been assumed while observing the event is relevant in assessing the weight to be assigned by the jury to his testimony.

3. Competent. He possesses minimum credibility. Alcoholism does not make a witness incompetent.

4. Competent. He possesses minimum credibility. Difficulty in recalling events does not make a witness incompetent.

5. Competent. He possesses minimum credibility. Conviction of a crime, even perjury, does not make a witness incompetent.

6. Not competent. A statement that as a truthful man I will tell the truth is neither an oath nor an affirmation. The witness neither declared, promised, nor even stated that he will testify truthfully; his representations thus fall short of being an affirmation.

7. Competent. He possesses minimum credibility. Absolute certainty of observation or recollection is not required. The use of phrases such as "I think", "I believe" or "my best recollection" does not make the testimony given inadmissible.

8. Competent. Rule 603 is satisfied. John has declared by affirmation that he will testify truthfully. Rule 603 does not require that for a witness to be competent he must feel a moral obligation to speak the truth. Nor is a belief in God required. John has adequately communicated that he understands the difference between a lie and the truth and the obligation to tell the truth.

9. Not competent. An attorney may not normally testify as a witness with respect to a significant contested matter in a trial where he represents one of the parties. Extrinsic evidence as to the prior inconsistent statement may be presented by Mr. Smith's attorney only if Mr. Smith's attorney seeks leave to withdraw from the case and is permitted by the court to do so.

10. Not competent. Under Rule 606(b) a juror is incompetent to attack a jury verdict on the grounds that it is a quotient verdict.

Direct Examination; Generally

Answers:

1. Yes. Rather than go through the routine of having a doctor, or other expert witness, state they do not recall followed by review of medical records followed by a question whether the doctor now recalls with respect to each and every minute detail contained in the medical records of a patient, as a matter of customary practice the doctor is permitted to freely consult the medical records of the patient as he or she testifies. In almost all cases the same medical records have been or will be admitted in evidence under the business record hearsay exception, Rule 803(6).

2. Yes. It is not necessary that the document shown to the witness to refresh his or her recollection be prepared by the witness. Any document or other item likely to refresh recollection may be employed, even an item never previously seen by the witness.

3. Yes. Pursuant to Rule 612, with respect to a document employed at trial to refresh a witness' recollection, the adverse

party is entitled to inspect the writing, to cross-examine the witness therein and to introduce in evidence those portions which relate to the testimony of the witness for the jury to consider in evaluating the credibility of the witness. Rule 612 does not make documents employed to refresh recollection admissible when offered by an adverse party as substantive evidence but only for purposes of impeachment.

4. Probably No. For plaintiff's counsel to be able to ask leading questions of the witness without first developing a foundation satisfying the "necessary to develop" requirement of the first sentence of Rule 611(c), plaintiff's counsel will have to convince that trial judge that the witness is hostile in law in that he is identified with an adverse party, Rule 611(c), third sentence. If the co-worker was himself injured in the accident, hostile in law status will clearly not have been shown. Even if the co-worker had not been injured, the mere fact of being a co-worker alone is unlikely to be sufficient to result in a trial judge granting plaintiff counsel's request for a declaration of hostile in law. Whether the co-worker did or did not cooperate with plaintiff's counsel with respect to being interviewed and more importantly with respect to preparing the co-worker to testify at trial are relevant facts. Most likely the trial judge will deny the plaintiff counsel's request but consider the foundation laid by counsel in support of his request for a hostile in law designation in deciding whether leading questions have been shown to be "necessary to develop the witness' testimony" based upon how the witness actually responds to non-leading questions when called to testify at trial.

5. No. The matter inquired of is an undisputed matter constituting background evidence where leading questions are permitted as a matter of customary practice under the rubic of "necessary to develop", Rule 611(c), first sentence.

6. Probably Yes. Plaintiff's counsel must argue that under Rule 615 plaintiff's mother's presence in court while her daughter testifies is essential to the presentation of the party's cause on the grounds that the daughter is in need of a support person in court when she testifies. Given that the plaintiff is fifteen and is the alleged victim of an accident, not a sexual battery, it is doubtful the trial court will grant plaintiff's request. Having the mother testify before the plaintiff makes it more likely that the trial court

will grant plaintiff's request to permit the mother to remain in the courtroom during her daughter's testimony.

7. No. A non natural party, in this case the corporation owning the truck, has a right to designate an officer or employee to remain in the courtroom at all times, Rule 615(2). Presumably the owner is an officer of the corporation even if not an employee.

8. No. A witness' recollection may not be refreshed with a leading question in open court that goes to the heart of a contested matter being presented to the jury.

9. Yes. Even though the question can not be answered "Yes" or "No", the structure of the question clearly suggests to the witness the answer desired by counsel.

10. No. A witness may not be required to present contemporaneously other portions of a conversation. Rule 106 only permits a party under certain circumstances to require contemporaneous presentation of other portions of a writing or recorded statement.

Leading Questions

Answer: Yes. The question to John is clearly a leading question suggesting the answer with respect to a matter of critical importance in the lawsuit. Under the facts as presented, the requisite foundation has not been established to permit leading questions on direct examination as "necessary to develop the witness' testimony" under Rule 611(c), first sentence. A nine year old child may not be lead simply because he is nine years old.

No. Barbara Green, John's mother, may be lead when called to testify by Mr. Smith's attorney. As a witness identified with an adverse party, i.e., her son, the trial court must declare her a hostile in law witness under Rule 611(c), last sentence; interrogation of a hostile in law witness may be by leading questions.

Refreshing Recollection

Answer: With respect to the number of lanes of traffic, a non-critical although relevant subject, John answered definitively "1" rather than said the he didn't recall the number of lanes of traffic in each direction. Whether a witness who answers definitively but in fact incorrectly may have his recollection refreshed is the subject of disagreement in reported decisions. It is sometimes stated that a party may seek to refresh the recollection of a witness only if the witness testifies that his recollection is exhausted and that he can't recall the matter forming the subject of the inquiry. Thus under such authority, if a witness replies in an absolute fashion, for example, that nothing else was said or nothing else happened, refreshment of recollection would not be permitted. However other decisions reach the sensible position that refreshing recollection is proper even if the witness gives a positive albeit unanticipated answer. As McCormick, Evidence § 9 at 37 (5th ed.1999) states, "The witness may believe that she remembers completely but on looking at the memorandum, she would recall additional facts." Counsel can sometimes avoid having to face the issue by incorporating lack of recollection in the question asked, such as "Do you recall whether anything else was said?" Where such a question would be inconvenient as a matter of form or where counsel does not wish to suggest to the jury that the witness has memory problems, counsel must fall back on a general instruction to the witness to respond to questions such as "Was anyone else present?" with the answer, "I don't recall."

The question to John following his testimony that he doesn't recall where Mr. Smith's car was when he first saw it, is objectionable when asked in open court. Counsel is in effect testifying before the jury as to a critical matter in the lawsuit under the guise of refreshing recollection. While it might sometimes be possible to refresh the witness' recollection outside the presence of the jury, on almost all occasions the proper procedure would be to show the witness a document and ask him whether he now recalls the matter he previously said he does not recall. Any document or for that matter any item that might refresh the recollection of the witness may be employed. The document or item used need not have been created by the witness nor even seen by the witness before.

The procedure employed in refreshing the recollection of the witness with a document is improper. The witness must be asked to read the document to himself. After he puts it down, he is then asked, "Do you now recall when you first saw the car driven by Mr. Smith?" It is improper to either read what is contained on the document to the witness in the form of a question as was done in the problem or to have the witness read the document himself to the jury.

The court has discretion to find that the witness' recollection has not been refreshed. However, to so find the court must determine that the witness lacks minimum credibility. As previously discussed, it is rare that a witness will be found by the court to lack minimum credibility.

It is worth emphasizing that *any* document may be employed to refresh recollection. If counsel was so brash, he could write on a piece of paper, "You idiot, I told you twenty times that John was also present." The tactical deficiencies of such an attempt to refresh recollection are highlighted by the specific provisions of Rule 612 dealing with opposing counsel's rights with respect to any document used by a witness at trial to refresh recollection.

One way to avoid the problem of refreshment of recollection before testifying is simply not to permit a witness to read any document that is not already in the possession of the adversary. Information contained in documents not in the possession of the adversary can be stated orally by counsel to the witness to refresh his recollection as part of the process of witness preparation. Since the witness will not have used the document itself to refresh his recollection, Rule 612 is inapplicable.

Cross Examination

Answer: Whenever a party calls a witness to testify it is direct examination. Of course, if the witness called is the adverse party or a witness identified with an adverse party such as the train engineer, the witness may be asked leading questions by the examining attorney, Rule 611 (c), third sentence, here plaintiff's attorney. When counsel for the railroad stands to examine the train engineer, it is cross-examination. Whenever the attorney for a party who is adverse to the party calling the witness to testify examines the witness, it is cross-examination. Cross-examination under such circumstances is in the nature of re-direct. Rule 611(c) provides that leading questions "ordinarily" should be permitted on cross-examination.

The two situations where leading questions should ordinarily not be permitted on cross-examination are where the court, in its discretion, permits inquiry on cross-examination into matters beyond the subject matter of direct examination, Rule 611(b) second sentence, and where cross-examination is of a witness who when called by the opposing party was a hostile witness, an adverse party, or a witness identified with an adverse party where direct examination may be by leading questions, Rule 611(c), third sentence. Since in the later situation as applied to the problem counsel for the railroad will be cross-examining an employee of the railroad leading questions are not permitted unless necessary to develop the witness' testimony.

Defense counsel must limit his examination to the deliberately very narrow scope of direct examination, i.e., the speed of the train and the speed limit for the train at the scene of the accident. All other matters within the personal knowledge of the train engineer fall outside the scope of direct examination. The trial court should not permit examination in the nature of direct examination beyond the scope of direct examination during cross-examination, Rule 611(b), second sentence, but should rather simply permit the railroad to recall the train engineer during its case in chief to obtain whatever additional testimony as to the accident is desired.

Impeachment; Generally

Answer: With respect to each of the seven questions that defense counsel desires to ask of Mary on cross-examination for the purpose of affecting the credibility of the witness, i.e., impeachment, the trial court must decide first whether the question may be asked and if so second whether extrinsic evidence, i.e., evidence offered other than through the witness herself, will be permitted and possibly even required. With respect to each and every question, since the cross-examiner desires to state an impeaching fact in each question, a good faith basis must be possessed by examining counsel as to the truth of underlying matter contained in each question. Innuendoes and insinuations of inadmissible or nonexistent matters are improper. Note that the requirement of a good faith basis applies only when the cross-examiner is effectively asserting in the form of a question the truth of a factual statement included within the question. If the cross-examiner is merely inquiring generally whether something is or is not true, a good faith basis is not required. Thus the question, "Your glasses were being repaired at the time of the accident, weren't they?" requires a good faith basis, while the question, "Were you wearing your glasses at the time of the accident?" does not. The principle of a good faith basis applies not only to questions challenging personal knowledge but to all modes of impeachment including the laying of a foundation for impeachment by means of a prior inconsistent statement. Moreover, with respect to prior inconsistent statement impeachment, the examining party must have the intent and ability to introduce extrinsic evidence establishing the making of the prior inconsistent statement as to a non-collateral matter in the event the making of the statement is not admitted by the witness. Assuming the presence of a good faith basis and the ability to introduce extrinsic evidence with respect to impeachment with any inconsistent statement bearing upon a non-collateral matter if the witness denies making the inconsistent statement, the trial court should rule as follows:

(1) Mental illness is a proper subject of inquiry. Cross-examination concerning hallucinations is relevant in assessing the acquisition of personal knowledge. Personal knowledge is a non-collateral matter; extrinsic evidence may be introduced.

(2) Even with a good faith basis that Mary is actually an alcoholic (not that she is rumored at work to be an alcoholic) most courts would not permit cross-examination. Alcoholism, as opposed to use of alcohol at the time of the event perceived or at trial, is generally not considered to be sufficiently probative in light of Rule 403 trial concerns to be admitted to attack personal knowledge.

(3) No glasses goes to the acquisition of personal knowledge. Cross-examination is thus proper. Personal knowledge is a non-collateral matter; extrinsic evidence may be introduced.

(4) Physical incapacity constitutes an injury and is thus an ultimate fact of consequence in determining damages. Cross-examination as to this non-collateral matter is proper as is extrinsic evidence in the form of contradiction or self-contradiction. If self-contradiction, i.e., prior inconsistent statement, extrinsic evidence establishing the making of the statement relating to a non-collateral matter must, not may, be introduced.

(5) Firing by an opposing party is relevant to establish bias. Bias is a non-collateral matter; extrinsic evidence may be introduced.

(6) Falsification of time records constitutes specific instances of conduct probative of untruthfulness, i.e., involves dishonesty or falsification—some element of active misrepresentation. Rule 608(b)(1) permits cross-examination but not the introduction of extrinsic proof; the matter is collateral.

(7) With respect to the prior inconsistent statement, all matters related are the proper subject of cross-examination. Prior inconsistent statements evidencing inconsistency of belief, blowing hot and cold, are relevant in assessing the weight to be given to the witnesses in court testimony. Prior inconsistent statement impeachment may be employed to attack any or all of the testimonial risks of perception, recordation and recollection, narration and sincerity. The distance at which she was standing and the weather at the time are related to personal knowledge, a non-collateral matter; extrinsic evidence may but need not be introduced. What Mary was wearing is a collateral matter relevant solely for purposes of contradiction; extrinsic evidence may not be introduced. Whether the light and bell signal were operating at the time of the accident is a matter relevant in the litigation for a purpose other than contradiction and is thus non-collateral. Whether the light and bell signal were working tends to directly establish a fact of consequence in the litigation. When a witness is impeached with a prior inconsistent statement bearing on a non-collateral matter, extrinsic evidence establishing the prior inconsistent statement must, not may, be introduced whenever the witness fails to admit making the prior inconsistent statement.

Prior Inconsistent Statements

Answer: The defense counsel need not show Mildred her written statement prior to any questions being asked. Rule 613(a) specifically abolishes whatever was left of such a common law requirement emanating from Queen Caroline's Case (Eng.1820). Rule 613(a) provides that in examining a witness concerning a prior statement made by the witness, whether written or not, the statement need not be shown nor its contents disclosed to the witness at that time, but on request the same shall be shown or disclosed to opposing counsel. Mildred is alleged to have stated to the defense investigation that she was walking home from work, not standing on the corner waiting for a friend. Cross-examination relates to the acquisition of personal knowledge as one is more likely to accurately observe and record surroundings while standing on a corner waiting than while walking home. Personal knowledge is a non-collateral matter; extrinsic proof is permitted but not required. The prior inconsistent statement allegedly made by Mildred as to the age of the perpetrator and that she was not sure what he was wearing concern a subject matter that circumstantially tends to establish a fact of consequence, i.e., identity. Recollection while testifying on direct examination as to clothing worn by the perpetrator is inconsistent with a prior statement by Mildred stating that she was not sure what he was wearing. Memory does not get better with time. The subject matter of the prior inconsistent statement, i.e., age and appearance bearing upon identity, is non-collateral, i.e. relevant for a purpose other than mere contradiction; extrinsic evidence is required, not merely permitted if Mildred fails to admit making the prior inconsistent statement on cross-examination. Failure to mention the plastic bag bearing the logo of the convenience store in a prior statement when it certainly would have been natural to do so is clearly inconsistent with trial testimony to that effect. A prior statement that the knife was thrown down a sewer is clearly inconsistent with in court testimony that the perpetrator threw the knife in a dumpster. The prior inconsistent statements concerning the plastic bag bearing the logo and concerning the knife also relate to a non-collateral matter; extrinsic evidence is required if Mildred fails to admit making the prior statement. Finally, a prior statement by Mildred that she was 60 to 100 feet away is marginally inconsistent when juxtaposed to her in court testimony of being

80 feet away, probably in the discretion of the trial court inconsistent enough upon application of the liberal test of inconsistency employed in the federal courts. The prior inconsistent statement as to distance when perceiving the event bears upon personal knowledge; it is thus treated the same as the prior statement that Mildred was walking home after work rather than standing on the corner waiting for a friend, i.e., extrinsic evidence may but is not required to be introduced if Mildred fails to admit making the prior statement. The foundation presented in the form of the question "Did you ever tell anyone else that the knife was thrown somewhere other than the dumpster," fails to satisfy the common law foundation requirement that before extrinsic evidence may be introduced on a non-collateral matter as to the existence of a prior inconsistent statement, the cross-examiner must direct the witness to the time, place, and circumstances of the statement, often called "persons present," along with the content of the statement. However, Rule 613(b) does not mandate that the traditional common law foundation be laid on cross-examination. Rule 613(b) provides extrinsic evidence of a prior inconsistent statement by a witness is not admissible unless the witness is afforded an opportunity at some time to explain or deny the same and the opposite party is afforded an opportunity to interrogate the witness thereon, or the interests of justice otherwise require. It is thus proper under Rule 613(b) for defense counsel to introduce in the defense case in chief through the investigator the written prior inconsistent statement of Mildred, provided Mildred remains under subpoena thus providing the prosecution, if it chooses, the opportunity to recall Mildred to provide her with an opportunity to admit, deny and/or explain with respect to the alleged prior inconsistent statement.

Contradiction by Other Evidence

Answer: Allen may be cross-examined as to whether the red car in fact did stop at the stop sign and as to whether Egg McMuffins were not available that morning at the particular McDonald's. Whether the car stopped at the stop sign is an ultimate fact in the case. Whether Allen had an Egg McMuffin is relevant to explore the quality of Allen's alleged personal knowledge in that an error as to one fact brings into question his testimony as to other facts.

Whether the red car stopped at the stop sign is a non-collateral matter. Robert may testify that the red car did in fact stop at the stop sign. Robert's testimony is relevant to establish what happened at the accident scene as well as to impeach Allen's contrary testimony. However, Audrey may not testify that McDonald's wasn't serving Egg McMuffins that morning because its delivery of Canadian bacon was delayed. What Allen ate or did not eat is a collateral matter, one not relevant in the litigation for a purpose other than contradiction. Extrinsic evidence on a collateral matter is inadmissible.

Untrustworthy Partiality

Answer: Assuming that Harry's attorney possesses a good faith basis inquiry is permissible into (a) membership in an animal rights groups as relevant to establish bias, (b) the affair with Sam as relevant to establish bias, (c) the $25,000 reward as relevant to establish interest, and (d) the plea agreement as relevant to establish interest. None of the foregoing is thus objectionable. As to whether a foundation must be laid on cross-examination prior to extrinsic evidence being offered on the non-collateral matter of untrustworthy partiality, while the ordinary practice of confronting Lori on cross-examination with the flyer announcing the $25,000 reward is to be encouraged, nothing in the federal rules of evidence actually requires that the witness be given at any time an opportunity to admit, deny, and/or explain much less than such opportunity be provided on cross-examination, i.e., Sarah may so testify.

Conviction of a Crime

Answer:

a) Craig:

(1) Craig's less than 10 year old conviction for armed robbery involves a felony, i.e., a crime punishable by death or imprisonment in excess of one year. The fact that he was released in 11 months is irrelevant as would have been the fact that he had received probation if that had been the case. Punishable, not

punished, defines a felony. Armed robbery does not involve dishonesty or false statement. Thus under Rule 609(a)(1) the prior conviction can be employed to impeach Craig, the defendant, if the court determines that the probative value of admitting evidence of the prior conviction outweighs the prejudicial effect to the accused. The probative value of a prior conviction is premised upon the assumption that a person who has shown a willingness to violate a serious law of society possesses a bad character for truthfulness and thus is more likely to lie as a witness when testifying. The unfair prejudice to the accused is the bad man inference, i.e., in spite of a limiting instruction to the contrary that the jury will infer that if the accused committed a crime once he committed the crime for which he is on trial or at least committed other crimes he has not been punished making it fair to punish him now.

The following factors should be considered by the trial court in applying the discretionary balancing test provided by Rule 609(a)(1) in determining whether the probative value of admitting the evidence upon the credibility of the criminal defendant outweighs its prejudicial effect:

(1) the nature of the prior crime;
(2) the length of the defendant's criminal record:
(3) defendant's age and circumstances;
(4) the likelihood that the defendant would not testify;
(5) the nearness or remoteness of the prior crime;
(6) defendant's subsequent career;
(7) whether the prior crime was similar to the one charged;
(8) the centrality of the issue of credibility; and
(9) the need for defendant's testimony.

To this one might add a tenth fact surrounding the conviction including whether or not the defendant pled guilty or was convicted after trial, and whether the defendant testified at the trial. Generally speaking, however, it appears that as a matter of trial convenience facts surrounding the prior conviction are not considered by the court.

Judges in practice uniformly admit prior convictions of the criminal defendant under Rule 609(a)(1) to impeach character for truthfulness.

(2) The less than ten year old misdemeanor conviction, i.e., a

crime punishable by one year or less imprisonment, for making false statements on a customs declaration, involves dishonesty or false statement, i.e., deceit, untruthfulness or falsification—some element of active misrepresentation. Such a conviction is made admissible to impeach every witness without application of a discretionary balancing test by Rule 609(a)(2).

(3) The over ten year old misdemeanor conviction for making false statements on a customs declaration form, a crime involving dishonesty or false statement, is inadmissible unless, as provided in Rule 609(b) the trial court determines, in the interest of justice, that the probative value of the conviction supported by specific facts and circumstances substantially outweighs its prejudicial effect. Applications of the discretionary balancing test provided in Rule 609(b) ordinarily results in the prior conviction being excluded, a likely result herein given the existence of a more recent prior conviction for the same offense made admissible to impeach Craig if he chooses to testify by Rule 609(a)(2). However, if the trial judge decided to admit the prior conviction to impeach, a finding of abuse of discretion on appeal is unlikely.

(4) Application of the discretionary balancing test mandated by Rule 609(a)(1) to be applied when a prior non remote felony conviction, i.e., roughly not more than ten years old, not involving dishonesty or false statement, here a battery conviction, is offered to impeach the criminal defendant when he testifies, is fairly likely to result in the prior conviction being excluded because of its age, the fact that it arose out of a domestic dispute, and the fact that two prior convictions have already been found admissible to impeach Craig if he testifies. It is worth noting that it appears that some trial judges tend to admit every prior conviction they can, especially if of the criminal defendant. Clearly, the trial court possesses discretion to make either ruling.

b) Harold:

(1) Harold is solely a witness in the case, not the criminal defendant. Rule 609(a)(1) provides that a non-remote felony conviction, i.e., roughly not more than ten years old, not involving dishonesty or false statement, here a battery conviction, is admissible to impeach subject to Rule 403. Thus the defendant has the burden of persuading the trial court under Rule 403 that the probative value of the less than 10 year old felony conviction

for battery is substantially outweighed by the danger of unfair prejudice. While the trial court has discretion to rule either way, a rule permitting impeachment is to be expected.

(2) The less than 10 year old conviction for defacing public property is a misdemeanor conviction not involving dishonesty or false statement. Such a prior conviction is inadmissible under Rule 609 to impeach.

(3) Rule 609(e) provides that a juvenile conviction is generally not admissible. The prosecution will be unable to persuade the court that the exception provided in Rule 609(e) with respect to juvenile adjudication of a witness other than the accused, i.e., that admission of the evidence is necessary for a fair determination of the issue of guilt or innocence, is applicable. This would be the case even if the juvenile conviction had not arose out of protests against abortion clinics.

With respect to Craig's and Harold's convictions, inquiry is permitted solely as to matters appearing on the public record including the court, date and nature of offense. Inquiry into related matters on redirect examination such as the circumstances surrounding the offense, length of time served, fact paroled and most importantly protestations of innocence are not permitted. On the other hand, Craig, the criminal defendant, will usually be permitted to testify to having pled guilty to a prior offense thereby suggesting his willingness to "own up" to what he does for the further inference that he is innocent of the current charge to which he pled not guilty, an extremely weak argument for Craig given that the jury will also hear about one or more prior convictions where he did not plead guilty. Craig may ask the trial court to employ the mere fact system instead of permitting disclosure of court, date and nature of the offense. Pursuant to the mere fact method, Craig would be asked on direct examination by his own counsel whether he was ever convicted of a felony and whether he was ever convicted of a crime involving dishonesty or false statement followed in each case by the question how many times. If Craig answers these questions accurately, then the prosecution is prohibited from conducting any inquiry with respect to Craig's prior convictions. It is extremely unlikely that a federal trial judge would employ the mere fact method rather than permit the nature of the prior offense to be disclosed to the jury.

Prior Acts of Misconduct

Answer:

(1) Falsifying time records is a specific instance of conduct probative of untruthfulness in that it involves dishonesty or false statement, i.e., some element of deceit, untruthfulness or falsification—some element of active misrepresentation. Inquiry on cross-examination of Tucker as to the specific instance of conduct, i.e., falsifying time records, is probative of character for untruthfulness for the further inference that Tucker is hereby more likely to lie as a witness will undoubtedly be permitted, in the discretion of the court, as provided in Rule 608(b)(1). Inquiry is limited to the underlying act, i.e. falsifying time records, and thus does include whether or not he was fired from his job for such conduct.

(2) Inquiry under Rule 608(b)(1), when permitted in the discretion of the court, must be as to the underlying act, i.e., armed robbery; inquiry as to an arrest is not permitted. In fact, since armed robbery does not involve dishonesty or false statement, defense counsel will be precluded by the trial court from cross-examining Tucker with respect to the armed robbery. If Tucker had also been convicted for armed robbery, admissibility of the prior conviction to impeach Tucker's character for truthfulness if he testified would be governed by Rule 609 and not Rule 608(b)(1).

(3) Failure to file income tax returns is a specific instance of conduct probative of untruthful character in that it involves dishonesty or false statement, i.e., involves some element of deceit, untruthfulness, or falsification—involves some element of active misrepresentation. The trial court, in its discretion, is therefore likely to permit inquiry, Rule 608(b)(1).

(4) Inquiry into the fact of an indictment is not permitted under Rule 608(b)(1); inquiry may only be made as to the underlying act and then only if the underlying act is itself probative of character for untruthfulness—involves dishonesty or false statement, i.e., involves some element of active misrepresentation—which embezzlement certainly does. The trial court will thus in the exercise of its discretion under Rule 608(b)(1) most likely permit

inquiry as to the embezzlement on cross-examination of Tucker. The fact that the embezzlement occurred 15 years ago is not preclusive. While remoteness is clearly relevant in determining the probative value of the specific instance of conduct as bearing on the current character of the witness for truthfulness, federal courts have frequently permitted inquiry of specific instances of conduct even more remote than 20 plus years.

(5) Fighting does not involve dishonesty or false statement—some element of active misrepresentation—and is thus not sufficiently probative of character for untruthfulness to be permitted by the trial court in its discretion to be employed under Rule 608(b)(1) to impeach.

(6) Turning back an odometer, although not criminal, involves an element of active misrepresentation and is thus sufficiently probative of character for untruthfulness to be permitted, in the discretion of the court, to be employed to impeach Rule 608(b)(1).

Rule 608(b)(1) permits inquiry on cross-examination of the witness only. The matter is considered collateral; extrinsic evidence as to the underlying matter inquired about on cross-examination is not admissible. The cross-examiner must thus take the answer given by the witness.

Character of Witness for Untruthfulness and Truthfulness

Answer: Rule 608(a) provides the evidence in the form of reputation or opinion testimony by a character witness as to the principal witness' character for truthfulness is admissible only after the character of the principal witness for truthfulness has been attacked by opinion or reputation evidence or otherwise. Since the prosecution has not called an opinion or reputation character witness to testify that Tucker possesses at the time of trial an untruthful character, Tucker will be permitted to call Dr. Pepper as a character witness only if Tucker's character for truthfulness was attacked in a manner on cross-examination constituting what Rule 608(a)(2) refers to as "or otherwise." Impeachment of the witness on cross-examination by means of a prior conviction, Rule 609, prior act of misconduct, Rule 608(b)(1), or a showing of coercion or corruption are all "or otherwise" attacks on character and thus make opinion or reputation testimony admissible in rebuttal. However, a showing of interest or bias does not constitute a sufficient attack upon character to permit introduction of evidence in support of the character of the witness for truthfulness. Supporting evidence in the form of opinion or reputation testimony for truthful character may also be admissible in situations where the witness has had his character for truthfulness assaulted upon cross-examination or by means of self-contradiction. With respect to cross-examination, the trial court must initially determine whether the net effect of the cross-examination constitutes a sustained direct attack on the witness' character for truthfulness. This is often a difficult decision. Even if the court finds that a sustained direct attack has occurred, whether opinion and reputation testimony for truthfulness becomes admissible is disputed. Where the witness is impeached by a prior inconsistent statement, a court in its discretion may allow subsequent proof of opinion or reputation for truthfulness where the impeachment raises an inference impinging truthfulness of the witness but not where such impeachment merely charges lack of memory or mistake. While the Advisory Committee's Note points out that whether contradiction constitutes a sufficient attack upon the character of the witness depends upon the circumstances, it has generally been held that mere contradiction by other evidence does not suffice.

An "or otherwise" attack on the character of Tucker on cross-examination has clearly occurred. His failure to file tax returns, Rule 608(b)(1), and a prior conviction for bank robbery, Rule 609(a)(1), are each alone sufficient to permit character testimony in support of Tucker's character for truthfulness to be admitted. In addition cross-examination of Tucker with respect to an alleged prior inconsistent statement concluding with a direct assault on veracity is sufficient alone to allow a court in the exercise of its discretion to permit character evidence to be admitted to rebut. Dr. Pepper is sufficiently familiar with Tucker in his capacity of college teacher and soccer coach to testify in the form of an opinion as to Tucker's character for truthfulness. Sufficient personal knowledge to render such an opinion may be acquired as a result of contact with the principal witness in any aspect of the principal witness' life. Only the opinion of the character witness held at or near the time of trial is relevant. Dr. Pepper states that he has had some contact with Tucker following Tucker's graduation from technical college one year earlier. All in all, a sufficient foundation has been laid to permit Dr. Pepper to opine as to Tucker's character for truthfulness at the time of the trial. If Dr. Pepper did not have any contact with Tucker following his graduation, or in fact only minimum contact of a very casual nature, it is questionable whether Dr. Pepper would be permitted to testify as a lot can happen during a person's first year following graduation from technical college.

Dr. Pepper may be cross-examined as to his extent of contact with Tucker both during and following college. In fact, the prosecution should request an opportunity to conduct a voir dire limited to the basis for Dr. Pepper's proposed character testimony prior to Dr. Pepper offering his opinion. In this manner, if an adequate basis is not present, Dr. Pepper will simply be dismissed as a witness without ever stating his opinion as to Tucker's character for truthfulness before the jury. Since the jury will not be aware of what Dr. Pepper would have testified to if permitted, addressing competency during voir dire is more than form over substance. The competency of Dr. Pepper to testify as a character witness may of course also be raised in a motion in limine before or at trial. Dr. Pepper may be cross-examined as provided by Rule 608(b)(2) as to specific instances of conduct which, in the discretion of the trial court, are probative of untruthfulness concerning the character for truthfulness of Tucker. The prior conviction of Tucker admissible to impeach Tucker himself, Rule 609(a)(1), is probative of truthfulness. With respect to the remaining specific instances of conduct of Tucker the prosecution desires to employ in cross-examination of Dr. Pepper, assuming the presence of a good faith basis:

(1) Falsifying time records involves active misrepresentation, i.e., involves dishonesty and false statement, i.e., deceit, untruthfulness or falsification and is thus probative of untruthfulness. A character witness testifying in the form of opinion testimony may be asked about firings, arrests, rumors, reports, indictments, etc., as these bear upon the extent of awareness of the character of the principal witness as well as the character witness' standard for character for truthfulness. A good faith basis as to the underlying act is required. Other than with respect to a prior conviction, specific instances of conduct may not be proved by extrinsic evidence, Rule 608(b). Cross-examination of a character witness testifying as to truthfulness or untruthfulness of a principal witness

is a collateral matter; the cross-examiner must take the witness' answer.

(2) Armed robbery not resulting in a conviction is not sufficiently probative of truthfulness to be inquired of on cross-examination of a character witness.

(3) Failure to file tax returns is an act involving dishonesty or false statement, i.e., deceit, untruthfulness, or falsification—involves some element of active misrepresentation, and may properly be inquired of on cross-examination of Dr. Pepper under Rule 608(b)(2).

(4) Embezzlement is similarly an act of dishonesty or false statement. Inquiry of Dr. Pepper as to whether he knows of or is aware of Tucker's indictment is permitted provided a good faith basis as to Tucker actually embezzling money from his uncle in 1996 in Orlando exists. The fact that the event occurred over 10 years ago is relevant but not preclusive. Inquiry as to a specific instance of conduct more remote than 10 plus years has been frequently permitted.

(5) A fight at a football game is not sufficiently probative of untruthfulness—does not involve active misrepresentation.

(6) Turning back an odometer, even though not illegal, is an act involving dishonesty or false statement, i.e., deceit, untruthfulness, or falsification—some element of active misrepresentation.

On direct examination Dr. Pepper may testify that he would believe Tucker under oath. On cross-examination Dr. Pepper may be asked if he had been aware of the specific instances of conduct probative of untruthfulness committed by Tucker inquired of during Dr. Pepper's cross-examination, whether his opinion as to Tucker's character for truthfulness would have changed. It is however improper to ask the character witness whether his testimony would change if he knew that Tucker, the defendant, had committed the acts for which he is on trial. Such a question possesses no probative value, assumes facts which are the subject of the litigation, and destroys the presumption of innocence.

As previously mentioned, if Dr. Pepper denies knowledge or awareness of any of the events mentioned during cross-examination or denies that such events actually occurred, extrinsic evidence with respect to the specific instances of conduct of the principal witness, other than conviction of crime as provided in Rule 609, is not admissible; the cross-examiner must take the witness' answer, Rule 608(b). The prohibition against introduction of extrinsic evidence encompasses evidence establishing the existence of the act, arrest, indictment, report, rumor, etc., as well as evidence establishing that the character witness heard or knew about any of the foregoing.

Religious Beliefs or Opinions

Answer: Harry can be asked whether he is an elder in the particular church that experienced the fire. Such a question raises an inference of bias in favor of the church and interest in the outcome of the case. Rule 610 bars only evidence of beliefs or opinions of a witness on matters of religion for the purpose of showing that by reason of their nature the witness' credibility is impaired or enhanced. While inquiry of Harry as to whether he is a member of the same religion as the church that experienced the fire also does not rely upon the beliefs or opinions of a witness on matter of religion to be relevant for the purpose of showing bias, such evidence is so marginally relevant as to be properly precluded in the court's discretion under Rule 403 on the grounds of misleading the jury and unfair prejudice. Religion should be kept out of litigation unless significantly probative for a purpose other than for the purpose prohibited by Rule 610.

Impeachment of a Party's Own Witness

Answer: Rule 607 provides that the credibility of a witness may be attacked by any party, including the party calling the witness. The prosecution is entitled to impeach Wes to the same extent as any witness called by the defendant employing leading questions addressed to personal knowledge and to impeach by virtue of a mode of impeachment with the sole exception of the mode of impeachment involving utilization of a prior inconsistent statement. Here the prosecution is restricted. The prosecution may not employ a prior inconsistent statement that is itself not admissible as substantive evidence to impeach a witness it has called if such cross-examination is a "mere subterfuge" for the "primary purpose of placing before the jury substantive evidence which is not otherwise admissible" when the party is aware prior to calling the witness that the witness will not testify consistent with the witness' prior statement. Application of the "mere subterfuge" "primary purpose" caveat focuses upon the content of the witness' testimony as a whole. Thus if the witness' testimony is helpful in establishing any fact of consequence significant in the context of the litigation, the witness may be impeached as to any other matter testified to by means of a prior inconsistent statement including matters the witness now simply claims not to recall. Because Wes testified to the red Pontiac firebird squealing away at the time of the robbery, under Rule 607 as interpreted Wes was not called as a "mere subterfuge" for the "primary purpose" of placing the prior inconsistent statement that is not substantively admissible before the jury. The realization that frequently the witness' lack of recollection is a result of defendant originated witness intimidation underlies this very favorable to the prosecution interpretation of Rule 607. Contrast the requirements of the common law as applied in the federal court prior to the adoption of the Federal Rules of Evidence of surprise and affirmative damage. The requirement of surprise and affirmative damage was applied to each portion of the witness' testimony separately. Since surprise was not present, impeachment would be precluded. Because affirmative damage in the sense of positive aid to the adversary was not present but rather merely disappointment occurred when Wes testified, even if the prosecution had been surprised, impeachment would not be permitted. Whatever the merits of surprise and affirmative damage, the federal courts apply the "mere subterfuge" "primary purpose" doctrine with respect to impeachment of a party's own witness with a prior inconsistent statement.

Refutation

Answer: The function of redirect examination is to meet new facts or rehabilitate a witness with respect to impeaching matter brought out on cross-examination through the introduction of evidence tending to refute, i.e., deny, explain, modify, qualify, disprove, discredit, repel or otherwise shed light upon evidence developed during cross-examination. The witness may be asked questions designed to explain apparent inconsistencies between statements made on direct and cross-examination; to deny or explain the making of an alleged prior inconsistent statement, Rule 613; to correct inadvertent mistakes made on cross-examination; to bring out circumstances repelling unfavorable inferences raised on cross-examination; to bring out prior consistent statements admissible pursuant to Rule 801(d)(1)(B); and to bring out other aspects of an event, transaction, conversation or document shedding light on those aspects previously developed during cross-examination. In order to accomplish these objectives, it is frequently necessary to direct the witness' attention to the exact subject matter of the testimony sought. Hence some questions which might be objectionable as leading if asked during direct examination will often be permitted on redirect examination as necessary to the development of the witness' testimony. It is also generally proper to employ a leading question incorporating particular factual matters where refutation takes the form of a denial or affirmation. However where refutation takes another form such as explanation, is it improper to incorporate the explanation or other testimony desired into the question itself. Harry should be asked on redirect "What, if anything, did you tell the investigator as to how far from the intersection you were standing when you saw the truck go through the red light?" Harry may not be asked about his ability to perceive, i.e., lighting conditions and line of sight, on redirect examination as cross-examination did touch upon this subject.

The function of recross is to meet new factual matters or rehabilitate a witness with respect to matters of credibility brought out for the first time during redirect examination. Inquiry merely repeating testimony developed during cross-examination is normally improper. The scope and extent of recross-examination rests in the discretion of the court. The question propounded on recross-examination "Didn't the investigator show you his notes of your conversation which indicated that you were 140 feet away and ask you if you had any corrections to make before he left?" is a proper question.

Court Calling and Interrogation of Witnesses

Answer: The court may ask questions of a witness, Rule 614(b). The trial judge must, however, avoid conveying to the jury his views regarding the merits of the case, the veracity of the witness, or the weight of the evidence. Throughout the trial the court must maintain an appearance of impartiality and neither become an advocate for a particular party nor display hostility to anyone. If the questions asked by the court are improper, the embarrassing position of counsel is obvious. Avoidance of these hazards confines the court largely to questions designed to clarify confused factual issues, to correct inadequacies of direct or cross-examination, to aid an embarrassed witness, or otherwise to insure that the trial proceeds efficiently and fairly. Here the trial judge clearly stepped over the line thus improperly entering the fray. A specific objection is required to preserve for appeal any alleged error with respect to the court calling or interrogating a witness, Rule 103. However, under Rule 614(c) the objection need not be made contemporaneously with the calling or interrogation if the jury is present. Thus counsel is relieved of the embarrassment attendant upon objecting to the court's action in the presence of the jury. The objection can be made at the next available opportunity when the jury is absent, or preferably at the first reasonable opportunity for a side bar conference. Objections so made will be considered timely under Rule 103(a)(1).

Exclusion and Separation of Witnesses

Answer: John's mother may remain in the courtroom if the court determines that her presence as a support person for her 9 year old son makes her presence essential to the presentation of the party's cause, Rule 615(3). A witness is entitled to review his own prior statements, deposition, etc., prior to testifying; John's mother reading John his prior statement is not improper. John, however, acted improperly to communicating with a witness who had just testified if the court's invocation of rule on witnesses included a separation order.

ARTICLE VII
OPINIONS AND EXPERT TESTIMONY

Opinion Testimony of Lay Witnesses

Answer: Harry may testify that he heard three loud gunshots if he possesses personal knowledge of facts as to which the supposed gunshots are being compared, i.e., that he has observed gunshots before. His testimony that the gunshots were from a pistol requires a similar foundation that Harry's past experience would permit him to distinguish between a pistol shot and any other firearm discharge. Harry's testimony that the man was running out of the bank and that he was of a certain height, etc., is rationally based upon the perception of the witness. It would be extremely difficult if not impossible as well as confusing to attempt to convey the idea of running in a more detailed form. The word "brandishing" is not particularly helpful to a clear understanding; a more detailed description should be required upon objection, i.e., he was carrying a pistol in his right hand and pointing it in various directions as he ran out of the bank. The fact that Harry believes the perpetrator is Hispanic but is not positive does not preclude admissibility of the witness' opinion testimony. Harry's testimony concerning running full out, leaping into the truck bed, and the truck spinning rubber as it sped away is admissible opinion testimony as well for the reasons stated above as is his testimony that the truck was probably a Ford. At this point Harry's testimony becomes unhelpful. He stops testifying to what he observed and begins to provide legal conclusions like "murdered people". He also then describes his feelings such as "I felt sick", it was "real horrible". For Harry's testimony to be relevant helpful opinion testimony Harry must describe what he observed rather than what he concluded and what he felt.

Qualifications of Experts

Answer: Aldo is probably not qualified to testify as an expert witness in his cousin's case. Although Aldo is qualified on the basis of knowledge, skill, experience and training to testify in an area of specialized knowledge, i.e., tile laying, all of Aldo's knowledge relates to warm weather climates. Tile work outside in cold climates where snow and ice require chipping, shoveling and salt use appears to be sufficiently distinct from Aldo's background to require a trial judge to find him unqualified. Aldo has in addition not been shown to be an expert in tile maintenance even in a warm climate—all one knows is that he is a tile layer. Obviously, before making a final determination in addition to learning about Aldo's exposure to tile maintenance, a trial judge would like to be informed as to whether in fact cold weather installation and maintenance of tile differs from warm weather installation and maintenance.

Bases of Opinion Testimony by Experts

Answer: Rule 703 provides that an expert witness may rely upon a fact not admitted into evidence in forming the basis of his opinion if the fact is of a type reasonably relied upon by experts in the particular field in forming opinions upon the subject. Reasonable reliance requires that the facts be sufficiently trustworthy for the reliance to be reasonable. The Advisory Committee's Note's reference to physician relying upon information provided by other medical personnel as an instance of reasonable reliance supports the notion that reasonable reliance requires that the not admitted evidence establishing the fact sought to be relied upon possess trustworthiness equivalent to an exception to the hearsay rule. Thus customary, regular and ordinary reliance by an expert in the particular field is insufficient to make the reliance reasonable; the fact that accidentologists customarily, regularly and ordinarily rely on statements of occurrence witness is to no avail. The oral statement of an occurrence witness is the classic illustration of inadmissible hearsay. If the fact had been reasonably relied upon, it could not be disclosed to the jury unless the trial court first determined that the probative value of the fact in assisting the jury to evaluate the expert's opinion substantially outweighs its prejudicial effect if the jury were to give the fact substantive effect. The jury would be instructed that they may consider the fact solely in evaluating the expert witness' basis for his opinion and not as substantive evidence as to the fact itself.

Disclosure on Direct Examination

Answer: Rule 705 provides that an expert may testify in terms of an opinion and give reasons therefor without first testifying to the underlying facts, data, or opinions, unless the court requires otherwise; a bare bones foundation is permitted. However, the necessity of making the expert appear to the jury to be extremely well qualified, with the opinion of the expert understandable and persuasive, almost invariably results in counsel posing additional questions which further qualify the expert and elicit his basis before requesting his opinion.

Disclosure on Cross-Examination

Answer: Every matter suggested in the problem is an area where cross-examination is proper. Obviously the expert may be cross-examined to explore bias in favor of iron manufacturers as well as personal interest because of her job with Ace Manufacturing defending product liability suits. Since Ace Marketing's expert relies upon the independent laboratory test results, inquiry concerning performance of such tests and their importance to the expert in reaching her conclusion is clearly proper. The same of course applies to the tests she herself did. Plaintiff's counsel may explore whether, and if so how, the non-existence of any fact, data or opinion in the existence of a contrary version of the fact, data, or opinion supported by the evidence, would affect the experts' opinion.

Opinion on Ultimate Issue

Answer: The objection should be overruled provided a proper foundation is laid by Bill as to what factors were taken into consideration in reaching the conclusion that the forklift design was defective and unreasonably dangerous. An opinion on an ultimate issue to be decided by the trier of fact is not objectionable, Rule 704(a), provided it is helpful, i.e., will assist the trier of fact to understand the evidence or to determine a fact in issue, Rule 702. An opinion by an expert as to the law is unhelpful as is an opinion that a particular party is correct and should win or that a particular witness is lying. With respect to questions that are a mixed questions of law and fact, the factual criteria underlying the legal meaning must first be explored thus making the legal meaning clear to the trier of fact. Thus here if Bill first explains his basis, including for example the availability of an alternative design that is economically and technologically feasible that would have avoided the accident, then an opinion on the ultimate issue, i.e., the forklift is defective and unreasonably dangerous, is admissible.

Mental State or Condition

Answer: The objection should be overruled provided a proper foundation is laid by Bill as to what factors were taken into consideration in reaching the conclusion that the forklift design was defective and unreasonably dangerous. An opinion on an ultimate issue to be decided by the trier of fact is not objectionable, Rule 704(a), provided it is helpful, i.e., will assist the trier of fact to understand the evidence or to determine a fact in issue, Rule 702. An opinion by an expert as to the law is unhelpful as is an opinion that a particular party is correct and should win or that a particular witness is lying. With respect to questions that are a mixed questions of law and fact, the factual criteria underlying the legal meaning must first be explored thus making the legal meaning clear to the trier of fact. Thus here if Bill first explains his basis, including for example the availability of an alternative design that is economically and technologically feasible that would have avoided the accident, then an opinion on the ultimate issue, i.e., the forklift is defective and unreasonably dangerous, is admissible.

"Gatekeeping" Under *Daubert* /*Kumho* /Rule 702: Determining Reliable"

Answer: The Fourth Circuit in Benedi v. McNeil-P.P.C., Inc., 66 F.3d 1378, 1384 (1995) stated as follows:

> Benedi's treating physicians based their conclusions on the microscopic appearance of his liver, the Tylenol found in his blood upon his admission to the hospital, the history of several days of Tylenol use after regular alcohol consumption, the liver enzyme blood level, and the lack of evidence of a viral or any other cause of the liver failure. Benedi's other experts relied upon a similar methodology: history, examination, lab and pathology data, and study of the peer-reviewed literature. We conclude that the district court did not abuse its discretion when it determined that the methodology employed by Benedi's experts is reliable under *Daubert*. We will not declare such methodologies invalid and unreliable in light of the medical community's daily use of the same methodologies in diagnosing patients.

Subjects of Expert Testimony

Answer: A forensic evidence expert may conduct a comparison analysis of a shoe print found at the scene and a shoe tied to the accused. A forensic evidence expert may conduct a DNA test on the hair and compare it to DNA obtained from the accused. An expert in gangs may testify as to the typicalness of the robbery to a particular gang's initiation rights to provide evidence of motive, to possibly explain an act which might appear unexplainable, and to help identify the perpetrator. The defense will probably not be permitted to introduce an eyewitness identification expert to testify about the reliability concerns with cross-racial identification on the grounds of lack of helpfulness—credibility issues arising from cross-racial identification are generally within the common knowledge of the jury. [If one buys this explanation, one probably already owns the Brooklyn Bridge.] The defendant will not be permitted to introduce the results of a polygraph—not sufficiently reliable and thus potentially misleading to the jury.

Court Appointed Experts

Answer: The argument in favor of court appointment centers on the fact that a neutral independent highly qualified expert is more likely to accurately and clearly inform the jury than any of the bought and paid for heavily screened and prepared experts presented by a party. The employment of a court appointed expert would also encourage settlement. On the other hand, does there really exist an expert who is neutral? Everyone has biases, professionally or otherwise. The fact of selection and financial reward is not the only kind of bias. Intellectual bias clearly permeates all contentious fields. Moreover, how is the trial court to find and secure such a god sent expert if god has in fact sent her. While these and other arguments in support and opposition to the court appointment of an expert are significant, the real question concerns disclosure of court appointment to the jury. If there is no disclosure, the court appointed expert carries no clout—just another expert testifying for a side. If there is disclosure, the court appointed expert carries far too much clout. In most if not nearly all cases, if qualified experts testify on both sides of a complex issue, a jury is very likely to go with the side favored by the expert they have been told was selected by the court. She is the one who in their minds is fair and neutral. Why would she lie? If she is court appointed, she must be a very good expert and thus unlikely to be wrong, etc. Rule 706(c) sidestepped the issue saying that in the exercise of discretion, the trial court may—not must—authorize disclosure to the jury of the fact that the trial court appointed the expert witness. In practice, court appointed experts are rarely employed to testify before the jury. Court appointed experts are employed more frequently to assist the judge in her handling of a case by providing the judge a better understanding of the positions being advocated by the experts for both sides testifying with respect to a matter of substantial complexity.

ARTICLE VIII
HEARSAY

DEFINITION OF HEARSAY

Rules 801(a)-(d)

Answers:

Yes. 1. This is the classic hearsay statement, i.e., an oral statement by an occurrence witness describing an event critical to determination of a civil or criminal case. Mary Jane is a person who made an oral assertion intended to assert that the truck went through the red light offered in evidence to prove that the truck went through the red light.

Yes. 2. See above. Here the statement only has two hearsay risks, i.e., sincerity and narration. Although there is arguably some perception and recordation and recollection risk, these risks are ordinarily not thought to apply when none of the five senses is employed. Here perception, if it is to be called perception, is internal.

No. 3. The notification is relevant for the fact said. The law attaches independent legal significance to the notification to cancel the uninsured motorist coverage. The communication is a legally operative act.

Yes. 4. The sign is a written assertion by a person offered in evidence to prove the truth of the matter asserted, i.e., "Acme Electrical Service" owns the truck. Note that Rule 902(7) provides a hearsay exception in the form of a rule of authentication providing that signs purporting to be affixed in the course of business are admissible to prove ownership.

No. 5. There is no out of court statement by a person. The reliability of the speedometer is assessed by Rule 901(b)(9) dealing with authentication of a process or system to show that the process or system produces an accurate result and the sufficient assurances of trustworthiness gatekeeping function imposed upon the trial judge for explanative theories of experts pursuant to *Daubert/Kumho/*Rule 702.

No. 6. There is no out of court statement by a person. The police officer is simply testifying to a matter based upon personal knowledge.

Yes. 7. The fact that an out of court statement offered to prove the truth of the matter asserted is in the form of a sworn writing does not alter its status as hearsay.

No. 8. Offering of a bribe is an operative act having independent legal significance when offered in a civil case to show consciousness of guilt. The very act of offering a bribe constitutes a crime.

No. 9. Flight is nonverbal conduct not intended as an assertion. Clearly the fleeing truck driver desires not to be observed; he clearly does not intend to assert anything by his flight.

10. The statement by Jim Harris to Ted Knight that the master cylinder had a leak is hearsay. The statement by Jim Harris to Roberta Jones that the master cylinder is bad is hearsay if offered to prove that the master cylinder was bad. It is not hearsay when offered for the effect being advised of a leaking master cylinder would have upon the reasonableness of the conduct of the listener in driving the car after being so advised. For this purpose, the statement is relevant by virtue of having been said. The reasonableness of driving the car is affected by the advice without regard to whether the master cylinder is in fact defective. The statements made by Roberta Jones acknowledging the advice and telling her son that the brakes are bad are hearsay when offered to prove that the brakes were in fact bad. Moreover both statements are also hearsay when offered a bearing upon the reasonableness of Roberta Jones' conduct in then driving the car. The statements of Roberta Jones asserting her belief that the brakes are bad are relevant only if the matter asserted is true, i.e., that Roberta Jones believed her

brakes to be bad. If Roberta Jones did not so believe, then the statement would have no bearing upon the reasonableness of her conduct. For example, she could have been kidding her son so that she could drive home slowly so as not to get home too early for a surprise birthday party. With respect to her response to Jim Harris, Roberta Jones could have believed that Jim Harris does unnecessary repairs and thus responded in the way she did to avoid confronting him. Since the risk of sincerity and also narration is present with respect to both statements of Roberta Jones, they are hearsay under Rules 801(a)-(d).

Prior Inconsistent Statements

Answer: Harry's affidavit and oral statement that was videotaped are not admissible under Rule 801(d)(1)(A) as neither was made at a trial, hearing, other proceeding (grand jury), or deposition. The presence of an oath even combined with videotaping providing certainty of making is not enough. Both statements admitted by Harry to have been made are relevant for the fact said and thus admissible as not hearsay when offered solely to impeach. If Harry had adopted his prior statements as true, the statements would then be current testimony on personal knowledge, i.e., not hearsay, and therefore admissible as substantive evidence. If Harry's prior statement that the light facing Sue Ann was green was made at either a deposition or before the grand jury, the prior inconsistent statement would be admissible as substantive evidence for its truth as defined as not hearsay under Rule 801(d)(1)(A) as well as to impeach.

Prior Consistent Statements

Answer: It is improper for Bob to testify on direct examination as to what he told his wife. Nor may his wife testify as to Bob's out-of-court statement. Bob's statement to his wife is a prior consistent statement that is not admissible unless offered to rebut an express or implied charge of recent fabrication or improper influence or motive. No such express or implied charge has been made in the trial at the time Bob is asked what he told his wife. Once Bob is cross-examined as to whether his son two weeks before trial became a business partner of the plaintiff, Ted, the earlier in time, i.e., before the alleged improper influence and improper motive is expressly or implicitly charged to have arisen (in this case two years earlier) is now admissible to rebut. A consistent statement made earlier in time, "before" the expressly or impliedly charged recent fabrication, improper influence, or improper motive is said to have arisen rebuts the express or implied charge. The consistent statement was made before such charge was asserted to have arisen and thus was made free of its influence. Because such a prior consistent statement possesses significant probative value in rebutting an attack upon the credibility of the witness, Rule 801(d)(1)(B) admits the prior consistent statement as substantive evidence by being defined as not hearsay. A prior consistent statement if, and only if, admitted substantive under Rule 801(d)(1)(B) may also be considered by the trier of fact as relevant to corroborate the in court testimony of the out-of-court declarant by showing the witness had earlier in time nearer the event when memory was fresher maintained the same position. The prior consistent statement is relevant for the fact said when offered to corroborate.

Prior Identification of a Person After Perceiving Him

Answer: The police officer may testify that Mary Sue identified the defendant as the man who stole her purse by picking out his picture in the mug book and by pointing him out at a line-up. Any prior out-of-court statement of a person who is a witness in court subject to cross-examination that is one of identification of a person made after perceiving the person again is defined as not hearsay, Rule 801(d)(1)(C). The statement must be made after perceiving the person again. Thus a statement made by Mary Sue in the process of reporting the purse snatching to the police that described the perpetrator or even possibly named the perpetrator is not encompassed with Rule 801(d)(1)(C). The declarant must be making the statement after perceiving him again after the event in question. In this case Mary Sue saw him again through his picture in the mug book and in person at the line-up. Both subsequent statements of identification are admissible when testified to by any witness with sufficient personal knowledge that the statement was made. Thus Rule 801(d)(1)(C) does not require that the witness providing the foundation testimony to the fact the statement was made be the declarant of the statement; anyone who heard the statement may so testify. Finally under Rule 801(d)(1)(C), it doesn't matter what the declarant says when asked about the underlying event, the alleged prior statement of identification, or as to the witness' ability to identify a person in open court as having done something. Thus the fact that the witness denies or claims not to recall the event, the identification and whether the person in court is the person who the declarant had observed earlier commit a specific act does not impact upon admissibility of the statement of prior identification when offered through another witness. Lack of recollection may be real or feigned. Feigned lack of recollection is frequently the result of the witness having been intimidated. Rule 801(d)(1)(C), by permitting admissibility in spite of the fact that the declarant asserts a lack of recollection, not only seeks to foster justice by permitting the jury to consider the prior statement of identification made by the witness as substantive evidence, Rule 801(d)(1)(C) also attempts to discourage the intimidation of witnesses by reducing its impact, i.e., the prior identification statement is admissible even if the witness feigns lack of recollection.

Statements of Party Made in Individual Capacity

Answer: Yes. A party's own statement is admissible as an admission of a party-opponent, Rule 801(d)(2)(A), even though the declarant lacked personal knowledge, possessed impaired mental capacity, and/or contains opinions and/or legal conclusions.

Plea of Guilty

Answer: In the federal court, a plea of guilty to a traffic ordinance is admissible as an admission of a party-opponent. Also admissible is the party's explanation for doing so. The argument that a plea of guilty to a traffic infraction should not be included within those statements declared not hearsay by Rule 801(d)(2)(A) because motivation to defend a traffic ticket is minimal or nonexistent, while accepted in many state courts, has fallen upon deaf ears in the federal court.

Statements of Party Made in Representative Capacity

Answer: Yes. Rule 801(d)(2)(A) provides that if an individual has a representative capacity such as an administrator, executor, trustee, guardian, or agent and the statement is offered against him in that capacity, the statement is admissible without reference to whether the individual was acting in a representative capacity in making the statement; all that is required is that the statement be relevant to representative affairs.

Persons in Privity or Jointly Interested

Answer: No. Rule 801(d)(2) alters the common law by omitting any provision declaring either a statement by a person in privity with another (as in the problem) or by one person jointly interested to be an admission by the other or others.

Manifestation of Adoption or Belief in Truth of Statement

Answer: Yes. Harry's original statement is admissible against him under Rule 801(d)(2)(A). Bob's response manifests an adoption in the truth of the statement, not expressly, but impliedly by relying on the content of Harry's statement to give meaning to his own statement, i.e., "I wish I was as confident that Adam won't get it either" and is thus an admission of a party-opponent under Rule 801(d)(2)(B). Both Harry's failure to respond to Bob's statement and John's failure to respond to both Harry's and Bob's statements constitute adoptive admissions by silence, i.e., by their silence Harry and John manifested an adoption or belief in the truth of the statement, Rule 801(d)(2)(B), i.e., the statements contained assertions of fact which if untrue both Harry and John would under the surrounding circumstances naturally be expected to deny. An illustration of a situation when a denial might not be expected is a young man being confronted by his elderly and venerated Chinese grandfather.

Vicarious Admissions

Answer: The security alarm repairman's statements are not admissible against the security alarm company as an admission of a party-opponent under Rule 801(d)(2)(C) as authorization to make a statement is lacking. In fact, the security alarm repairman was instructed and signed a statement acknowledging that he was specifically not authorized to make statements concerning his driving. However, under Rule 801(d)(2)(D), authorization to speak is not required and specific directions not to speak are ineffective. Pursuant to Rule 801(d)(2)(D), a statement by a party's employee concerning a matter with the scope of employment made during the existence of the relationship is admissible against the employer party as an admission of a party-opponent. The only way to prevent the particular statement being considered from being an admission of a party-opponent is for the security company to install a monitoring device on the truck that indicates the occurrence of a collision. The security company then has a person send a message back to the truck flashing a red sign and making an announcement firing the truck driver. If the firing occurs prior to the statement, the statement would not have been made during the existence of the employment relationship and thus not an admission of a party-opponent. The purpose of this provision is to prevent disgruntled ex-employees from subsequently making statements harmful to the employer to get even. Rule 801(d)(2) provides that the content of the security alarm repairman's out-of-court statements are admissible to establish the existence of the employment relationship and the scope thereof, i.e., that he was on the job when the accident occurred, but are not alone sufficient when offered for such purposes.

Statements by Coconspirator

Answer: A, B, and C are all present during the conversation. A's own statement is admissible against him under Rule 801(d)(2)(A). B's statement is an adopted admission of A's statement, Rule 801(d)(2)(B), as well as being an admission of a party-opponent in its own right, Rule 801(d)(1)(A). Both A's silence and C's silence constitute an adoptive admission by silence, Rule 801(d)(2)(B). Thus the coconspirator hearsay exception is not required to admit the statements made by or in the presence of A, B, or C. The coconspirator hearsay exception is required to admit either A's or B's statement against E because E, not being present, neither made nor adopted any of the statements. Both A's and B's statements are admissible against E when testified to by D if the court determines that it is more probably true than not true, Rule 104(a), that A, B and E were members of the conspiracy and that the statements of A and B were made during the course of and in furtherance of the conspiracy. The contents of A's and B's statements are to be considered but are not alone sufficient to establish the existence of the conspiracy and the participation therein of A, B and E.

HEARSAY EXCEPTIONS; AVAILABILITY OF DECLARANT IMMATERIAL

Present Sense Impression

Answer: Margaret's recorded statement meets the requirements of Rule 803(1). It is a statement describing an event made while the declarant was perceiving the event or immediately thereafter. While personal knowledge of Margaret would need to be established, under Rule 602 the content of the statement taken in conjunction with surrounding circumstances will suffice. There is no confrontation clause issue. The statement is nontestimonial having been made to someone other than a government official, i.e., Margaret's friend, Sally.

Excited Utterance

Answer: Not sure. Best guess is that although a close case given the facts because it involves a sexual battery, even though an adult rather than a child, most trial courts would admit the women's statements of the rape under Rule 803(2). The issue is whether she had time for reflective thought or conversely whether the statement was made under the stress of excitement caused by the alleged rape. Excitement is said to still the capacity from reflective thought thus making the statement trustworthy. The fact that her statement was made in response to a question, especially a non leading question is not dispositive.

Nor is the fact that (1) although she had the opportunity she didn't make a prompt complaint prior to returning home and (2) she did not tell her mother until asked "What happened". Given the nature of the startling event, a trial court would be justified in finding that the foregoing facts adequately support a finding that her statement was made while still under the stilling influence of the startling event.

Then Existing Mental, Emotional, or Physical Condition; Intent as Proof of Doing Act Intended; Statement as Proof of Fact Remembered or Believed; Will Cases

Answer: Bob's statement that he loves his wife is admissible under Rule 803(3) as a statement of the existing mental, emotional, or physical condition. From the evidence that he loved his wife a week before the crash under the concept of continuity in time, the jury can infer that he loved his wife at the moment of his death. Bob's statement that he and Ralph intended to go to Boston on business is a statement of current state of mind expressing an intent to do a future act admissible under Rule 803(3) as evidence both of his current intent and as evidence that he did in fact go to Boston on business. Moreover, although various theoretical arguments as developed in the text and also in the discussion of Rule 805 in the text infra can forcefully be raised to the contrary, Bob's statement is admissible under Rule 803(3) as evidence of both Ralph's current intent and as evidence that Ralph did in fact go to Boston on business. Rule 803(3) neither in text nor legislative history speaks authoritatively when it comes to the admissibility of Bob's statement as to Ralph's intent while the United States Supreme Court's opinion in Mutual Life Insurance v. Hillmon (1892), clearly sanctions admissibility.

Answer: The man's statement is admissible because it satisfies the requirements of Rule 803(3). It is not the job of the judge to determine trustworthiness of statements that on their face meet the requirements of the current state of mind hearsay exception, nor as mentioned within the suggested answer to a problem dealing with Rule 803(2), with respect to any denominated hearsay exception except Rules 803(6) (7), (8) and (10). Necessity here plays a part. The state of mind of an individual is often critical in deciding a matter and that person's expression of her statement of mind is almost always the most probative evidence available. Any rule that attempts to have the trial judge admit only those statements the court finds credible would be unworkable as being unpredictable, uninformed, arbitrary, etc. In short, the common law correctly recognizes that while people will sometimes lie about their current state of mind, justice is best served by letting all such statements into evidence and asking the jury to sort them out. Thus "I love you" said to the woman in a bar is just as admissible as "I love you" said to her by her mother. Rule 403 does not serve to exclude statements possibly made in "bad faith" in that in evaluating probative value under Rule 403, the trial judge is required to view probative value most favorably to the proponent of the evidence after first assuming that the jury finds that the out-of-court statement was made.

Answer: The statement is admissible under the hearsay exception provided in Rule 803(3) to prove that the victim *believes* that Mark has broken the legs of two other store owners for the inference that the money paid to Mark was as the result of extortion. However, the statement is not admissible under Rule 803(3) or any not hearsay definition, Rules 801(d)(1) and (2), or other hearsay exception, Rules 803, 804 and 807, to prove that Mark in fact did break the legs of two other store owners. Under such circumstances a limiting instruction, Rule 105, is required to insure that assertions as to particular facts contained in the statement will be considered by the jury solely as bearing upon the declarant's state of mind, etc., and not for the truth of the factual matter asserted. If the unfair prejudice to a party likely to result from the substantive consideration by the trier of fact of such factual assertion in spite of the giving of a limiting instruction substantially outweighs the probative value of the evidence as to declarant's state of mind, etc., considered in light of the need for such evidence, exclusion under Rule 403 is appropriate.

Statements for Purposes of Medical Diagnosis or Treatment

Answer: The plaintiff will call the nurse at trial to testify to plaintiff's statements made to her that satisfy the requirements of Rule 803(4). Patient's statement that she is in great pain and that her left ankle felt broken are statements describing present pain and symptoms made for purposes of medical diagnosis or treatment. Her statements as to her age and of having previously sprained the left ankle several times and that it never hurt that much before is a statement of medical history also made for purposes of medical diagnosis or treatment. The plaintiff's statement that she was hit by a car while rollerblading on Lincoln Road at an intersection is a statement of the general character of the cause of her condition admissible as well under Rule 803(4). If plaintiff were to offer in addition through the nurse her statement that the car that hit her was a Dominos pizza delivery car, that statement would fail to meet the requirements of Rule 803(4) as the identity of the car goes well beyond a statement of the inception or general character of the cause of plaintiff's expressed condition and thus is not reasonably pertinent to medical diagnosis or treatment. If Dominos was to offer through the nurse the plaintiff's statement that she went through a don't walk sign, etc., the statement will not be admitted under Rule 803(4) in that it is a statement of fault not reasonably pertinent to medical diagram in treatment. Of course with the nurse on the stand, the plaintiff's statements as to rollerblading through the don't walk sign is admissible as a not hearsay admission of a party-opponent when elicited by Dominos, Rule 802(d)(2)(A).

Recorded Recollection

Answer: The list meets the requirements for recorded recollection as specified in Rule 803(5). The husband remembers now remembering at the time the list was made shortly after discovering the robbery when his memory was fresh that the list was accurate, but does not remember now what he remembered when he made the list with his wife. As structured the husband and wife each reviewed the list for accuracy and either alone could lay a sufficient foundation as both had personal knowledge of the items that were missing. Thus the wife's testimony is unnecessary. Compare the foregoing to a situation where one party is examining items located on a high shelf for inventory purposes yells down to his partner the description and quantity of items recorded by the partner. Here the testimony of both persons will be needed as neither can adequately alone lay a foundation as to the accuracy of the inventory list they collectively created. When admitted, the list of items stolen should be read into evidence in the presence of the jury but as specified in Rule 803(5) may not itself be received as an exhibit unless offered by an adverse party.

The one way to look at Rule 803(5) is that it requires a witness to state with respect to the document, "I remember now remembering then, but I don't remember now what I remembered then."

Records of Regularly Conducted Activity; Business Records

Answer: The records custodian is qualified to lay the foundation required for the admissibility of the hospital record as a business record under Rule 803(6). It is not required that the custodian have personal knowledge of the matters recorded, or of the persons creating the records, or the medical procedures regularly followed. The custodian even though she had not been working at the hospital when the records were created and never saw them before the day of trial by examination of this particular hospital record when compared with other hospital records with which she is familiar can answer "Yes" to the questions "Was it the regular course of business to make these records?" "Were these records kept in the ordinary course of business?" "Were these records made at or near the time of the matter recorded?" and "Was the record made by a person within the business with knowledge of, or made from information transmitted by a person within the business with the knowledge of, the acts, events, conditions, opinions or diagnosis appearing in it?"

The observations of the ambulance driven at the scene, the examination of the worker's elbow, the taking of vital statistics, and other results of the physical examination all fall with the business records hearsay exception, Rule 803(6), as the ambulance driver was under a business duty to do and record each such item. The business duty of the ambulance driver is everything pertinent to medical diagnosis or treatment and nothing more. The statement of the worker that his elbow really hurts is admissible under Rules 803(4) and 803(6). Same is true for the empty pallet sliding off the forklift onto his arm—inception or general character of the cause or external source, Rule 803(4). The statements by the worker that the pallet was at a 20 degree level, that the pallet slide over the guard, that the guard should have been higher, and that if it was higher he wouldn't have got hurt are not pertinent to medical diagnosis of treatment, Rule 803(4). Since such standard also defines the scope of the ambulance driver's business duty, Rule 803(6) is not available even to prove the statement was made.

This same analysis applies to the statements by the worker to the attending emergency room physician. The initial quoted statement in the hospital records concerning the empty pallet sliding off the forklift breaking the worker's arm is admissible multiple level hearsay, Rule 803(4) and 803(6), as it presents the inception or general character of the cause or external source. However, the paraphrased inclusion in the hospital report where the worker makes a damaging admission of culpability is not admissible in the form of a hospital record under Rule 803(6) as such a statement of fault is not pertinent to medical diagnosis or treatment. Defense counsel will have to call the attending emergency room physician or anyone else who has personal knowledge of the worker's damaging admission of a party-opponent to testy to the existence of the statement which of course is admissible as not hearsay under Rule 801(d)(2)(A).

The recording of information by the emergency room transmitted by the ambulance satisfies Rule 803(6) as does his report to the extent described above. The fact that the ambulance driver works for someone in this case other than the hospital does not defeat admissibility. The two entities, the ambulance and the hospital, work as one. Each relies upon information furnished by the other in its day-to-day operations and surrounding circumstances clearly indicate trustworthiness. Thus the custodian of the hospital records may lay a foundation from the ambulance records found in the patient's file.

Obviously, the records of medical diagnosis and treatment done by hospital employees upon the worker's arrival at the hospital satisfy all of Rule 803(6)'s requirements of regular, regular, at, personal knowledge. The MRI report received on the medical internet is not a record generated by the hospital itself. Here, however, like the ambulance report because the hospital relies upon this records and concurs in its recommendation upon making its own assessment, the MRI is treated the same as any other part of the patient's medical file. The same would hold true for laboratory reports prepared by outside agencies.

Answer: The conduct of an investigation of an accident for the purpose of determining causation and thus informing decisions on prevention is a regularly conducted activity of the warehouse. The investigation was conducted in an appropriate manner and appears with the presence of testing to be more thorough then some. All of the employees are under a business duty to cooperate with the human resources department investigation. The fact that forklift accidents do not happen on a regular basis is not controlling—the proper question is whether similar accident investigations are conducted regularly when an accident does occur. Obviously the real question is whether the fact that the warehouse has an incentive to find the worker at fault in anticipation of being sued for personal injuries arising from the incident means that the investigation report should be excluded—the source of information or the method of circumstances of preparation indicates lack of trustworthiness, Rule 803(6). Rule 803(6) provides that when the "source of information or the method or circumstances of preparation indicate lack of trustworthiness," a business record, otherwise admissible, will not be received in evidence. As the Advisory Committee's Note indicates, the question of the motivation of the declarant is particularly troubling especially when the question of motivation arises in conjunction with a business record that is prepared if not solely for the purpose of litigation with at least an eye toward litigation.

Documents made in anticipation of litigation are generally held inadmissible under Rule 803(6).

Absence of Entry in Records of Regularly Conducted Activity

Answer: The business records of B & B Brake Service of the brake work performed on the particular Acme Trucking Company truck involved in the accident are admissible under Rule 803(7) to prove the nonoccurrence of an event, i.e., rebuilding the brakes of the truck involved when it had 50,000 miles, because rebuilding of brakes is the kind of matter as to which a record is regularly made and preserved by the B & B Brake Service.

Public Records and Reports

Answer: The police report containing a description of the fleeing perpetrator and the car employed are under Rule 803(8)(B) "matters observed pursuant to duty imposed by law to which matters there was a duty to report." However, Rule 803(8)(B) also provides that in criminal cases such matters observed by police officers or other law enforcement personnel are excluded. This exclusion applies regardless of whether or not the police officer testifies at trial.

Answer: The defendant may introduce the forensic examination under Rule 803(8)I which provides a hearsay exception in civil actions and proceedings and against the government in criminal cases for factual findings resulting from an investigation made pursuant to authority granted by law, unless the sources of information or other circumstances indicate lack of trustworthiness. The term "factual finding" includes not only what happened, but how it happened, why it happened, and who caused it to happen.

Answer: The certified copy of the DNA report is not admissible against John. Rule 803(8)I excludes "factual findings" resulting from a governmental investigation when offered against the defendant in a criminal case. Some courts would permit the admissibility of the DNA report upon the testimony of the supervisor of the "unavailable" laboratory technician as an "other qualified witness" under Rule 803(6). While lower court cases express some disagreement, an overwhelming number of opinions have for different reasons found forensic laboratory reports to be nontestimonial under *Crawford/Davis*.

Records of Vital Statistics

Answer: Yes. Rule 803(9) provides a hearsay exception for records of birth if the record was made to a public office pursuant to requirement of law. The record of birth is admissible to prove any matter contained thereon such as the name of the father.

Absence of Public Record or Entry

Answer: Yes. Rule 803(10) provides a hearsay exception to prove the absence of a record, here a gun permit, as well as to prove the nonoccurrence or nonexistence of a matter of which a record is regularly made and preserved by a public officer or agency in the form of a certificate in accordance with Rule 902.

Statements in Ancient Documents

Answer: The letter is admissible under Rule 803(16) providing a hearsay exception for statements in a document in existence twenty years or more the authenticity of which is established. Under the facts of the case, Mary Flower is able to lay a sufficient foundation to authenticate the letter as provided in Rule 901(b)(8) by showing that (a) its condition creates no suspicion concerning its authenticity, (b) it was in a place where it would be likely to be if authentic, and (c) it has been in existence 20 years or more at the time it is offered. In both Rules 803(16) and 901(b)(8) the common law time period of 30 years is reduced to 20 years.

Market Reports, Commercial Publications; Mortality Tables

Answer: The books used by the auto repairman to price the cost of parts for the job fall within the hearsay exception provided in Rule 803(17) for published compilations generally used and relied upon by the public or persons in particular occupations.

Learned Treatises

Answer: Counsel should be permitted to proceed with his cross-examination if his representation is modified to state that plaintiff's expert will testify that the article "The Ins and Outs of Knee Surgery" rather than the publication as a whole—the 2006 A.H. Wells Annual—is a reliable authority in the field. Periodicals, compilations, etc., may be generally reliable but a particular article within it may not or vice versa. On cross-examination counsel may employ a published treatise, article in a periodical, etc., provided that it is established as a reliable authority. If the witness refuses to acknowledge that the treatise, article in a periodical, etc., is a reliable authority, Rule 803(18) provides that counsel may request the court to take judicial notice of that fact. Since counsel knows the court will refuse, counsel will proceed immediately to the third and last option—a representation that counsel's own expert if he or she has not already done so will testify that the treatise or article in the periodical, etc., is a reliable authority in the field. The trial judge does not have a gatekeeping role here. Assume that an expert on cross-examination states that the article is totally bogus yet the proponent's expert testifies that the same article is a reliable authority. Under such circumstances the court must permit the cross-examination to proceed and let the jury sort out what weight if any to be given to the article. As provided in Rule 803(18) the article may be read into evidence through the testimony of the witness on direct examination or by being included in a question posed on cross-examination but may not be received as an exhibit.

Judgment of Previous Conviction

Answer: The conviction may not be employed under Rule 803(22) for two reasons. First, the conviction was for a misdemeanor and Rule 803(22) provides a hearsay exception for introduction of a judgment of conviction to prove any fact essential to sustain the judgment only if the judgment adjudged the defendant guilty of a crime punishable by death or imprisonment in excess of one year, i.e., a felony. Second, Rule 803(22) provides that a judgment of conviction may not be offered by the government in a criminal prosecution for purposes other than impeachment if the judgment is against a person other than the accused. Thus the judgment against Alfred, even if it had been a felony, could not be introduced against Sam to prove any fact essential to sustain Alfred's judgment, i.e., Alfred stole a box of pocket knives.

HEARSAY EXCEPTIONS, DECLARANT UNAVAILABLE

Definition of Unavailability

Answer: Harry, age 11, is clearly unavailable, i.e., his testimony is unavailable. He testifies to "a lack of memory of the subject matter of the declarant's statement," Rule 804(a)(3) and an attempt to refresh recollection with a writing, Rule 612, proved unavailing. Harry appears simply too upset and probably frightened to be able and willing to testify.

Former Testimony

Answer: Bob's testimony is admissible against Mike when offered by John in the second action. Mike was a party to the first action with an opportunity and similar motive to develop the testimony in the first action by cross-examination. Although the first case involved only $2,500 which makes the incentive to prepare and defend less compelling, Mike probably was already aware that John suffered significant personal expenses and that a win by him in the first suit would be influential in settling any claim matter subsequently brought by John. Moreover, as a practical matter the cost of preparation to cross-examine a red light-green light witness who is a neutral occurrence witness will most likely be the same or very similar regardless of the amount at stake in the litigation. Mutuality is not a requirement of Rule 804(b)(1), i.e., John can offer Bob's testimony against Mike even if Mike can not offer Harry's testimony in the first action against John. With respect to Mike offering Harry's testimony in the first action against John in the second action, the issue is whether Mike can offer Harry's testimony against a party to the second action who was not himself a party to the initial lawsuit. Rule 804(b)(1) says no in a criminal case, but yes in a civil case if the party in the first action is a predecessor in interest to the party in the second action against whom the testimony is being offered provided that the party to the first action had an opportunity and similar motive to develop the testimony in the first action. While predecessor in interest as a matter of plain meaning appears to limit admissibility to cases in which the party is the first action "preceded" the party in the second action in the sense of being in privity of interest, case law defines predecessor in interest much more broadly to encompass anyone who shares a sufficient "community of interest." Community of interest will be found whenever it is fair to impose upon the party in the second action who was not a party in the first action the selection of representation, tactics, state of preparation, and totality of information present with respect to the party in the first action. Since John and Mary were married, imposing this responsibility is fair.

Statement Under Belief of Impending Death

Answer: This is a classic dying declaration. Sam has a settled hopeless expectation of death. He need not believe in God or an afterlife. The rationale is that no matter what, one doesn't want to die with a lie on one's lips and probably also that there is no such person as an atheist in a foxhole. That Sam expects to die is evidenced by the content of his statements made while he was clutching his stomach as his blood flows onto the floor. The circumstances coupled with the content of his statement is sufficient to support a finding that Sam has personal knowledge, Rule 602, when he says Harold Silverman murdered me, a statement concerning the cause or circumstances of what Harold believed to be impending death. The portion of his statement, "He murdered me" made while pointing at Harold Silverman is admissible in the prosecution for homicide and in a civil action to collect on the insurance policy. However Rule 804(b)(2) does not provide a hearsay exception for the remainder of Sam's statement—"I'm sure happy I changed the beneficiary on my insurance policy from Harold to my mother. That S.O.B. will get nothing. Tell my mother I lover her"—in that such statement does not concern the cause or circumstance of what the declarant believed to be his impending death. The fact that the statement imputes a motive for Harold to murder Sam because of his change of beneficiary is too removed an act to constitute cause or circumstances of impending death. Harold's statement "Tell my mother I lover her" would, of course, fall within the hearsay exception provided in Rule 803(3) for then existing mental, emotional, or physical condition.

Statement Against Interest

Answer: The statement against penal interest by Tim to the police that "the marijuana is mine but the crack is Alfie's" is a "testimonial" statement as defined in *Crawford* and *Davis*. As such, since Tim is not available to testify at trial and no prior opportunity for cross-examination existed for Alfie, Tim's statement is barred from admissibility by the confrontation clause when offered by the prosecution.

The confrontation clause does not govern the admissibility of Tim's statement to the bartender that both the crack and marijuana was his, as Alfie, the criminal defendant, is offering the statement. Alfie's attempt to admit the statement under Rule 804(b)(3) as a statement of an unavailable declarant which so far tended to subject the declarant to criminal liability that a reasonable person in the declarant's position would not have made the statement unless he believed it to be true should be successful. When Alfie offers Tim's statement to the bartender that both the marijuana and the crack was his, the entire statement is sufficiently against penal interest to be admitted under Rule 804(b)(3) provided in addition corroborating circumstances clearly indicate the trustworthiness of the statement. Applying the factors suggested as appropriate in the Advisory Committee's Note to a once proposed amendment to rule 804(b)(3), it appears that Alfie ought to be able to establish sufficient corroborating circumstances to have Tim's statement to the bartender admitted into evidence.

Statement of Personal or Family History

Answer: Mary's statement to her daughter Marilyn that Marilyn's great grandfather was once a priest in a small town outside Bari, Italy, is admissible under Rule 804(b)(4)(B) as a statement concerning a matter of legitimacy, ancestry or other similar fact of family history of another person by a person, Mary, related to the other person, Marilyn, by blood.

Forfeiture by Wrongdoing

Answer: For the statement to the police by Pete the store clerk to be admissible under Rule 804(b)(6), the trial court must find that it is more probably true than not the defendant has engaged in or acquiesced in wrongdoing that was intended to, and did, procure the unavailability of Pete. There is in fact no evidence of an overt act constituting wrongdoing. All the prosecutor has is a statement by the defendant that the store clerk will not testify. That could be his belief that circumstances having nothing to do with him will result in Pete not testifying. The defendant didn't even threaten Pete in any way. Even if Ace had said "I will make sure that the store clerk will not testify," absent evidence of actual wrongdoing, as against a statement of intent to possibly engage in wrongdoing, Pete's statement should not be admitted under Rule 804(b)(6). Someone said something about something is simply not enough to deprive the accused of his constitutional right to confront witnesses against him and to permit statements that are hearsay and not admissible pursuant to a hearsay exception to be admitted against him.

* * *

Hearsay Within Hearsay

Answer: The statement by Beatrice meets the requirements of an excited utterance. Her statement that her sister told her she intended to travel with her husband on Cheapo Airlines to Chicago relates to the startling event. As we know after September 11, 2001 if not before, observation on television may constitute a startling event. Beatrice's statement was made under the stress of excitement caused by observing the report of the airline crash. Lucy's statement that she and her husband intended to fly Cheapo Airlines to Chicago on the morning in question meets the requirements of Rule 803(3) which, as interpreted in light of Mutual Life Insurance v. Hillmon, provides a hearsay exception not only for the state of mind of Beatrice for the inference that she in fact acted in conformity therewith but for the state of mind of her husband for the inference that he acted in conformity therewith. Beatrice spoke with her sister the day before the airline crash. Given the totality of circumstances, any concern over whether Beatrice had personal knowledge and was accurately conveying the content of Lucy's statement appears satisfied. In addition as previously stated the statement of Lucy meeting the hearsay exception provided in Rule 803(3) relates to the startling event underlying the hearsay exception provided for Beatrice's statement by Rule 803(2). Accordingly, Rule 805 is satisfied and the statement by Beatrice is not excluded under the hearsay rule.

Attacking and Supporting Credibility of Declarant

Answer: Harry is unavailable as provided by Rule 804(a)(3) in that Harry's attendance in the civil automobile accident litigation could not be compelled by process and reasonable means failed to secure his attendance. His deposition testimony meets the requirements of Rule 804(b)(1):

> Testimony given by a witness at another hearing of the same or a different proceeding, or in a deposition taken in compliance with law in the course of the same or another proceeding, if the party against whom the testimony is now offered, or, in a civil action or proceeding, a predecessor in interest, had an opportunity and similar motive to develop the testimony by direct, cross, or redirect examination.

Pursuant to Rule 806, Harry's credibility may be attacked by any evidence which would be admissible for such a purpose if declarant had testified as a witness. Evidence that Harry is red green color blind attacks his capacity to acquire personal knowledge, Rule 602. Evidence that Harry was recently fired from his job at a small company operated by plaintiff's brother in which plaintiff had a small financial interest is admissible to establish untrustworthy partiality in the form of bias, Rule 607. The prior statement by Harry that he never saw the color of the traffic light, only the crash, is a prior inconsistent statement that may be employed to impeach, Rule 613. The fact that Harry was never provided an opportunity to explain or deny the prior inconsistent statement as required by Rule 613(b), and could have been provided such an opportunity at the deposition, plaintiff's lawyer being knowledgeable of the prior inconsistent statement at that time, does not preclude the prior inconsistent statement being proved at trial to attack Harry's credibility. Rule 806 specifically provides that evidence of a statement or conduct by the declarant at any time, inconsistent with the declarant's hearsay statement, is not subject to any requirement that the declarant may have been afforded an opportunity to deny or explain.

Residual Exception

Answer: Janice's statement that "Mr. Larry hurts me where I pee pee" is an out-of-court statement offered in evidence to prove the truth of the matter asserted, Rules 801(a)-(c)—all four hearsay risks are present. Janice's statement made at least the morning after the day in which the incident may have occurred—it could have been earlier—following a calm afternoon and evening during which time Janice did not mention Mr. Larry's conduct fails to meet the requirements for an excited utterance—the statement was clearly not made while under the stress caused by the startling event. The requirements of Rule 803(2) are not satisfied where a person is simply reminded of a supposed startling event for any reason and then blurts out a statement relating to the startling event under the stress of their self-created excitement in supposedly recalling the event. Obviously sufficient capacity for reflective thought existed during the interim period. Janice's statement does not meet any definition of not hearsay provided by Rules 801(d)(1) and (2) nor does it meet the requirements of any other hearsay exception found in Rules 803 or 804. Janice's statement should, however, be admitted under Rule 807 provided proper notice is given. Her statement is clearly offered as evidence of a material fact, is more probative on this point than other available evidence, and its introduction serves the general purposes of the rules of evidence and the interests of justice. Janice's statement, very importantly, does possess equivalent circumstantial guarantees of trustworthiness. She volunteered in child like language in an excited mental state a description of an event a child of her age would not know might be sexually gratifying to another person. No motive to fabricate appears present; Janice previously enjoyed her day care experience. In determining the presence of equivalent circumstantial guarantees of trustworthiness, it would be up to the court deciding Janice's case as to whether or not to take into consideration in determining the presence of equivalent circumstantial guarantees of trustworthiness the corroborating circumstances testimony by

Janice's doctor that her vaginal area was bruised and sore. Whether in a criminal case corroborating circumstances may be considered is currently unclear as *Davis* overruled *Roberts* effectively overruling *Wright* and *Lilly* as well, the two United States Supreme Court cases precluding consideration of corroborating circumstances under the confrontation clause.

The Confrontation Clause

Answer: Mabel is unavailable under Rule 804(a)(1) on the ground of privilege. Mabel's initial statement made to her friend Sally contains a collateral statement that is neutral in content—Tony and I robbed the bank. I robbed the bank is a statement against penal interest, the appended collateral statement about Tony is neutral in that it does not tend to enhance or diminish Mabel's role. Since the parts of both of her statements dealing with Tony are non-self-inculpatory to Mabel, under *Williamson* they are not admissible against Tony pursuant to Rule 804(b)(3) in the federal court. However, because *Williamson* involved a Supreme Court interpretation of a federal rule of evidence pursuant to the court's supervisory power over the federal courts, and was not based upon the confrontation clause or any other constitutional provisions, *Williamson* is not binding on state courts. Thus state courts adopting the Wigmore contagious theory which admits all collateral statements against penal interest of the unavailable declarant as well as state courts employing a balancing approach, given that the first collateral statement was neutral while the second was clearly disserving to Mabel, would admit both her statements against Tony under the state hearsay exception equivalent to Rule 804(b)(3). Since Mabel's statement was made to her friend Sally and not a police officer or other governmental official, the statement is "nontestimonial" under *Crawford* and *Davis*. As such the fact that Mabel is unavailable to testify at trial thus precluding cross-examination by Tony does not preclude admissibility. Moreover, since *Davis* declares that *Roberts* has been overruled, the confrontation clause no longer requires any further determination that the statement against penal interest of Mabel to Sally, not being firmly rooted, possesses "particularized guarantees of trustworthiness." On the other hand, Mabel's testimony before the grand jury is "testimonial," the primary purpose upon receipt of the statement was anticipation of criminal litigation. A "testimonial" statement is barred by the confrontation clause when the out-of-court declarant is not available at trial for cross-examination.

ARTICLE IX
AUTHENTICATION AND IDENTIFICATION

ILLUSTRATIVE TESTIMONIAL FOUNDATIONS

Testimony of Witness With Knowledge

Answer: Authentication of the blender will require the laying of chain of custody. No one person can testify that the blender pieces contained in the bag came from the blender that harmed Harold and that they are now in the same condition as they were immediately following the accident. If Harold's daughter had been home and had come into the kitchen immediately after the accident, the unique character of the broken blender would permit her alone to provide an adequate foundation for its admissibility. Nevertheless, Harold's attorney might still prefer to employ a chain of custody rather than rely upon the jury accepting Harold's daughter's testimony that she can recall the shape of the pieces of the blender and that they are now in the same condition as they were when she gathered up the pieces and placed them in the brown shopping bag. To lay a chain of custody foundation to introduce evidence sufficient to support a finding that the matter is what Harold claims it to be, Rule 901(b)(1), Harold, Harold's daughter, the investigator, and the expert witness should be called to the witness stand. Harold, after testifying as to the accident, would testify as to the location and condition of the blender pieces following the accident. He would testify that they remained as they were following the accident until he left for the hospital. Harold's daughter would testify to picking up all the pieces and placing them in the brown shopping bag and putting the bag in a closet. She will also testify that the bag was where she had left it in the closet when she retrieved the bag and gave it to the investigator. The investigator will simply testify that he received the bag from Harold's daughter, that he did not open the bag and that the contents were in the same condition when he gave it to the expert as when he got it from Harold's daughter. The expert will testify to opening the bag, doing his thing, and returning all the pieces to the bag. He will also testify that he did not alter the blender pieces in any way during his examination and thus the contents of the bag are in the same condition at trial as they were when received from the investigator. It normally would not be necessary for Harold, Harold's daughter, Harold's wife, or the maid to testify that they didn't touch the brown paper bag while it was stored in the closet. However, if the maid was working the day of the accident since her job includes cleaning up, she might under such circumstances be called to testify that she did not touch any of the blender pieces between the time of the accident and Harold's daughter's return home from work, although such testimony, it is suggested, is not necessary to lay a sufficient chain of custody foundation to admit the blender considering the absence of an assertion by the defense of alteration, change in condition, or substitution.

Nonexpert Opinion on Handwriting

Answer: The store detective's testimony is clearly sufficient evidence of authentication. The store detective observed Mark write the document, Rule 901(b)(1). The store detective is not testifying based upon having seen Mark's handwriting at a time other than when he wrote the confession and making a comparison. Thus Rule 901(b)(2) is not involved. Bruce, on the other hand, is attempting to lay a foundation from the admission of Mark's alleged confession through non expert opinion testimony as to the genuineness of handwriting based upon having observed Mark's handwriting in the past under circumstances not dealing with preparation for litigation, i.e., when in summer camp ten years ago. Remarkably little familiarity constitutes evidence when viewed most favorably sufficient to permit a jury to find that it is more probably true than not that Mark wrote the confession, Rule 901(b)(2). Bruce's testimony meets this standard. If whether a particular witness wrote a particular document is critical to the litigation, counsel would be well advised to corroborate authentication testimony as weak as Bruce's.

Comparison by Trier or Expert Witness

Answer: The prosecution will call a police officer to testify to having observed Mary dead at a given location. The police officer will also testify that the body was moved to the coroner's office. The coroner will testify to receiving Mary's body and as part of the autopsy procedure removing a bullet. The coroner will state that he placed the bullet in an evidence bag, sealed it, labeled it, and delivered it to the forensic crime unit of the local police department. Another police officer will testify to finding a gun in Bob's car, placing the gun in an evidence envelope, labeling it, and delivering the gun to the forensic crime unit of the local police department. An expert witness will testify to removing both the bullet and the gun, still in their evidence envelopes, from the evidence locker at the forensic crime unit. He will testify to discharging the gun into water and collecting the bullet. He will then testify to comparing the bullet retrieved from the water shot from the gun found in Bob's car with the bullet removed from Mary by the coroner. The expert will testify that the exemplar taken from the water and the bullet that killed Mary was discharged from the same weapon, i.e., gun found in Bob's car. Ordinarily it will not be required to call as a witness or show the unavailability of others who had access to the gun or bullet while in the evidence locker. Moreover, it ordinarily will not be necessary to do either with respect to still others who had access to either the bullet or the gun such as the persons who moved the body to the coroner, police officer who checked in the gun at the forensic unit, etc., etc. Moreover, an actual break in the chain of custody will not result in exclusion of the evidence when the chain of custody established to have occurred viewed as a whole supports the improbability of alteration, substitution, or change of condition.

Distinctive Characteristics and the Like

Answer: The most obvious way to authenticate the letter is to require that Toyota admit or deny as part of the pleading and/or discovery process whether the letter was sent by them. Another method would be to compare items such as ink, paper, etc., to establish that the letter in question is consistent with other letters that Toyota admits mailing to Toyota car owners or others. In addition Rule 901(b)(4) provides that appearance, contents, substance, internal patterns, or other distinctive characteristics may be sufficient to support a finding when taken in conjunction with surrounding circumstances that the matter in question is what its proponent claims, Rule 901(b)(4). Given the fact that the letter employed the name Toyota and its symbol plus very importantly that the letter included not only a statement that Jeannette owns a Toyota Tundra but includes as well its vehicle identification number, Rule 901(b)(4) is satisfied. As an additional circumstances tending to show authentication, it is not likely that someone would go to all the effort required to forge such a letter given that it is difficult to see any significant benefits flowing to a forger from such conduct.

Voice Identification

Answer: Claudia heard the thief's voice when her purse was stolen. She can testify based upon hearing the voice at that time that a particular person whom she heard speak at the line up was the person who spoke to her when her purse was stolen. Rule 901(b)(5) provides that voice identification may be by opinion testimony based upon hearing the voice at any time under circumstances connecting it with the alleged speaker.

Answer: (1) Melvin can testify that the tape recording fairly and accurately reflects the conversation that took place between Tom, Jamal and himself in the park with respect to the sale of drugs and identify who is speaking. Melvin was there, i.e., he possesses personal knowledge, Rule 602, and can thus testify identifying the voices on the tape recording, Rule 901(b)(5).

(2)(a) The tape recording may be authenticated by the testimony in part of the police officer who remained and listened to the conversation as it was being recorded. The police officer must testify that the directional microphone can pick up and transmit conversations accurately when operating properly and that it was operating properly in this case. The police officer must then testify that the tape recording fairly and accurately reflects the conversation he heard as it was being transmitted. Finally, someone else must testify identifying the voices on the tape recordings as Tom or Jamal as this police officer can identify only Melvin's and Barry's voice on the tape recording.

(b) Now the prosecution lacks a witness who can testify that the tape recording fairly and accurately reflects the conversation heard either live (Melvin) or simultaneously with it being taped (police officer who remained). With both police officers having gone to Melvin's aid, the prosecution must now lay additional foundation to admit the tape recording. It must establish that the tape recorder is capable of accurately recording the transmission from the directional microphone when both are operating properly and that both were operating properly at the time in question. This is established by testimony that both were tested before Melvin arrived at the park and that the test recording accurately reflected what had been said. In addition, the prosecution must establish a chain of custody from the tape itself since it is subject to alteration, substitution, or change in condition and no person can testify on personal knowledge that the tape to be played at trial accurately reflects the conversation. Finally, evidence must be offered identifying who was speaking at each moment of the recorded conversation.

Telephone Conversations

Answer: The first telephone call is an incoming telephone call. A mere assertion by the speaker as to his identity, being hearsay, is not a sufficient showing of his identity. Toots cannot recognize the voice of the person calling. Moreover the telephone call does not meet the requirements for the reply doctrine. While Rule 901(b)(4) provides that the contents, etc., taken in conjunction with circumstance may constitute a sufficient foundation of identification, given the content of the communication at hand and the fact that the $500 was paid to a post office box that can't be connected to AVDTA, it is suggested that Rule 901(b)(4) is not satisfied. Toots would probably need to show at a minimum that AVDTA has done telephone solicitations at same time for Rule 901(b)(4) to be satisfied. The second telephone call is outgoing. Rule 901(b)(6) provides that an outgoing telephone call is sufficiently authenticated by evidence that the call was placed to a number assigned at the time by the telephone company to a particular business and the conversation that resulted for the telephone call related to business reasonably transacted over the telephone.

Public Records and Reports

Answer: If the clerk testifies that the sprinkler system inspection report offered in evidence is an original report authorized by law to be filed and in fact filed in a public office, the clerk will have laid a sufficient foundation of authentication for the sprinkler system inspection report, Rule 901(b)(7). However, the independent inspector's company's sprinkler inspection report is hearsay not falling within any hearsay exception; Rule 803(8) covers solely records, reports, statements or data compilations prepared by the public office or agency itself, not reports filed with the public agency as authorized by law.

Ancient Documents or Data Compilation

Answer: One way would be to find a newspaper in the library reporting that Joe DeMaggio's 56 game hitting streak has ended. The newspaper having been located in the library where it would be expected to be found would be in such condition as to create no suspicion concerning its authenticity and would show on its face that it is 20 years or more old, Rule 901(b)(8). A hearsay exception for ancient documents is provided by Rule 803(16).

SELF-AUTHENTICATION

Answer:

(1) The tag stating that the hot water heater was manufactured by XXX Gas Hot Water Heater Company of Oakville, Ohio is self-authenticating when offered to prove origin of the hot water heater, Rule 902(7).

(2) Rule 902(6) provides that printed material purporting to be a newspaper is self-authenticating. However, the newspaper itself was not produced at trial. It is suggested that a writing is not self-authenticating when a witness in court testifies that a given

document she observed out of court was a newspaper. The rational of sufficient indicia of reliability requires actual production in court of the item claimed to be self-authenticating. If the actual item is not produced, authentication should proceed under Rule 901 rather than Rule 902. The requirement of actual production of the item under Rule 902 operates independently of the Original Writing Rule, Rule 1002. Of course, even if properly authenticated, the newspaper story remains hearsay not falling within a not hearsay definition or hearsay exception.

(3) Rule 902(5) provides that books purporting to be issued by a public authority, here the State of Ohio Occupational Health and Safety Department, are self-authenticating. The contents of the book appears to meet the requirements of Rule 803(8)(C).

(4) Copies in Carla's hands of service orders dealing with her hot water when authenticated upon personal knowledge by Carla, Rule 901(b)(1) remain inadmissible under the hearsay rule; Carla is not operating a business. However, Carla can request that the company that performed the service on the hot water heater provide a duplicate of the service records accompanied by a written declaration from the records custodian or other qualified witness in the form required by Rule 902(11). The duplicate, accompanied by said declaration, would not only be self-authenticating, Rule 902(11), but also admissible under Rule 803(6), the business records exception to the hearsay rule.

(5) A certified copy of the inspection report of the gas hot water heater by the city inspector would be self-authenticating under Rule 902(4), and admissible. Rules 803(8)(B) and (C) would provide a hearsay exception for matters observed by the city inspector and for his conclusion that nothing was wrong with the gas hot water heater However, Carla's statements of prior failure of the pilot light when contained in the inspection report creates a multiple level hearsay problem with no hearsay exception being available to admit Carla's statement to prove the truth of the matter stated.

ARTICLE X
CONTENTS OF WRITINGS, RECORDINGS AND PHOTOGRAPHS

Nature of An Original

Answer: There are three originals. Although there is one ink and two carbon copies, an "original" of a writing is the writing itself or any counterpart intended to have the same effect by the person executing or issuing it, Rule 1001(3); the intent of the signer was to create three originals.

The copy retained is the customer copy, already an original evidencing purchase of equipment by credit card, becomes an original business record in its own right as well when incorporated into the customer's business records in the ordinary course of business. Copies of the credit card transaction when made in the regular course of a regularly conducted business activity are also original business records as is the information entered from the credit card slip into the computer system. In short, internally generated records made in the ordinary course of business are original business records.

Requirement of An Original

Answer: To prove the content of a writing, recording, or photograph, the original writing, recording, or photograph is required, except as otherwise provided by the Federal Rules of evidence or by Act of Congress, Rule 1002. Thus in order for the Original Writing Rule to apply, the contents of a writing, recording, or photograph must be sought to be proved. If the contents are not sought to be proved, then evidence other than the original writing, recording, or photograph is admissible without reference to Rule 1002.

When a happening or transaction itself assumes the form of a writing, recording, or photograph, as with a deed or a written contract, proof of the happening or transaction necessarily involves the contents of the writing, recording, or photograph and calls for application of the Original Writing Rule. If, however, the happening or transaction does not take the form of a writing, recording, or photograph, it may be proved by other evidence even though a writing, recording, or photograph was made. The proof is directed to the occurrence of the happening or transaction and not to the contents of the writing, recording, or photograph. The Original Writing Rule, Rule 1002, applies in this situation only when the happening or transaction is sought to be proved by the writing, recording, or photograph, not when it is sought to be proved by other evidence.

The alleged beating exists in a form other than a writing, recording, or photograph. Accordingly, the presence of the videotape does not preclude the plaintiff from testifying or the passerby from testifying as to what was observed on the video camera screen. The original of the video tape is admissible. A copy of the original tape of the alleged beating, being a duplicate, Rule 1001(4), would be admissible under Rule 1003 to the same extent as the original unless a *genuine* question is raised as to the authenticity of the original. Whether a *genuine* question is present cannot be determined from the facts provided. The passerby's husband could only testify as to the content of the videotape if the original videotape is unavailable under Rule 1004. Rule 1004(1) provides that an original is unavailable if "destroyed", which could include "eaten" by the videotape machine.

Admissibility of Duplicates

Answer: Petunia is not in business. Therefore the copy she made of the contract is not an original but merely a duplicate, an exact mechanical reproduction, Rule 1001(4). A duplicate is admissible to the same extent as an original unless a genuine question is raised as to the authenticity of the original, Rule 1003(1). Here XYZ Corporation raises a genuine question as to the authenticity of what Petunia claims to be the original as it states that the date of delivery on what Petunia claims to be the contract has been modified deliberately.

Admissibility of Other Evidence of Contents

Answer: Before Irwin can introduce secondary evidence of the contract with A, B, and C, Irwin must establish that all four of the original copies he claims once existed are unavailable as provided for in Rule 1004. If he is successful, relevant evidence of any kind as to the contents of the original contract may be introduced including the copy given to his friend; no degrees of secondary evidence are recognized by Rule 1004. As to Irwin's own original contract for the van conversion, his testimony will establish that it was lost in good faith, Rule 1004(1). B's disposition testimony establishes that if there was an original contract, even though B can't recall whether there was one or not, it was destroyed in an accidental fire several months ago, Rule 1004(1). A's deposition testimony establishes that A asserts no contract ever existed. Irwin by his pleadings put A on notice that the contents of the van conversion contract would be the subject of proof at the hearing and A, stating that the contract never existed, clearly won't produce the original at trial, Rule 1004(3). Customary practice is to give formal written notice, denominated a notice to produce, in advance of the hearing, describing the particular exhibit and calling upon the opposing party to produce the writing, recording or photograph at the hearing without regard to whether notice had previously been given in the pleadings or otherwise. A notice to produce served on a party is without compulsive force. It is designed merely to account for nonproduction of the writing, recording, or photograph by the proponent, and thus enable him to use secondary evidence of the item's terms. The original contract for the van conversion Irwin will testify was given to C is not obtainable by any available judicial process or procedure, Rule 1004(2); C's attorney represents that C is no where to be found. Since all four originals have been accounted for, Irwin may introduce into evidence any secondary evidence establishing its existence, i.e., the copy of the contract originally given to his friend.

Public Records

Answer: Rule 901(b)(7) provides for authentication of a public record by testimony of a witness with personal knowledge, here

Melvin, that a writing authorized by law to be recorded or filed and in fact recorded or filed in a public office, or a purported public record, report, statement, or data compilation, in any form, is from the public office where items of this nature are kept. Employment of a handwritten copy instead of the original, a certified copy of the original, or even a duplicate as defined in Rule 1001(4), is in accordance with Rule 1005; the handwritten copy is a copy "testified to be correct by a witness who has compared it with the original", Rule 1005.

The compared copy is not always a duplicate obtained by photocopying the original public record. Sometimes mechanical reproduction of the official record or recorded or filed writing is not available at the public office. Under such circumstances, it is common for a person to handcopy the document and then compare the handwritten copy with the original. On other occasions, particularly with respect to recorded or filed documents, the party may have retained a duplicate which can be compared with the original.

Summaries

Answer: The AAA Bentley's expert witness hired by Sam will review all the books and records relating to lost inventory, damage repair, and business interruption. Because business interruption insurance provides compensation for lost profits, virtually all of Sam's business records along with other facts, data, and opinions must be analyzed by the AAA Bentley expert witness. Eventually a report accompanied by a chart, summary, or calculator will be prepared. Both will be disclosed to the insurance company. In addition, as provided in Rule 1006, the originals or duplicates of all facts, data, or opinions reviewed by the AAA Bentley expert, principally Sam's business records, will be made available to the insurance company for examination or copying, or both at a reasonable time and place. In all likelihood the insurance company will both dispute the accuracy of the AAA Bentley expert report's conclusions as well as have an expert of its own examine the aforesaid facts, data, and opinions and most likely prepare a report of their own, possibly including a chart, summary or calculation. Any report and/or chart, survey or calculation must be disclosed to Sam if the insurance company's expert witness is going to testify at trial. Since Sam's voluminous business records and other facts, data, and opinions consulted in creating the chart, summary, or calculation cannot conveniently be presented in court, Rule 1006 provides for presentation in the form of the chart, summary, or calculation, prepared by the respective experts. The court may but is very unlikely to order the facts, data, or opinions contained in the voluminous writings, recording, or photographs reviewed by the experts to be produced in court.

Functions of Court and Jury

Answer: The hospital claims that the hospital business record admitting form it is offering is the original filled out and signed by Joanne on the morning of her surgery. As such the hospital will introduce evidence sufficient to support a finding that the admitting form is what it purports to be, Rule 901(b)(1), that it is the original admitting form, and that it is admissible to prove its content under Rule 805 by virtue of Rule 803(6), business records, and Rule 803(4), statements for purpose of medical treatment. Upon this foundation, the trial judge must admit the hospital exhibit of what appears to be an original admitting form into evidence. Admissibility of secondary evidence on the part of Joanne is more complicated but equally certain to be permitted by the trial court. Joanne claims that there was an original but that the sole copy of the original was destroyed by the hospital when it was altered to read "9" instead of "1". This is established through the testimony of the nurse. Under Rule 1008, the trial judge then assumes the existence of an original which said "1" in deciding whether Joanne has established that such original, if it ever existed, is unavailable under Rule 1004(1), i.e., alteration constituting destruction. Since the hospital states that such an original stating "1" never existed, and Joanne's evidence sufficiently established that if it existed it no longer exists, the original admitting form, if it ever existed, stating "1" is agreed by both parties now not to exist. Accordingly, secondary evidence in the form of the nurse's testimony as well as introduction of the properly authenticated duplicate made by the nurse is now admissible. Either or both are admissible; Rule 1004 does not provide for degrees of secondary evidence. In accordance with Rule 1008, the jury must then decide whether the hospital admitting form signed by Joanne stated and still states as the hospital claims states "9", or whether on the basis of the nurse's testimony and the document asserted by the nurse to be an accurate copy of the admitting form as it existed right after Joanne's surgery, whether the original admitting form stated "1".

EVIDENCE FINAL ESSAY EXAMINATIONS

EXAM 1 — ANSWERS

Answer 1: (40 points)

John's statement to Ed must be analyzed under Rule 803(1), present sense impression. The part of the statement that the truck ran a red light "describes" the event. However the part of the statement to the effect that the light's been stuck on red all day long neither "describes" or "explains" an event; the statement "relates" to an event, a concept limited to Rule 803(2), excited utterances. Moreover it looks backwards thus failing to satisfy the rationale for trustworthiness underlying Rule 803(1)—contemporaneous reporting of personal knowledge of an instant event. John's statement was made "after finishing tightening the water hose", presumably an event that took a few seconds to less than a minute, and thus "or immediately thereafter." What if the statement was made 5 minutes, 10 minutes or 1 hour after perceiving the event? What is the length of a "short lapse" of time constituting "or immediately thereafter"? Ed did not see the accident and thus cannot testify to corroborate the truth of what John asserted. Pursuant to Rule 803(1) Ed's testimony, even though John does not testify, that John told him the truck ran a red light is admissible.(15)

Alice's statement to her mom meets the requirements of an excited utterance, Rule 803(2). The entire statement, even that part that states that the red light was stuck all day, relates to the startling event. Alice made her statement while under the stress of excitement caused by the event.(10)

The statement by the unidentified man appears to have been made upon personal knowledge under the continuing excitement caused by the startling event and thus also meets the requirements of Rule 803(2). The fact that the man is unidentified does not affect admissibility, only the assessment of weight to be assigned by the trier of fact. Rule 403 will not serve to exclude. The reason Rule 403 is not employed is that evaluation of whether an in-court declarant is telling the truth is not one of the functions undertaken by the court in evaluating probative value versus trial concerns. In evaluating probative value under Rule 403, the trial judge in such a situation is required to view probative value most favorable to the proponent of the evidence after first assuming that the jury finds that the out-of-court statement was made.(15)

Answer 2: (40 points)

(a) The testimony of the clerk in the dry cleaning store is evidence of another crime being offered to establish Dennis' knowledge that the $20 bills presented at Wal-Mart were counterfeit and of his intent to pass them off as genuine, Rule 404(b). While successfully paying with a counterfeit $20, if adequately established, is relevant to show knowledge and intent, the evidence of the clerk in the dry cleaning store is not sufficient, as stated, to permit a jury to find that it is more probably true than not true that Dennis was the person who paid with the three counterfeit $20 bills, Rule 104(b). Presumably the dry cleaning store took in many $20 bills that day.(10)

(b) The testimony of the clerk in the clothing store as to conduct of Dennis with respect to a $20 bill is relevant to establish knowledge and intent with respect to the $20 bills presented at Wal-Mart based upon the law of chances, Rule 404(b). Here the prosecution through the testimony of the clothing store clerk can present an adequate foundation supporting a finding that Dennis presented on a prior occasion counterfeit $20 bills as payment.(10)

(c) Evidence that a very sophisticated copying machine capable of producing counterfeit bills was found in Dennis' garage is admissible under Rule 404(b) to show plan and preparation and thus absence of mistake or accident making the evidence relevant to establish knowledge and intent. The fact that possession of the copying machine was not criminal is insignificant; Rule 404(b) applies to other crimes, wrongs, or acts.(10)

(d) Evidence of a final judgment adjudging a person guilty of a crime punishable by imprisonment in excess of one year satisfies the requirements of the hearsay exception provided in Rule 803(22) when offered to prove any fact essential to sustain the judgment in a criminal case against the same person who was the subject of the prior conviction. Evidence of the prior conviction for manufacturing and distributing counterfeit bills is admissible under Rule 404(b) to show knowledge, intent and absence of mistake or accident.(10)

Answer 3: (20 points)

(a) The original writing rule is applicable. The defamation alleged to have occurred exists solely in the form of a writing and photograph. Thus Margaret to prevail clearly must prove the content of a writing and photograph. Rule 1002 requires under such circumstances that an original is required, except as otherwise provided in the Federal Rules of Evidence or by Act of Congress.(10)

(b) The original is the 500 copies distributed to the students. Since Mary did everything by herself, the sole publication of the allegedly defamatory writing and photograph was distribution of the 500 copies to the students. Although not significant here, a digital photograph is data stored on a computer or other similar device, i.e., a computer disk, an original of which is any printout or other output readable by sight, Rule 1001(3). The 500 copies each become an original for purpose of the Original Writing Rule because their distribution constituted the allegedly defamatory publication.(10)

Answer 4: (20 points)

(a) The police officer should label the otherwise fungible beer bottle by placing a tag, scratching, or otherwise marking the beer bottle.(5)

(b) The beer bottle may be authenticated without employing a chain of custody because the police officer is able to identify the beer bottle by its tag or markings.(5)

(c) The bartender and the police officer. (5)

(d) The bartender must testify to having observed X hit Y over the head with the beer bottle and then place it upon the bar counter. The bartender must testify to having picked up the beer bottle from the counter that it was in her possession up until the police officer arrived, and that the bartender handed the beer bottle to the police officer in the same condition that it was when it came into her possession. The police officer must testify that the beer bottle in court is the same beer bottle she received from the bartender in the same condition it was when received. (5)

EXAM 2 — ANSWERS

Answer 1: (20 points) Mary's attorney would like to admit the results of Ace's own test results contained in a report that concludes that there is significant risk of injury when several empty pallets are moved in the warehouse on a forklift. Post occurrence tests and reports have generally been held to fall outside the ban of Rule 407 on the ground that neither is actually a remedial measure that would have made the injury less likely to occur although other decisions question whether post occurrence tests and reports can be freely admitted without in practice substantiality undermining the policy supporting the exclusion of subsequent remedial measures as represented in Rule 407. (5)

On the other hand, both the actual installation of mesh guards on all forklifts and the placement of a warning on the forklift against removal of the mesh guard are inadmissible under Rule 407 to prove a defect in the forklift, a defect on the forklift's design, or the need for a warming; both installation of a mesh guard and the warning notice are measures taken after an event, i.e., the accident injuring Mary, that, if taken previously, would have made the injury less likely to occur, Rule 407. (5)

When the expert for Ace testifies at trial that the forklift that injured Mary is not unreasonably dangerous by virtue of not having a mesh guard and that a mesh guard would impede the driver's line of sight, Mary's attorney will offer the subsequent installation of the mesh guard and the warning notice for a purpose other than to prove a defect in the product, a defect in the product's design, or need for a warning. When the expert opines that a mesh guard would impede the driver's line of sight, the expert is controverting the feasibility of precautionary measures thus making evidence of installation of the mesh guard by Ace on all new warehouse forklifts admissible on the issue of feasibility of precautionary measures. (5)

Whether evidence of subsequent installation of the mesh guards and inclusion of a warning notice is admissible for the other purpose of impeachment should be decided in the negative. Most decisions correctly prohibit impeachment when the evidence introduced by a defendant, here through the testimony of an expert witness, goes no further than to maintain that nothing improper occurred. This is to prevent the impeachment exception effectively destroying the rule excluding evidence of subsequent remedial measures so as to encourage such measures to be taken. On the other hand, if the evidence offered by the defendant during its case in chief goes beyond what is necessary, here that the forklift is not defective and unreasonably dangerous by virtue of not having a mesh guard and presumably on cross-examination of the expert that a warning with respect to moving empty pallets was not necessary, and asserts that a party's conduct was the "safest", or "most reasonable" or "best designed product possible" then impeachment by means of the subsequent remedial measure is in order. (5)

Answer 2: (20 points) Yes, the victim is a competent witness.

The witness clearly possesses minimum credibility, i.e., a juror could reasonably believe that the witness possesses personal knowledge, Rule 602, i.e., could observe, record, recollect, and recount with respect to the event in question. (5)

Competency of a witness to testify requires a minimum ability to observe, record, recollect and recount as well as an understanding of the duty to tell the truth. Where the capacity of a witness has been brought into question, the ultimate question is whether a reasonable juror must believe that the witness is so bereft of his powers of observation, recordation, recollection and narration as to be so untrustworthy as a witness as to make his testimony lack relevancy. One can refer to the seventy year old witness as a negligible human being—lots of very good reasons to doubt his testimony but a competent witness nevertheless. As the Advisory Committee's Note indicates, no mental or moral qualifications for testifying as a witness are specified—"the question is one particularly suited to the jury as one of weight and credibility." (10)

While the witness will not swear an oath he will affirm, i.e., promise to tell the truth, which also satisfies Rule 603. (5)

Answer 3: (20 points) The plaintiff's statements are hearsay when offered to prove that the truck ran a light, that her chest hurt badly, or that she loved her husband. (5)

None of these statements nor the statement "I'm still alive" are hearsay when offered to show she survived the accident. The mere utterance of a coherent thought makes the statement relevant, i.e., the statement is relevant for the fact said, and thus not hearsay, even the very statement "I'm alive". (5)

The statements made by the occurrence witness are relevant to show negligence, i.e., who ran the red light, and to corroborate such statement by tending to establish that the occurrence witness has maintained her position that the truck ran a red light consistently from the moment of observation through her testimony at trial. (5)

The out-of-court statement to her husband when offered to prove that the truck ran a red light is hearsay under Rules 801(a)-(c), i.e., an out-of-court oral statement of a person intended as an assertion offered is evidence to prove the truth of the matter asserted. Both the matter intended to be asserted, Rule 801(a), and the matter asserted sought to be proven, Rule 801(c), is that the truck ran a red light. The occurrence witness' statement does not meet the requirements of Rule 801(d)(1)(B), prior consistent statement of an in court witness, in that it was not offered to rebut an expressed or implied charge against the declarant of recent fabrication or improper influence or motive. (5)

Thus over objection, only the in court testimony of the occurrence witness and any of the statements by the injured lady when offered to show that she survived the accident are not hearsay under Rules 801(a)-(d).

Answer 4: (20 points) The statement testified to by the police officer at trial is a hearsay statement not admissible pursuant to any hearsay exception. The statement made to a police officer is also "testimonial" under *Crawford/Davis* as it was received by the police for the primary purpose of establishing or proving a past event potentially relevant to later criminal prosecution. Confrontation clause errors properly preserved are subject to harmless error analysis. (10)

However, since defense council did not object, the error will be reviewed on appeal under the plain error standard. The accused thus has the burden of establishing that the alleged error was "error," it was "plain," and affected "substantial rights." In addition, the accused must establish that the error "seriously affect[s] the fairness, integrity, or public reputation of judicial proceeding." (5)

Defense counsel's objection, "I object," to the admissibility of the victim of the shooting raised solely the objection of relevancy, not the Rule 403 objection for unfair prejudice appropriate for the situation. Thus, the error once again was not properly preserved below and is subject to the plain error standard of review as set forth above. (5)

Answer 5: (20 points) Where the item is not readily identifiable because it is fungible, such as where narcotics are involved, the object must be authenticated by means of a chain of custody. Chain of custody ideally consists of testimony of continuous possession by each individual having possession, together with testimony by each that the object remained in substantially the same condition during its presence in his possession. All possibility of alteration, substitution or change of condition, however, need not be eliminated to establish an adequate chain of custody. For example, normally an object may be placed in a safe to which more than one person had access without each such person being produced. Similarly an actual break in the chain of custody will not result in exclusion of the evidence when the chain of custody established to have occurred viewed as a whole supports the improbability of alteration, substitution or change of condition. Overall, the more authentication is genuinely an issue, the greater the need to negate the possibility of alteration, change in condition, or substitution. The prevailing standard is that the proponent of the evidence established to the court that there is a reasonable probability that no modification occurred. Upon such a showing, a presumption of regularity as to the chain of custody arises. The requirements of a chain of custody has been more rigorously applied in criminal than in civil cases. The prosecution to lay a sufficient foundation need not produce each and every person mentioned in the problem. Only the absence of Officer Jones or C.S.I. Blue would a practice result in exclusion of the evidence—the absence of any of the others would not prevent the prosecution from establishing to the court that there is a reasonable probability that no modification occurred. (15)

C.S.I. Blue tested only one of the bags, not all ten as he should have. Thus, there is no evidence showing that the remaining nine bags contained cocaine. (5)

Answer 6: (20 points) Mary may testify as to what she observed and may employ opinion testimony in the process provided it is rationally based on her perception and helpful. Her experience permits her to identify the outfit of the Over My Dead Body Gang. Stomped is a helpful opinion describing severe kicking but murdered execution style is an unhelpful conclusion. Mary can and should testify more specifically as to what she had observed, i.e., presumably a boy placing a gun behind the left ear of Robert and shooting him. (10) Officer Evans, as an expert in gang behavior generally and specifically with respect to the Over My Dead Body Gang, Rule 702 may testify to explain to the jury this gang's culture with respect to obtaining revenge to help explain the motive for Robert's murder, to help explain an otherwise seemingly unexplainable act, and as evidence of identity. (10)

EXAM 3 — ANSWERS

Answer 1: (40 points) The 2001 prior conviction for armed robbery of a liquor store constitutes other crime, wrong, or act evidence, Rule 404(b), admissible to prove identity on the theory of modus operandi. The two events are sufficiently unique and similar as to create a signature—the person who did one did the other. (10)

While a certified copy of the prior conviction itself, Rules 803(8)(A), 902(4) and 1005, constitutes evidence sufficient to support a finding, Rule 104(b), other evidence must be presented to establish the actual facts surrounding the 2001 conviction and their uniqueness and similarity to the armed robbery for which Harry is now on trial. (10)

The 2001 conviction is potentially admissible under Rule 609 if Harry testifies to impeach his character for truthfulness. The 2001 conviction is for a crime punishable by death or imprisonment in excess of one year not involving dishonesty or false statement. It is admissible to impeach Harry if he testifies provided that the court determines that the probative value of admitting the evidence outweighs its prejudicial effect to the accused. In practice, such impeachment is almost certainly going to be permitted. (10)

Harry's 1999 conviction for perjury involves dishonesty or false statement and is less than ten years old. As such, it is usable to impeach Harry if Harry testifies under Rule 609(a)(2) with no judicial discretionary balancing test being applied (10).

Answer 2: (20 points) No. The alleged error is not properly preserved. Pursuant to Rule 103(a) the trial court did not make a "definitive ruling on the record" excluding the evidence. Any ruling that does not state it is "definitive" is not definitive. (10)

As such, the plaintiff must make an offer of proof at trial to preserve the error for appeal. Plaintiff sometime during trial should make a request to the court to permit the expert to testify. If the request is denied at trial, an offer of proof satisfying Rule 103(a)(2) must be made making it known to the court the substance of what would be testified to by the expert if permitted to testify. The court may direct that the offer of proof be taken in question and answer form, Rule 103(b), or permit another method of presenting the offer such as a prepared statement signed by the witness. (10)

Answer 3: (40 points) Mabel's 911 call requesting police assistance meets all of the requirements for the excited utterance hearsay exception, Rule 803(2). However, under *Crawford/Davis*, the statement by Mabel to the 911 operator is "testimonial." Since Mabel does not testify subject to cross-examination the confrontation clause bars admissibility. Mabel's statement describes a past event that is over—the perpetrator was leaving the scene. Thus, there is no ongoing emergency and the primary purpose of the governmental authority in receiving the statement was to establish a past event potentially relevant to later criminal prosecution, *Davis*. (10)

Mary's statement to the police describing the robber is hearsay not meeting the requirements of any hearsay exception. (5)

As to Mary's prior statement of identification of Juan at the line up, if Mary is called at trial to testify in spite of the fact that she testifies to a lack of current recollection of the description of the perpetrator, she is available for cross-examination for both Rule 801(d)(1)(C) and confrontation clause purposes. United States v. Owens, 484 U.S. 554 (1988). (10)

Mary's identification of Juan at the line-up constitutes a statement by a declarant who testifies at the trial, subject to cross-examination concerning the statement and the statement is one of identification of a person after perceiving the person again, Rule 801(d)(1)(C). (10)

A police officer is permitted to testify on personal knowledge to the identification even if the declarant of the statement fails to so testify at trial, as would happen with Mary. (5)

Answer 4: (20 points) Bob has sufficient ongoing business dealings to identify the voice on the telephone ordering the widgets as Harry's. Their prior business dealings present circumstances sufficient to support a finding of an ability to recognize the voice as Harry's even though they never met, Rule 901(b)(5). (10)

The same is true as to the signature on the September 14, 2000 contract. The prior business dealings gave Bob sufficient familiarity with Harry's signature to authenticate the September 14, 2000 contract as having been signed by Harry, Rule 901(b)(2). (10)

EXAM 4 — ANSWERS

Answer 1: (20 points) The statement of the occurrence witness to the police officer is admissible as double level hearsay, Rule 805, as a public record, Rule 803(8), incorporating an excited utterance, Rule 803(2). Counsel for defendant Mr. Smith wants John's counsel to introduce another portion of the same police report at the same time the prior statement of the occurrence witness is being introduced under Rule 106 on the basis that such additional portion ought in fairness be considered contemporaneously. Since the second statement of the occurrence witness that John was doing wheelies on the sidewalk as he approached the intersection does serve to shed light on the initially offered statement, the trial judge should grant defense counsel's request. (5)

The second statement by the occurrence witness is not itself otherwise admissible as it is hearsay and does not meet the requirements of the excited utterance hearsay exception, Rule 803(2), or any other hearsay exception. The second statement nevertheless may be presented contemporaneously as authorized by Rule 106 and the doctrine of "door opening." (5)

The ambulance report deals with the issue of damages and not liability as does the initial statement contained in the police report offered by John's counsel. The ambulance report fails to satisfy the requirement of Rule 106 because it is not another writing which ought in fairness be considered contemporaneously. (5)

Rule 106 does not apply to oral statements. (5)

Answer 2: (40 points) Under Rule 404(a)(1) Robert may call Mary Powell as a character witness for the purpose of proving action in conformity with character to testify in the form of reputation or opinion evidence only, no specific instances of conduct, Rule 405(a), regardless of whether Robert testifies or not. Mary can testify more or less that she has known Robert for about 20 years, that they are close friends, and that in her opinion his character for peacefulness is good. Peacefulness is the relevant character trait for a person charged with assault and battery. (10)

If Mary is called as a character witness under Rule 404(a)(2), she can be asked on cross-examination as to her knowledge of relevant prior specific instances of conduct, such as a prior assault and battery conviction, 405(a). Such questions go to both the basis of Mary's opinion and her standard for believing a person to be of good character for peacefulness. (10)

If Robert testifies in his own defense and the prior assault and battery conviction is employed under Rule 609(9)(1) to impeach his character for truthfulness, such impeachment would constitute an "or otherwise" attack, Rule 608(a). Accordingly, Robert's testimony could then be supported by evidence in the form of opinion or reputation only as to character for truthfulness by Mary Powell, who could conclude her testimony by stating that she would believe Robert when he testifies under oath. (10)

Pursuant to Rule 608(b)(2) Mary Powell may be cross-examined as to specific instances of conduct probative of truthfulness, in the discretion of the court. It is extremely likely that the trial court would permit cross-examination of Mary Powell as her knowledge and evaluation against her standard for character for truthfulness of the 5 year old assault and battery conviction of Robert. (10)

Answer 3: (20 points) First, move to reopen the receipt of evidence and seek permission to recall an expert witness to testify that the value of the cocaine was in excess of $10,000. (5)

Second, ask the trial court to take judicial notice of the fact that cocaine over a certain weight of a certain purity is valued in excess of $10,000. (5)

It is unlikely that the street value of a quantity of cocaine is generally known within the territorial jurisdiction of the trial court, Rule 201(b)(1). Thus, it will be necessary to resort to sources whose accuracy cannot reasonably be questioned to accurately and readily determine the value of the cocaine in question, Rule 201(b)(2). (5)

If the court takes judicial notice, it must instruct the jury that it may, but is not required, to accept as a fact that the cocaine in question is valued in excess of $10,000. (5)

Answer 4: (20 points) Rule 408 provides that evidence of furnishing or offering or promising to furnish— accepting or offering or promising to accept—a valuable consideration in compromising or attempting to compromise a claim which was disputed as to either validity or amount, is not admissible to prove liability for or invalidity of the claim or its amount. Evidence of conduct or statements made in compromise negotiations is likewise not admissible. Rule 408 does not require the exclusion of any evidence otherwise discoverable merely because it is presented in the course of compromise negotiations. (5)

Rule 408 also does not require exclusion when the evidence is offered for another purpose, such as proving bias or prejudice of a witness, negating a contention of undue delay, or proving an effort to obstruct a criminal investigation or prosecution. (5)

The completed compromise between Allen and Z, while inadmissible under Rule 408 to prove liability for the claim, is admissible, subject to Rule 403, when offered to impeach Z's representative's testimony that Y produced a metal press that was defective and unreasonably dangerous because of bias and possible interest arising by reason of the settlement. The more Z appears to have settled cheaply, the more likely the settlement will be admitted to impeach. Allen's attorney will not be permitted to introduce X's company records indicating prior similar accidents occurring with identical automatic metal pressing machines bought from Y and installed by Z, nor the copies of letters of complaint sent by X to Y and Z demanding machine modification nor the document detailing all measures X had taken prior to Allen's accident to address the problem, including a log of letters sent to Y and Z, changes in operational procedures to reduce the risk of injury, etc., that Allen's attorney received from X as part of compromise negotiations to prove liability for the claim; Rule 408(a)(2) provides that statements made in compromise negotiations are not admissible. (5)

However, Rule 408 does not require the exclusion of any evidence "otherwise discoverable" merely because it is presented in the course of compromise negotiations. The document detailing all measures X had taken prior to Allen's accident to address the problem including a log of letters, changes in operational procedures to reduce risk, etc., is a document created solely for purposes of compromise negotiations and is not "otherwise discoverable." However, X's company records indicating former prior accidents occurring with identical automatic metal pressing machines bought from Y and installed by X and copies of letters of complaint sent by X to Y and Z demanding machine modifications are "otherwise discoverable" documents existing independent of compromise negotiations. These documents, once otherwise discovered, may be employed to the extent permitted by the Federal Rules of Evidence by Allen's attorney at trial. (5)

Answer 5: (20 points) Evidence in the form of lay witness testimony as to handwriting may be offered, Rule 901(b)(2). (5)

In addition or alternatively, an expert or the trier of fact may authenticate the signature on the affidavit as Greedy's by comparing it to a specimen of Greedy's handwriting that has been authenticated, Rule 901(b)(3). (5)

In addition, Rule 901(8) provides that authentication may be accomplished by introduction of evidence that a document or data compilation, in any form, (A) is in such condition as to create no suspicion concerning its authenticity, (B) was in a place where it, if authentic, would likely be, and (C) has been in existence 20 years or more at the time it is offered. (10)

EXAM 5 — ANSWERS

Answer 1: (40 points) A certified copy, Rules 902(4), 1005, 803(8)(B), of the police report may be offered into evidence. The police report contains matters observed pursuant to duty imposed by law as to which matters there was a duty to report. As such the police report is potentially admissible in the civil case, Rule 803(8)(B). The police report portion containing the officers physical findings and authentication of puctures falls squarely within Rule 803(8)(B). (10)

However, the statements of the four witnesses interviewed by the police officer creates a multiple level hearsay problem as to which there is no hearsay exception from the second level, i.e., the witnesses statements. (10)

With respect to the statement of the defendant, such a statement is an admission of a party opponent, Rule 801(d)(2)(A) treated as not hearsay under the Federal Rules of Evidence. Thus the police report containing the admission is admissible under Rule 803(8)(B). (10)

In the criminal prosecution, the police report is inadmissible when offered by the prosecution. Rule 803(8)(B) specifically excludes from the breath of admissibility matter observed pursuant to duty exposed by law as to which matters there was a duty to reports offered in criminal cases by the government containing matters observed by police officers or other law enforcement personnel. (10)

Answer 2: (20 points) A presumption in a criminal case operates merely as an instructed inference advising the jury that they may but are not required to draw a certain inference, i.e., Mary Jones possessed the illegal weapons. The jury should be instructed in addition that if they draw such an inference, then they are to consider that inference with all the other evidence in the case in deciding whether the government has convinced them beyond a reasonable doubt that Mary Jones possessed the illegal weapons. (10)

The instruction requiring that the jury "must find" that Mary Jones possessed the illegal weapons if they find beyond a reasonable doubt her presence in the car, created an unconstitutional mandatory criminal presumption. As stated, the instruction directs the jury to reach a certain conclusion. In a criminal case, the jury may never be constitutionally instructed that they must find an element of the offense against the accused under any circumstances. It is also unconstitutional to shift he burden of prediction or both the burden of production and the burden of persuasion to the criminal defendant as to an element of a criminal case by means of a presumption. (10)

Answer 3: (40 points)

1) No. An opinion as to the guilt or innocence of the accused is an unhelpful opinion on the ultimate issue barred by Rule 704(a). Same for lay and expert witness. (10)

2) No. Rule 704(b) specifically precludes an opinion by a lay or expert witness as to whether the criminal defendant did or did not have the mental state constituting an element of the crime charged. The police officer is however permitted to testify that the cocaine was intended for distribution. (10)

3) Yes. A police officer may testify explaining to the jury the inner working of a particular gang. The police officer must be qualified as an expert witness for this purpose. (10)

4) No. It is improper for any witness to testify that another witness is lying. (10)

Answer 4: (20 points) Harold's statement to the police is hearsay—an out-of-court statement offered in evidence to prove the truth of the matter asserted, Rules 801(a)-(c). Harold's statements when offered into evidence would be offered for the inference that he acquired his memory in a manner consistent with the events implicit in his statement—he went there first with his parents. As so offered, all four hearsay risks are present. Even though the facts asserted by Harold as to the location are independently established by finding the televisions, the statement remains hearsay. (5)

Moreover, the statement is hearsay neither falling within any not hearsay by definition provided by Rules 801(d)(1) or (2) nor within any hearsay exception provided in Rules 803 or 804. The statement, however, assuming proper notice is provided, meets the requirements of Rule 807. The statement is clearly offered as evidence of a material fact—a fact important in the litigation; the statement is more probative on the question of Harold's parents stealing the 30 television sets than any other available evidence; and the general purpose of the rules of evidence and the interests of justice will be best served by admission of the statement into evidence—a proviso of little, if any, practical importance. Finally and very importantly, the statement by Harold possesses equivalent circumstantial guarantees of trustworthiness to those statements meeting a hearsay exception provided in Rules 803 and 804. There is a strong certainty that Harold's statement was actually made and equally strong assurance that Harold had personal knowledge of the matter related—the location of the 30 televisions. Although Harold is not available for cross-examination, at his age he appears relatively free from bias—if he possesses any untrustworthy partiality it most certainly would be in favor of not against his parents. Leading questions weren't employed and the declarant never recanted. (10)

Nevertheless, while the requirements of Rule 807 are satisfied, the requirements of the confrontation clause as interpreted in *Crawford* and *Davis* are not. Harold's statement was made to a police officer received with the primary purpose being anticipation of criminal prosecution. Harold's statement is thus classified as "testimonial"; "testimonial" statements of declarants' who do not testify at trial subject to cross-examination by the criminal defendant are barred under the *Crawford/Davis* interpretation of the confrontation clause. (5)

EXAM 6 — ANSWERS

Answer 1: (20 points) Pursuant to Rule 412 which governs the admissibility of evidence relating to the alleged victim in civil and criminal cases involving alleged sexual misconduct, character testimony in the form of reputation or opinion testimony is inadmissible (unless exclusion would violate an accused's constitutional right); Rule 412(a)(2) precludes evidence offered to prove the alleged victim's sexual predisposition. Evidence of specific instances of conduct involving sexual behavior are similarly inadmissible (unless exclusion would violate an accused's constitutional right) to prove that the alleged victim engaged in other sexual behavior, Rule 412(a)(1), except in criminal cases when offered to prove the source of semen, injury or other physical evidence or if the specific instance of conduct involved sexual behavior between the alleged victim and the accused offered to prove consent, Rules 412(b)(1)(A) and (B). Samantha's alleged conduct with the football team meets neither of the exceptions. Nor do the two remaining specific instances of conduct meet either of these two exceptions. (10)

However, both remaining specific instances of conduct may meet the exception in criminal cases provided in Rule 412(b)(1)(C) for evidence the exclusion of which could violate the constitutional rights of the defendant. Evidence of falsely reporting a sexual battery is very probative of the alleged victim's sincerity. It is an act of dishonesty—a false statement—involving an element of active misrepresentation. See Rule 608(b)(1). Cross-examination of Samantha as to having falsely previously reported a sexual battery should be permitted if the falsity of the report is adequately established, which appears to be the case—three unbiased alibi witnesses. (5)

Even more clearly John's testimony as to observing Samantha leaving Bill's house and his subsequent conversation with her must be admitted pursuant to Rule 412(b)(1)(C). Samantha's conduct, if true, provides a very substantial motive for her to fabricate the charge of rape and to single out John as the rapist, i.e., she knew where he was at the relevant time, etc. (5)

Answer 2: (30 points) John's statement to Ed must be analyzed under Rule 803(1), present sense impression. The part of the statement that the truck ran a red light "describes" the event. However the part of the statement to the effect that the light's been stuck on red all day long neither "describes" or "explains" an event; the statement "relates" to an event, a concept limited to Rule 803(2), excited utterances. Moreover it looks backwards thus failing to satisfy the rationale for trustworthiness underlying Rule 803(1)—contemporaneous reporting of personal knowledge of an instant event. John's statement was made "after finishing tightening the water hose", presumably an event that took a few seconds to less than a minute, and thus "or immediately thereafter." (5)

Ed did not see the accident and thus cannot testify to corroborate the truth of what John asserted. Pursuant to Rule 803(1) Ed's testimony, even though John does not testify, that John told him the truck ran a red light is admissible. (5)

Alice's statement to her mom meets the requirements of an excited utterance, Rule 803(2). The entire statement, even that part that states that the red light was stuck all day, relates to the startling event. Alice made her statement while under the stress of excitement caused by the event. (10)

The statement by the unidentified man appears to have been made upon personal knowledge under the continuing excitement caused by the startling event and thus also meets the requirements of Rule 803(2). The fact that the man is unidentified does not affect admissibility, only the assessment of weight to be assigned by the trier of fact. Rule 403 will not serve to exclude. The reason Rule 403 is not employed is that evaluation of whether an in-court declarant is telling the truth is not one of the functions undertaken by the court in evaluating probative value versus trial concerns. In evaluating probative value under Rule 403, the trial judge in such a situation is required to view probative value most favorable to the proponent of the evidence after first assuming that the jury finds that the out-of-court statement was made. (10)

Answer 3: (20 points) Rule 803(8)(C) provides that factual findings resulting from an investigation conducted pursuant to authority granted by law are not admissible as a public record when offered by the government in a criminal case. (10)

Under the confrontation clause, a vast majority of lower court decisions have concluded employing numerous rationale that forensic laboratory reports are not testimonial under *Crawford/Davis*. (10)

Answer 4: (30 points)

a. There is only one original as the intent of the parties was that the contract would be completed only upon receipt by John, the offerer, of a fully executed copy of the offer, Rule 1001(3). (5)

b. There is one duplicate. It is the xerox copy made by Sam prior to mailing the original to John, Rule 1001(4). (5)

c. No. There is clearly a genuine question as to the authenticity of the original, Rule 1003(1), as John claims never to have received a fully executed purchase order. (5)

d. Yes. There is only one original. Sam claims it is in John's possession which John denies. Sam's attorney would, in addition to notice provided in the pleading, serve a notice to produce on John's attorney who will continue to state that he cannot produce an original because a fully executed copy of the purchase order never came into John's possession, Rule 1004(3). (5)

e. Yes. Sam must testify to having signed and mailed a fully executed copy of the purchase order to lay a foundation for its existence. With the evidence having been introduced, the trial judge will assume John actually received the fully executed purchase order, and then rule that since Rule 1001(3) has been satisfied, the original, if it ever existed, is determined by the court to be unavailable. (5)

f. Any secondary evidence of the content of the original may now be introduced by Sam; Rule 1004 does not provide for degrees of secondary evidence. Thus Sam may testify to having executed the purchase order and/or introduce the duplicate copy of the fully executed purchase he claims to have made. (5)

The jury must decide whether Sam did in fact sign a copy of the purchase order and mail it to John and finally whether the fully executed original purchase order was in fact received or not received by John.

Answer 5: (20 points) It is possible to argue that since the car rental agreement form bearing the name Irwin Stuckey is found in Irwin Stuckey's apartment, that the appearance, content, substance, internal patterns, or other distinctive characteristics, taken in conjunction with circumstances provide sufficient evidence of authentication, Rule 901(b)(4). Many cases support such an argument. (10)

However, what is actually involved is employment of the contents of a document to prove the truth of the matter asserted. Pursuant to Rule 104(b) and Rule 901(a) only admissible evidence may be considered in determining whether a sufficient foundation has been laid; the contents of the document being offered is itself inadmissible hearsay. Counsel could, and should, employ 18 USCA § 3505 applicable to foreign documents in criminal cases and obtain a foreign certification of a copy of a business record from Budget Rent A Car, Bogota, Colombia, of the Irwin Stuckey car rental. (10)

EXAM 7 — ANSWERS

Answer 1: (40 points) With respect to the robbery of Sybil, her testimony as to what happened to her is arguably relevant as to the robbery charge with respect to Brenda for a purpose other than as proof of character for conformity, i.e., to establish identity. However, where evidence of a prior offense is offered to establish that the commission of both crimes were committed by the same individual, referred to as evidence of modus operandi, under Rule 404(b) the two offenses must be so nearly identical and *unusual and distinctive* in method as to ear-mark them both as the handiwork of the same person—be like a signature. The two robberies were neither sufficiently identical nor sufficiently unusual and distinctive to meet the foregoing test. (10)

Rule 413 provides that in a criminal case in which the defendant is accused of an offense of sexual assault, evidence of the defendant's commission of another offense or offenses of sexual assault is admissible, and may be considered for its bearing on any matter to which it is relevant, including but not limited to, the character of the defendant in order to show action in conformity therewith. Rule 413 is subject to Rule 403. Harry, the defendant, alleged act in pulling down Sybil's pants does not, however, constitute the commission of an offense of sexual assault required by Rule 413. Absent is the "contact" required in Rule 413(d)(2)-(3), or the infliction of death, bodily injury or physical pain on another person required by Rule 413(d)(4)—emotional distress, embarrassment, humiliation, etc., are not encompassed in subsection (4).

[With respect to Rule 413(d)(1), 18 USCA § 2245 provides:

§ 2245. Definitions for chapter

As used in this chapter [18 USCS §§ 2241 et seq.]—

* * *

(2) the term "sexual act" means—

(A) contact between the penis and the vulva or the penis and the anus, and for purposes of this subparagraph contact involving the penis occurs upon penetration, however slight;

(B) contact between the mouth and the penis, the mouth and the vulva, or the mouth and the anus; or

(C) the penetration, however slight, of the anal or genital opening of another by a hand or finger or by any object, with an intent to abuse, humiliate, harass, degrade, or arouse or gratify the sexual desire of any person; and

(3) the term "sexual contact" means the intentional touching, either directly or through the clothing, of the genitalia, anus, groin, breast, inner thigh, or buttocks of any person with an intent to abuse, humiliate, harass, degrade, or arouse or gratify the sexual desire of any person;

(4) the term "serious bodily injury" means bodily injury that involves a substantial risk of death, unconsciousness, extreme physical pain, protracted and obvious disfigurement, or protracted loss or impairment of the function of a bodily member, organ, or mental faculty;]

* * *

As stated § 2245(3) is not satisfied as the perpetrator did not have contact through Sybil's clothing with any of the prescribed areas of Sybil's body. Moreover, Harry's conviction for exposing himself in public also fails to qualify as an offense of sexual assault. Finally, fondling the penis of a four year old boy is an act of child molestation. As drafted, although Rule 413 can be argued to include acts of child molestation because a child is a person, it appears that Rule 413 sanctions solely admissibility of other offenses of sexual assault in a criminal case in which the defendant is accused of an offense of sexual assault, and not offenses of child molestation. The fact that Rule 415 refers to both sexual assault and child molestation argues in favor of the construction that sexual assault does not include child molestation. (10)

Okay, let's assume when Sybil was attacked the perpetrator also removed her panties and in the process came in contact with her buttocks with the intent to obtain sexual gratification, 18 USCA § 2245(3); Rule 413(d)(1). Now what? Whether to admit under Rule 413 the sexual assault on Sybil in removing her panties in a prosecution for the sexual assault of fondling Brenda's breasts through her clothing illustrates the true difficulty in applying Rule 403 in determining whether evidence of another offense of sexual assault should be admitted under Rule 413. If admitted, the evidence would tend to establish that

Harry is a sexual deviant, i.e., Harry possesses the pertinent character trait of lustful disposition. What types of sexual assaults qualify where the crime charged is fondling an adult female? Does rape of a female? Does sodomy of a male? If Rule 414 was invoked in a case for fondling the penis of a four year old boy, is consensual sex with a 12 year old girl admissible? How about non consensual anal sex with a 9 year old girl? The purpose behind Rules 413-415 was to make all of the foregoing admissible because each evidences a depraved sexual behavior and thus the character trait of lustful disposition. If each and every one of the foregoing is not admissible, where do you draw the line? Finally, is application of Rule 403 to Rules 413-415 extremely likely in practice to be form over substance even more than can now be said of application of Rule 403 to evidence offered under Rule 404(b)? In short, the attack on Sybil qualifies under Rule 413, it should not and will not be excluded on the basis of Rule 403. (20)

Answer 2: (20 points) The rifle is simply inadmissible because it was not tied in any way to the crime. There is no evidence that a rifle was used in the crime. The rifle is in fact being offered as other crimes, wrongs, or acts evidence to show a character for violence for the inference that the accused acted in conformity therewith in committing the crime for which on trial. Evidence of specific instances of conduct to show character for conformity is prohibited by both Rule 404 and Rule 404(b). (10)

Defense counsel did not preserve error for appeal. A party who loses a motion in limine to exclude evidence must object to the introduction of such evidence at trial to preserve error on appeal unless the court in ruling on the motion in limine states that his ruling is "definitive," Rule 103(a). No such indication was made by the trial judge. (10)

Answer 3: (40 points)

1 (a). Betty's testimony in the form of an opinion, i.e., always sat in the front row near the windows, is evidence of the habit of person admissible under Rule 406, whether corroborated or not and regardless of the presence of eyewitnesses, to prove that Betty's conduct on the day of the robbery was in conformity with the habit, i.e., she was seated in the front row near the

windows. Sally's testimony is similarly admissible under Rule 406 provided Sally is aware of a sufficient number of instances constituting a sufficiently regular pattern of the seating behavior in the history class of her classmate Betty. (20)

1 (b). Arrests are never admissible constituting an unhelpful opinion. What would be required to lay an adequate foundation with respect to each prior purse theft is evidence sufficient to supporting a finding viewed most favorably by a reasonably jury as to the existence of the facts, i.e., more probably true than not true, constituting the prior purse snatchings, Rule 104(b). The only person apparently in a position to present such evidence as to each of the other prior instances of conduct is the alleged victim thereof. Evidence of the prior purse thefts is arguably relevant for a purpose other than to prove the character of the accused in order to show action in conformity therewith (a prohibited purpose), i.e., to establish identity. However, where evidence of a prior offense is offered to establish that the commission of both crimes were committed by the same individual, referred to as evidence of modus operandi, the two offenses must be so nearly identical and *unusual and distinctive* in method as to ear-mark them both as the handiwork of the same person—be like a signature. Purse snatching from behind does not come close to meeting the foregoing test. Thus the testimony of the two prior victims along with evidence of Harry's prior arrests is inadmissible. (20)

Answer 4: (20 points) The statement is admissible as an excited utterance under Rule 803(2). (5)

Although "bad faith" is certainly a real risk with respect to what turns out to be a wholly self-serving statement by Jim that Dennis is after him with a knife, it is the jury's role to decide what weight if any is to give to the statement. Only Rules 803(6), (7), (8) and (10) of the denominated hearsay exceptions provide that the court is to exclude a statement otherwise meeting the requirements of a hearsay exception if the source of information or the method or circumstances of preparation indicate lack of trustworthiness. If the explicit requirements of any other denominated hearsay exception are met, the trial judge must admit the statement into evidence. (15)

APPENDIX A

Hearsay and Not Hearsay Under Federal Rules of Evidence 801(a)-(d)

A. THE HEARSAY RULE

1. An Overview - Rule 802 - Hearsay Rule - Hearsay is not admissible except as provided by these rules or by other rules prescribed by the Supreme Court pursuant to statutory authority or by Act of Congress.

As stated by McCormick, Evidence § 246 at 584 (Cleary ed. 1972), the common law defined hearsay as "testimony in court, or written evidence, of a statement made out of court, the statement being offered as an assertion to show the truth of matters asserted therein, and thus resting for its value upon the credibility of the out-of-court asserter." Absent an exception to the rule against hearsay, a hearsay statement is excluded on the ground that the trier of fact is not in a position to assess the accuracy of the statement, and with it the weight to be assigned to the matter asserted as true in the out-of-court statement: the hearsay statement was not made by the witness under oath, in the presence of the trier of fact observing the witness' demeanor, subject to contemporaneous cross-examination.

Article VIII of the Federal Rules of Evidence generally approaches hearsay in the traditional manner of a definition, Rules 801(a), (b) and (c), explored in detail in Subsection 2 infra, and a rule excluding hearsay, Rule 802, subject to certain exceptions under which evidence is not required to be excluded. Hearsay is not admissible except as provided by "these rules" or by other rules prescribed by the Supreme Court pursuant to statutory authority or by Act of Congress, Rule 802. In some instances hearsay is admissible pursuant to an exception without regard to the availability of the declarant as a witness, Rule 803, while in other instances the hearsay exception requires that the declarant be unavailable, Rule 804. Rule 807 provides a residual exception for hearsay statements not otherwise admissible under either Rule 803 or Rule 804 but having equivalent circumstantial guarantees of trustworthiness. Provision is also made for hearsay within hearsay, Rule 805 and for attacking and supporting the credibility of the hearsay declarant, Rule 806. Article VIII departs from the common law in Rule 801(d)(1) by treating certain prior statements by a witness as defined as not hearsay, and in Rule 801(d)(2) by treating admissions of a party-opponent as defined as not hearsay rather than as a hearsay exception. Illustrative of non-evidence rules of the Supreme Court prescribed pursuant to statutory authority creating hearsay exceptions are Fed.R.Civ.Proc. 56, affidavits in support of motions for summary judgment and Fed.R.Crim.Proc. 4(a), affidavits to show grounds for issuing warrants. The admissibility of depositions continues in part to be governed by Fed.R.Civ.Proc. 32(a) and Fed.R.Crim.Proc. 15. Out-of-court statements that are either not hearsay pursuant to Rules 801(a)-(c) or are exempt from the bar of the rule against hearsay through definition as not hearsay, Rules 801(d)(1) and (2), or fall within a hearsay exception, Rules 803, 804, and 807, to be admitted into evidence must, of course, still meet other requirements for admissibility, such as relevance, authenticity, and when the contents of a document are sought to be proved, the Original Writing Rule, Rule 1002. While hearsay is not admissible except as provided, it is nevertheless incumbent upon the party opposing the introduction of an inadmissible hearsay statement to properly object, Rule 103(a). In the absence of an objection to hearsay, the jury may consider hearsay for whatever value it may have; such evidence is to be given its natural probative effect as if it were in law admissible.

The Introductory Note: The Hearsay Problem of the Advisory Committee describes the approach taken as follows:

The factors to be considered in evaluating the testimony of a witness are perception, memory, and narration. Morgan, Hearsay Dangers and the Application of the Hearsay Concept, 62 Harv.L.Rev. 177 (1948), Selected Writings on Evidence and Trial 764, 765 (Fryer ed. 1957); Shientag, Cross-Examination: A Judge's Viewpoint, 3 Record 12 (1948); Strahorn, A Reconsideration of the Hearsay Rule and Admissions, 85 U.Pa.L.Rev. 484, 485

(1937), Selected Writings, supra, 756, 757; Weinstein, Probative Force of Hearsay, 46 Iowa L.Rev. 331 (1961). Sometimes a fourth is added, sincerity, but in fact it seems merely to be an aspect of the three already mentioned.

In order to encourage the witness to do his best with respect to each of these factors, and to expose any inaccuracies which may enter in, the Anglo-American tradition has evolved three conditions under which witnesses will ideally be required to testify: (1) under oath, (2) in the personal presence of the trier of fact, (3) subject to cross-examination.

(1) Standard procedure calls for the swearing of witnesses. While the practice is perhaps less effective than in an earlier time, no disposition to relax the requirement is apparent, other than to allow affirmation by persons with scruples against taking oaths.

(2) The demeanor of the witness traditionally has been believed to furnish trier and opponent with valuable clues. Universal Camera Corp. v. N.L.R.B., 340 U.S. 474, 495-496, 71 S.Ct. 456, 95 L.Ed. 456 (1951); Sahm, Demeanor Evidence: Elusive and Intangible Imponderables, 47 A.B.A.J. 580 (1961), quoting numerous authorities. The witness himself will probably be impressed with the solemnity of the occasion and the possibility of public disgrace. Willingness to falsify may reasonably become more difficult in the presence of the person against whom directed. Rules 26 and 43(a) of the Federal Rules of Criminal and Civil Procedure, respectively, include the general requirement that testimony be taken orally in open court. The Sixth Amendment right of confrontation is a manifestation of these beliefs and attitudes.

(3) Emphasis on the basis of the hearsay rule today tends to center upon the condition of cross-examination. All may not agree with Wigmore that cross-examination is "beyond doubt the greatest legal engine ever invented for the discovery of truth," but all will agree with his statement that it has become a "vital feature" of the Anglo-American system. 5 Wigmore § 1367, p. 29. The belief, or perhaps

hope, that cross-examination is effective in exposing imperfections of perception, memory, and narration is fundamental. Morgan, Foreword to Model Code of Evidence 37 (1942).

The logic of the preceding discussion might suggest that no testimony be received unless in full compliance with the three ideal conditions. No one advocates this position. Common sense tells that much evidence which is not given under the three conditions may be inherently superior to much that is. Moreover, when the choice is between evidence which is less than best and no evidence at all, only clear folly would dictate an across-the-board policy of doing without. The problem thus resolves itself into effecting a sensible accommodation between these considerations and the desirability of giving testimony under the ideal conditions.

The solution evolved by the common law has been a general rule excluding hearsay but subject to numerous exceptions under circumstances supposed to furnish guarantees of trustworthiness. Criticisms of this scheme are that it is bulky and complex, fails to screen good from bad hearsay realistically, and inhibits the growth of the law of evidence.

Since no one advocates excluding all hearsay, three possible solutions may be considered: (1) abolish the rule against hearsay and admit all hearsay; (2) admit hearsay possessing sufficient probative force, but with procedural safeguards; (3) revise the present system of class exceptions.

(1) Abolition of the hearsay rule would be the simplest solution. The effect would not be automatically to abolish the giving of testimony under ideal conditions. If the declarant were available, compliance with the ideal conditions would be optional with either party. Thus the proponent could call the declarant as a witness as a form of presentation more impressive than his hearsay statement. Or the opponent could call the declarant to be cross-examined upon his statement. This is the tenor of

Uniform Rule 63(1), admitting the hearsay declaration of a person "who is present at the hearing and available for cross-examination." Compare the treatment of declarations of available declarants in Rule 801(d)(1) of the instant rules. If the declarant were unavailable, a rule of free admissibility would make no distinctions in terms of degrees of noncompliance with the ideal conditions and would exact no quid pro quo in the form of assurances of trustworthiness. Rule 503 of the Model Code did exactly that, providing for the admissibility of any hearsay declaration by an unavailable declarant, finding support in the Massachusetts act of 1898, enacted at the instance of Thayer, Mass.Gen.L.1932, c. 233 § 65, and in the English act of 1938, St.1938, c. 28, Evidence. Both are limited to civil cases. The draftsmen of the Uniform Rules chose a less advanced and more conventional position. Comment, Uniform Rule 63. The present Advisory Committee has been unconvinced of the wisdom of abandoning the traditional requirement of some particular assurance of credibility as a condition precedent to admitting the hearsay declaration of an unavailable declarant.

In criminal cases, the Sixth Amendment requirement of confrontation would no doubt move into a large part of the area presently occupied by the hearsay rule in the event of the abolition of the latter. The resultant split between civil and criminal evidence is regarded as an undesirable development.

(2) Abandonment of the system of class exceptions in favor of individual treatment in the setting of the particular case, accompanied by procedural safeguards, has been impressively advocated. Weinstein, The Probative Force of Hearsay, 46 Iowa L.Rev. 331 (1961). Admissibility would be determined by weighing the probative force of the evidence against the possibility of prejudice, waste of time, and the availability of more satisfactory evidence. The bases of the traditional hearsay exceptions would be helpful in assessing probative force. Ladd, The Relationship of the Principles of Exclusionary Rules of Evidence to the Problem of Proof, 18 Minn.L.Rev. 506 (1934). Procedural safeguards would consist of notice of

intention to use hearsay, free comment by the judge on the weight of the evidence, and a greater measure of authority in both trial and appellate judges to deal with evidence on the basis of weight. The Advisory Committee has rejected this approach to hearsay as involving too great a measure of judicial discretion, minimizing the predictability of rulings, enhancing the difficulties of preparation for trial, adding a further element to the already over-complicated congeries of pretrial procedures, and requiring substantially different rules for civil and criminal cases. The only way in which the probative force of hearsay differs from the probative force of other testimony is in the absence of oath, demeanor, and cross-examination as aids in determining credibility. For a judge to exclude evidence because he does not believe it has been described as "altogether atypical, extraordinary. * * * " Chadbourn, Bentham and the Hearsay Rule: A Benthamic View of Rule 63(4)(c) of the Uniform Rules of Evidence, 75 Harv.L.Rev. 932, 947 (1962).

(3) The approach to hearsay in these rules is that of the common law, i.e., a general rule excluding hearsay, with exceptions under which evidence is not required to be excluded even though hearsay. The traditional hearsay exceptions are drawn upon for the exceptions, collected under two rules, one dealing with situations where availability of the declarant is regarded as immaterial and the other with those where unavailability is made a condition to the admission of the hearsay statement. Each of the two rules concludes with a provision for hearsay statements not within one of the specified exceptions "but having comparable [equivalent] circumstantial guarantees of trustworthiness." Rules 803(24) and 804(b)[(5)] [now Rule 807]. This plan is submitted as calculated to encourage growth and development in this area of the law, while conserving the values and experience of the past as a guide to the future.

For the convenience of the reader, the definition of hearsay, Rules 801(a), (b), and (c), and the two categories of statements exempt from the bar of the rule against hearsay, Rule 802, through definition as not hearsay, i.e. prior statement of witness, Rule

801(d)(1), and admission by party opponent, Rule 801(d)(2), are each treated separately in the sections which follow. With respect to each of the three segments comprising Rule 801, presentation of the text of the rule is followed by commentary addressed to the various subsections comprising the particular segment of Rule 801 under consideration.

2. The Definition of Hearsay — Rules 801(a), (b), and (c)

The following definitions apply under this article:

(a) Statement. A "statement" is (1) an oral or written assertion or (2) nonverbal conduct of a person, if it is intended by the person as an assertion.

(b) Declarant. A "declarant" is a person who makes a statement.

(c) Hearsay. "Hearsay" is a statement, other than one made by the declarant while testifying at the trial or hearing, offered in evidence to prove the truth of the matter asserted.

Hearsay is defined in Rule 801(c) as a statement, other than one made by a declarant while testifying at the trial or hearing, offered in evidence to prove the truth of the matter asserted, i.e., the content of the statement. A statement, Rule 801(a), is (1) an oral or written assertion or (2) nonverbal conduct of a person, if it is intended by him as an assertion. The term "assertion" includes both matters directly expressed and matters necessarily implicitly being asserted. A declarant is simply a person who makes a statement, Rule 801(b). Thus documentary evidence as well as the oral assertions of a witness, whether or not recorded, may fall within the definition of hearsay. The definition of hearsay contained in Rule 801 conforms with that of the common law. Specific applications of the definition of hearsay are presented in the sections that follow.

The four risks to be considered in evaluating the testimony of a witness are (1) perception in the sense of capacity and actuality of observation by means of any of the senses, (2) recordation and recollection (sometimes called memory), (3) narration (sometimes called ambiguity), and (4) sincerity (sometimes called fabrication).

> "When a witness testifies about an event he is saying that he perceived a particular fact, remembered it up to the moment of testifying and is now accurately expressing his memory in words. Error, deliberate or unconscious, can enter this process anywhere between the initial perception and the in-court narration. For instance, the witness may not have perceived the event at all, or he may have seen it without understanding, or his impression may have been affected by his emotional and intellectual condition at the moment, or he may have seen it so fleetingly that no accurate impression has remained. Or even if he accurately perceived the event when it occurred, the passage of time may have dulled his recollection or replaced the remembered facts with others. He may be deliberately lying in court, or be honestly mistaken, or be incapable of translating his memory into language that will have the same meaning to his listeners." 4 Weinstein's Evidence ¶ 800[01] at 800-9-800-10 (1984).

To encourage the witness to testify to the best of his ability regarding each of the four risks, and to expose inaccuracies in the witness' testimony, a witness possessing minimum credibility is required to testify at trial as to a matter within his personal knowledge (1) under oath or affirmation, (2) in person, so that the trier of fact may observe the witness' demeanor, and (3) subject to contemporaneous cross-examination.

Each of the four risks associated with evaluating the accuracy of a witness' in-court testimony are present as well when an out-of-court statement is offered to prove the truth of the matter asserted. Thus the trier of fact must evaluate risks of perception, recordation and recollection, narration, and sincerity when determining the trustworthiness of a hearsay statement. When the statement offered for the truth of the matter asserted was made out of court, however, the trier of fact, where ascertaining inaccuracies, does not have the benefit of having the declarant before it, under oath, and subject to contemporaneous cross-examination. Hearsay is excluded because of the absence of these tests for ascertaining trustworthiness.

"An understanding of the hearsay rule requires an elementary consideration of the conditions which under our adversary system are imposed upon a witness testifying in open court and of the mental processes which the trier of fact must use in valuing testimony.

If we assume that P, the proponent of the witness W, desires to persuade the trier T, to find the existence of fact A, P, through his attorney, will utter a series of sounds to which W will respond with another series of sounds. T must interpret these sounds and in doing so, must rely upon his sense of hearing aided by his sense of sight and his capacity for understanding and interpreting W's language. Suppose that he determines that the sounds uttered by W make up the sentence, 'I perceived A.' In order to put a proper value on this utterance as tending to prove the existence of A, T must either consciously or instinctively go through the following mental operations: (1) He must ask whether W by the use of this sentence means to convey to T what T would have meant if T had used the same words. If not, just what does he mean to convey? The answer will depend upon T's deduction as to W's use of language. (2) If T decides that W wants to have T believe that W perceived A, T must then ask whether W believes what he had said to be the truth. If not, T will not use the utterance as evidence of its truth. If so T has concluded that W believes that he now remembers that he perceived A. (3) But what about the validity of this belief? Does W really remember or is he deceiving himself by attributing to himself the experience of another? If he has had a personal experience, how much of what he relates is he remembering and how much is he reconstructing? T must determine to what extent, if at all, he can rely upon W's memory. (4) After determining how far W's memory is reliable, T must then decide to what extent W's mental impression at the time of his perception corresponded to what was then open to his perception. T's decision will depend upon his conclusion as to W's capacity and opportunity for accurate perception, and the stimuli for using that capacity at the relevant time. All this means only that T must use his own capacity for accurate observation and his ability to interpret what is happening in his presence and must determine to what extent he can rely upon W's use of language, sincerity, memory and perception.

Now if T decides that the series of sounds uttered by W make up the sentence: 'Declarant told me that he perceived A,' it is obvious that T's mental operations will concern only W's auditory experience and will furnish no basis for a conclusion by T as to Declarant's use of language, sincerity, memory, or perception in his communication to W, except possibly what T can gather from W's description of the details of W's auditory experience. In a word, upon the issue of the existence or non-existence of A, Declarant is the witness and W is only the means by which Declarant's testimony is brought to T. W is telling only what he heard Declarant say, and W's testimony is hearsay.

Since we are assuming that the investigation as to the existence of A is in an Anglo-American court, Declarant, if present, would not be heard unless he spoke under oath or an equivalent sanction and subject to cross-examination. It would seem too close for argument that P cannot avoid the imposition of these conditions upon his witness by the device of transmitting Declarant's testimony through W. And, generally speaking, he cannot do so. Hearsay is prima facie inadmissible." Morgan, Basic Problems of Evidence 243-44 (1961).

The essential factor underlying the rule excluding hearsay is the inability to conduct cross-examination.

"The primary justification for the exclusion of hearsay is the lack of any opportunity for the adversary to cross-examine the absent declarant whose out-of-court statement is introduced into evidence." Anderson v. United States, 417 U.S. 211, 220, 94 S.Ct. 2253, 41 L.Ed.2d 20 (1974).

"Emphasis on the basis of the hearsay the rule today tends to center upon the condition of cross-examination. All may not agree with Wigmore that cross-examination is 'beyond doubt the greatest legal engine ever invented for the discovery of truth,' but all will agree with his statement that it has become a 'vital feature' of the Anglo-American system. 5 Wigmore, § 1376, p. 29. The belief, or perhaps hope, that cross-examination is effective in exposing imperfections of perception, memory, and narration is fundamental. Morgan, Foreword to Model Code of Evidence 37 (1942)." Advisory Committee's Introductory Note: The Hearsay Problem.

"Morgan ['Hearsay Dangers and the Application of the Hearsay Concept,' 62 Harv.L.Rev. 177, 186 (1948)] analyzed the protective function of cross-examination and concluded (1) that while the fear of exposure of falsehoods on cross-examination is a stimulus to truth-telling by the witness, actual exposure of willful falsehood is rarely accomplished in actual practice and (2) that the most important service of cross-examination in present day conditions is in affording the opportunity to expose faults in the perception and memory of the witness." McCormick, Evidence § 245 at 583 (Cleary ed. 1972).

The definition of hearsay contained in Rules 801(a)-(c) together with the four risks relating to trustworthiness of a statement with which the hearsay rule is concerned is depicted in the following "Stickperson Hearsay" diagrams. Figure A portrays the hearsay risks associated with an oral statement of an out of court declarant. Figure B portrays the hearsay risks associated with the introduction of a written or recorded statement of an out of court declarant.

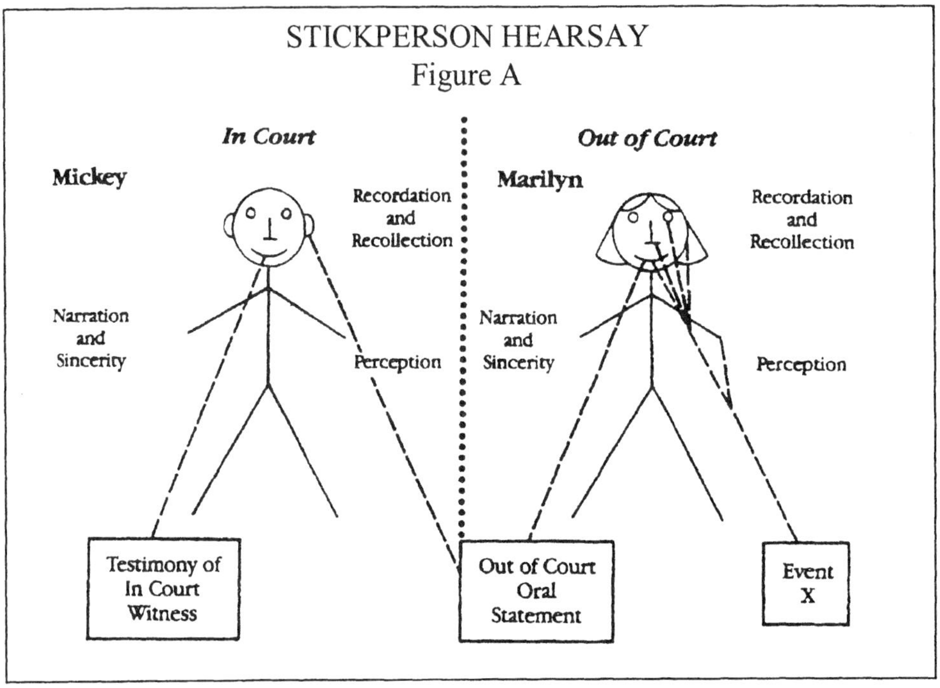
STICKPERSON HEARSAY
Figure A
In Court
Out of Court
Mickey
Marilyn
Recordation and Recollection
Narration and Sincerity
Perception
Recordation and Recollection
Narration and Sincerity
Perception
Testimony of In Court Witness
Out of Court Oral Statement
Event X

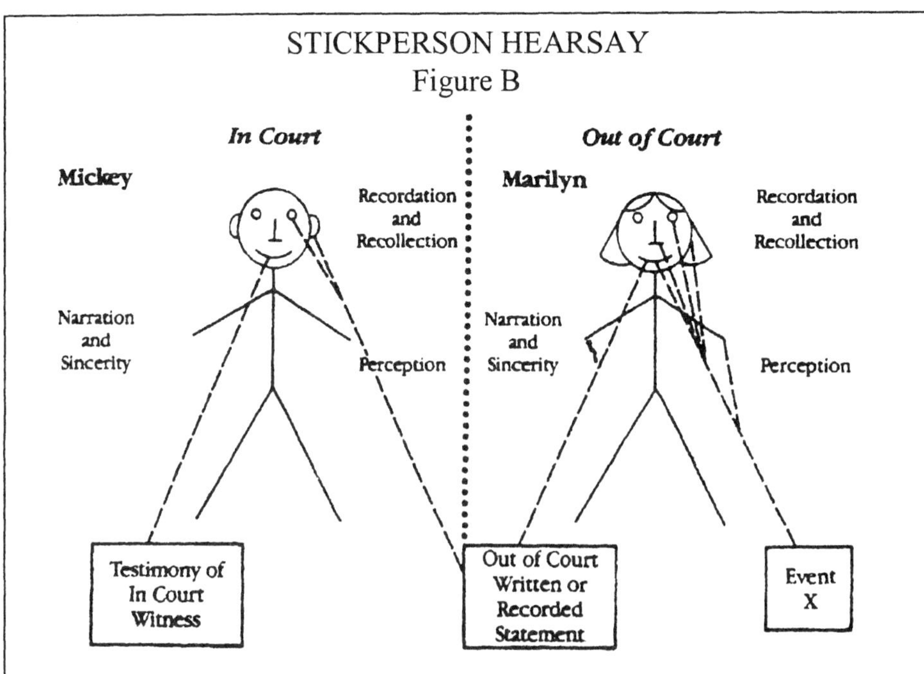
STICKPERSON HEARSAY
Figure B
In Court
Out of Court
Mickey
Marilyn
Recordation and Recollection
Narration and Sincerity
Perception
Recordation and Recollection
Narration and Sincerity
Perception
Testimony of In Court Witness
Out of Court Written or Recorded Statement
Event X

Figure A represents Mickey testifying in court, under oath, subject to contemporaneous cross-examination repeating the contents of a conversation with Marilyn during which she described in detail what she had previously perceived-referred to in the diagram as Event X. Figure B represents Mickey authenticating in court a written or recorded statement of Marilyn detailing the same Event X. Thus the testimonial risks associated with in court testimony (Mickey) and the hearsay risks associated with an out of court statement (Marilyn) can be appreciated by beginning at the left of either diagram and following the dashed lines of Mickey and then Marilyn. The dashed lines of Mickey represent the risks associated with an in court declarant testifying as to a fact of which he has personal knowledge, in this case the *making* of the oral, written or recorded statement by Marilyn. The dashed lines of Marilyn represent the risks associated with an out of court declarant's hearsay statement, i.e., a statement that must either be believed by the declarant to be true or in fact be true in order to be relevant in the context of the particular litigation.

In both Figure A and Figure B, testimony of Mickey repeating or authenticating a statement by Marilyn relevant without regard to the truth of the matter stated, or Marilyn's belief in the truth of the matter stated, is represented by the movement from the left of the diagram along the dashed lines *to* the dotted line. Testimony of Mickey repeating or authenticating a statement by Marilyn relevant only if believed by her to be true or only if the matter asserted is in fact true is represented by movement from the left of the diagram along the dashed lines to the right of the dotted line. Only if relevance of the statement requires movement beyond the dashed lines of Mickey along the dashed lines of Marilyn either into her head alone (belief-two hearsay risks) or further down the other side (Event X-four hearsay risks) is the statement hearsay. Such statement is offered to prove the truth of the matter asserted, Rule 801(c). Thus anytime a statement's relevance depends upon movement along the dashed lines of the diagram from the in court testimony of Mickey to the right of the dotted line, the statement is hearsay. Conversely, to the extent that the statement is relevant simply by virtue of Mickey repeating his personal knowledge of the making of the oral statement (Figure A) or authenticating the written or recorded assertion of Marilyn (Figure B), since movement proceeds from the in court testimony of Mickey along the dashed lines only *to* the dotted line, the statement of Marilyn is not hearsay. Such statement is not being offered to prove the truth of the matter asserted but solely for the fact it was said.

Determining whether a statement offered at trial for a particular purpose is hearsay thus involves solely a search for the presence of hearsay risks (belief-two hearsay risks or Event X-four hearsay risks). If such hearsay risks are present the statement is hearsay. *No assessment of the magnitude of hearsay risks present is undertaken.* Magnitude of hearsay risks bears solely upon whether the hearsay statement is felt sufficiently trustworthy to be admitted pursuant to an exception to the rule against hearsay.

The term "matter asserted" as employed in Rule 801(c) and at common law includes both matters directly expressed and matters the declarant necessarily implicitly intended to assert. When the declarant necessarily intended to assert the inference for which the statement is offered, the statement is tantamount to a direct assertion and therefore is hearsay. The declarant necessarily intends to assert, i.e., implicitly asserts, matters forming the foundation for matters directly expressed in the sense that such additional matters must be assumed to be true to give meaning to the matters directly expressed in the context in which the statement was made. To illustrate, the question "Do you think it will stop raining in one hour?" contains the implicit assertion that it is currently raining. The fact that it is currently raining is a necessary foundation fact which must be assumed true for the question asked to make sense.

With respect to the statement "it will stop raining in an hour," "[i]n

> addition to the express assertion, there is in that case a necessary implication of an assertion that it is now raining and will continue to rain for an hour. As far as the intent of the speaker is concerned, while it is principally to give his thought as to the cessation of the rain, it is incidentally without doubt to assert its present existence and continuance. It is due only to a chance use of words that he did not say 'the rain that is now falling will continue for an hour,' in which case the express and implied assertion would have been undoubtedly the same. It would seem, therefore, that ... implied assertions are hearsay, ..." Seligman, "An Exception to the Hearsay Rule," 26 Harv.L.Rev. 146, 150-151 n.13 (1911).

Under the definition of hearsay contained in Rule 801(a)-(c) when a statement offered to prove the truth of the matter asserted is made "other than ... by the declarant while testifying at the trial or hearing," the statement is hearsay without regard to whether or not the out of court declarant is available to testify or actually testifies at the trial or hearing at which the out of court statement is offered. Therefore the definition of hearsay in Rules 801(a)-(c) applies to all statements not made at the trial or hearing and thus not made subject to contemporaneous cross-examination before the trier of fact. When the out of court declarant does in fact also testify at trial, cross-examination, or direct and redirect examination, at that time provides an opportunity for the party opposing the truth of the out of court statement to explore the truth of the out of court statement before the trier of fact. Nevertheless, general admissibility of prior statements of in court witnesses is not provided for in the Federal Rules of Evidence. Rule 801(d)(1) does exempt from the operation of the rule against hearsay by definition as not hearsay certain prior inconsistent statements, Rule 801(d)(1)(A), and certain prior consistent statements, Rule 801(d)(1)(B). In addition statements of prior identification of a person after perceiving him are also exempted as not hearsay, Rule 801(d)(1)(C). The reasons for limiting the definition of not hearsay to only certain situations involving prior statements of an in court witness subject to later cross-examination are discussed in Section B infra.

Notice that in deciding whether a statement falls within the definition of hearsay, it is irrelevant whether the statement was self-serving or disserving at the time of being either made or offered. It is similarly irrelevant in deciding whether a statement falls within the definition of hearsay as to whether the statement is being offered as direct or circumstantial evidence.

Occasionally, whether the party against whom a statement is offered was present when the statement was made has a bearing upon whether the statement is hearsay under Rules 801(a)-(c) or is defined by Rule 801(d)(2) as "not hearsay". Thus, an oral statement offered to show notice cannot have been effective as such unless it was made in the presence of the person sought to be charged with notice. Similarly, the presence of the party is essential if it is claimed that she admitted the truth of an oral statement by failing to deny it. In general, however, the presence or absence of the party against whom an extrajudicial statement is offered has no bearing upon either its status as hearsay or its admissibility, and an objection based on such absence betrays a basic lack of understanding of the nature of hearsay. Accordingly, in the great majority of situations, the objection "not in the presence of the defendant," and the converse in support of admissibility, "in the presence of the defendant," both frequently heard in criminal prosecutions, fail to address questions relevant to determining admissibility under the hearsay rule.

Under Rule 103, a party who does not make a timely objection cannot complain of the admission of hearsay. The question remains, however, of the weight and probative value of hearsay so admitted. The almost infinite variety which hearsay assumes precludes any answer except that hearsay will be considered and given its natural probative effect.

(a) Nonverbal Conduct Intended as an Assertion

Nonverbal conduct may on occasion clearly be the equivalent of an assertive statement, that is, done for the purpose of deliberate communication, and thus classified as hearsay, Rule 801(a)(2). Nodding "Yes" or "No", pointing to identify the picture of the perpetrator in a mug shot book, pointing out the perpetrator in a lineup, and the sign language of the hearing impaired are as plainly assertions as are spoken words. So too is a videotape of the injured plaintiff recreating the accident which caused his injuries.

(b) Nonverbal Conduct Not Intended as an Assertion

Nonverbal conduct not intended as an assertion is not hearsay, Rule 801(a)(2). The provision of Rule 801 declaring nonverbal conduct not intended as an assertion not hearsay resolves a long-time controversy among commentators. The controversy, however, has only been rarely the subject of judicial decision, frequently because the hearsay question has not been perceived. When the issue is whether an event happened, evidence of conduct from which the actor's belief may be inferred from which in turn the happening of the event may be inferred, bears at least a superficial resemblance to an out of court statement by the actor that he believed the event occurred. An analysis in terms of the principal danger which the hearsay rule is designed to guard against, i.e., lack of opportunity to test by cross-examination the capacity and actuality of his perception as well as his recordation, recollection, narration, and sincerity, however, leads to a rejection of the analogy between such an inference, sometimes called an "implied assertion," and an express allegation. When a person acts without intending to communicate a belief, his veracity is not involved. Furthermore there is frequently a guarantee of the trustworthiness of the inference to be drawn because the actor has based his actions on the correctness of his belief. Consider for example a person who is observed opening an umbrella, offered for the inference that it is raining. While the inference to be drawn from such nonverbal conduct is the same as in the case of a direct assertion that it is raining, the fact remains that the intent to assert is absent and thus the all important danger believed to be inherent in hearsay with respect to sincerity is absent as well. While the risk of sincerity is removed, the objection still remains that the accuracy of the actor's perception and recollection are untested by cross-examination as to the possibility of honest mistake. However risks of error in these respects are more sensibly factors to be used in evaluating weight and credibility rather than grounds for exclusion. Practical necessity also supports treating nonverbal nonassertive conduct as falling outside the definition of hearsay. Consider the illustration of a car stopped at a traffic light offered for the inference that the light was red. Treatment of such conduct as hearsay would too often exclude highly trustworthy and probative evidence. Resort to the residual exception of Rule 807 is an inappropriate response to a frequently recurring situation.

The court must be satisfied of the probative value of the proffered proof in light of trial concerns. Thus the inference of belief drawn from the nonassertive conduct and/or the inference drawn from such belief when offered to prove the truth of the fact impliedly being asserted may be too ambiguous to warrant submitting the evidence to the jury; its probative value may be so slight in comparison with the possibility of confusing and misleading the trier of fact that exclusion pursuant to Rule 403 is proper. Thus if the person opening an umbrella was known to be both exiting a store that sells umbrellas and superstitious concerning the opening of umbrellas indoors, ambiguity associated with the offering of such evidence to establish that it was raining at the time would certainly be enhanced. Whether exclusion is warranted under Rule

403 of course would depend upon examination of all relevant circumstances.

When nonverbal conduct is at issue, it is not always perfectly clear whether an assertion was intended by the person whose conduct is in question. Consider the conduct of men and women during courting. If evidence of conduct is offered on the theory that it is not intended as an assertion and hence not hearsay, the burden of showing that an assertion was intended is on the party objecting to the evidence. The question of intention to assert is a preliminary one for the court, Rule 104(a). Even if the person intended to make an assertion, such as punching someone who insulted your companion, the person's conduct may itself be relevant to establish the same fact of consequence in the litigation and if so is not hearsay for such purpose.

Nonverbal conduct not intended as an assertion and thus not hearsay under Rule 801(a)(2) is frequently, but incorrectly, treated as an admission of a party opponent. Illustrations include flight, silence, and the fabrication, destruction, or suppression of evidence. Such evidence may be excluded upon application of Rule 403.

(c) Oral or Written Conduct Not Intended as an Assertion

Considerations present with respect to nonverbal nonassertive conduct support the position taken in Rule 801(a)(1) that oral or written conduct not intended as an assertion is not hearsay. Examples of such conduct are screams of pain, outbursts of laughter, singing a song or uttering or writing an expletive. Of course any of the foregoing may be intended as an assertion.

(d) Statements Offered Other Than to Prove the Truth of the Matter Asserted; Verbal Act; Characterizing Act; Effect on Listener; Impeachment

Hearsay does not encompass all extrajudicial statements but only those offered for the purpose of proving the truth of matters asserted in the statement, Rule 801(c). Therefore when the mere making of the statement is the relevant fact, i.e., tends to establish a fact of consequence, Rule 401, hearsay is not involved. Such statements are frequently said to be offered solely for the fact said and not for the truth of the matter asserted, i.e., the truth of their contents.

Verbal act. As to one group of extrajudicial statements falling outside the category of hearsay, the statement itself, the verbal act, has independent legal significance or gives rise to legal consequences, sometimes referred to as an operative act. Thus testimony by an agent as to a statement by the principal granting him authority to act as agent is not hearsay. Other illustrations include statements constituting contracts, canceling of an insurance policy, constituting an anticipatory breach, constituting the crime (e.g., selling drugs, solicitation, threatening someone's life, offering a bribe), directions issued by a police officer directing traffic, a stop sign at an intersection, statements offered as evidence of defamation, evidence offered that a statement has been made so as to establish a foundation for evidence showing the statement was made as part of a fraudulent scheme and is false, and statements offered to place in context other statements otherwise admissible made in a conversation.

Characterizing act. Also included in the group of statements comprising operative legal acts are assertions which relate to and characterize a particular act. Thus for example, where an instrument designating the executive's wife as his beneficiary was unclear as to whether she was to be the beneficiary of his insurance policy or of a six months gratuity payment, oral statements accompanying delivery of the instrument resolving the ambiguity were not hearsay.

Effect on listener. Another group falling outside the category of hearsay consists of statements made by one person which become known to another offered as a circumstance under which the latter acted and as bearing upon his conduct. For example a law enforcement official explains his going to the scene of the crime by stating that he received a radio call to proceed to a given location or to explain why an investigation was undertaken or other subsequent action, such testimony is not hearsay. However if he becomes more specific by repeating definite complaints of a particular crime by the accused, this is so likely to be misused by the jury as evidence of the fact asserted that the content of the statement, absent special circumstances enhancing probative value, such as the policeman shot a person leaving the bank after being advised that a bank clerk had been shot, should be excluded on the grounds that the probative value of the statement admitted for a non-hearsay purpose is substantially outweighed by the danger of unfair prejudice, Rule 403. Other illustrations of a statement being offered for the purpose of showing the probable state of mind of the listener include being placed on notice or having knowledge. Thus, in a negligence action to recover damages for personal injury sustained in a fall, a statement to a customer of a food store by the manager that the floor in aisle 2 is wet is not hearsay when it is offered to show the unreasonableness of the customer's conduct in skipping down aisle 2.

The same statement offered to show the floor was wet, of course, is hearsay. Similarly threats made to the defendant bearing on the reasonableness of his apprehension of danger or conversely providing a motive for action are not hearsay when offered for such purpose. In addition, the victim's fearful state of mind is an element in proving extortion. The testimony of victims as to what others say to them and the testimony of others as to what they said to the victim are admitted, not for the truth of the information in the statements but for the fact that the victim heard them from which one can infer the state of mind of a reasonable person having heard such statements. Similarly where the defendant alleges duress as a defense, statements threatening her and her two small children are not hearsay when offered to show her state of mind; in a prosecution for income tax violation, evidence as to advice received by the defendant at a tax protestors' meeting is not hearsay when offered to prove intent. Instructions to an individual to do something, such as a mother telling her son "Wait here, I'll be right back", are also not hearsay. Evidence relevant for its effect on the listener is subject to exclusion under Rule 403, after taking into consideration the giving of a limiting instruction.

A statement which is not hearsay when offered for its effect on listener is hearsay as defined in Rules 801(a)-(c) when offered to prove the truth of the matter asserted. The giving of a limiting instruction is appropriate. Thus a statement by Harry to John that Sam is the person who keyed John's car is not hearsay when offered as relevant to establish John's motive, and thus relevant to prove that John was the person who slashed Sam's tires, but hearsay when offered to prove that Sam in fact keyed John's car.

Impeachment. Prior statements of a witness inconsistent with the witness' in-court testimony offered solely to impeach, Rules 607 and 613, are not hearsay.

3. Problem Areas in Defining Hearsay

(a) Circumstantial Evidence

The employment of circumstantial evidence has occasionally over the years given rise to discussion of the application of the rule against hearsay. Such discussions have tended to be confusing and more often than not theoretically unsound. The reason for such inaccuracy may be attributed primarily to the fact that in most such instances while the evidence under consideration was highly probative, highly necessary and highly trustworthy, no applicable hearsay exception existed. Under such circumstances, it is not surprising that both the courts and commentators "squeezed" and thereby distorted the proper application of the definition of hearsay for the sake of admissibility of the evidence in the case at hand. With the enactment of the residual hearsay exception, Rule 807, resort to distortion of the hearsay definition in the interests of justice in the case at hand is no longer required. It should no longer be tolerated.

Hearsay questions arising with respect to evidence employed circumstantially, while varied, may for purpose of analysis conveniently be discussed in connection with certain relatively distinct and recurring situations. As will be developed, whether evidence is direct or circumstantial is irrelevant in determining whether the evidence falls within the rule against hearsay.

Mechanical traces. Presence of something upon a person or premises may constitute circumstantial evidence giving rise to an inference that a person did an act with which these circumstances are associated. Such items, referred to by 1A Wigmore, Evidence §§ 149-160 (Tillers rev.1983) as mechanical traces, include (1) the presence upon a person or premises of articles, fragments, stains, or tools, (2) brands on animals or timber, or (3) tags, signs and numbers on automobiles, railroad cars or other vehicles or premises and (4) postmarks, fingerprints and footmarks. Mechanical traces are frequently relevant as circumstantial evidence looking backwards to show that some act was or was not done. Hearsay questions arise only when the relevancy of the circumstantial evidence, such as a tag or sign, derives solely from the truth of the mechanical trace. Take for example the situation of a tag bearing the name "Bill Snow" on a briefcase containing narcotics. Since the relevancy of the tag to identify the defendant whose name is Bill Snow with the briefcase to which the tag is attached derives from the truth of the assertion made on the tag, i.e., this briefcase belongs to Bill Snow, the tag is hearsay. To say that the tag is a mechanical trace admissible as "circumstantial evidence of ownership" improperly ignores the definition of hearsay. To say that the tag is extremely probative and trustworthy evidence of ownership is simply to say that hearsay evidence may be extremely probative and trustworthy.

To be distinguished is the situation where the relevancy of the mechanical trace does not derive from the truth of the statement itself. Consider a book of matches bearing the name Red Fox Inn found on the defendant accused of a murder committed at the Red Fox Inn. If authenticated solely as having been taken off the person of the defendant, the matchbook is hearsay since its relevancy depends on the acceptance of the assertive statement on the matchbook that its origin is the Red Fox Inn. Now assume that the owner of the Red Fox Inn testifies that the matchbook found on the defendant is identical to the matchbooks he places on tables for use by customers. At this juncture, the relevancy of the matchbook is no longer dependent on the truth of the matter asserted but is based upon personal knowledge and the process of comparison. This point can be more easily appreciated by changing the cover of the matchbook to a modern design bearing no lettering at all. When the owner of the Red Fox Inn testifies that this matchbook is identical to those distributed at his bar, the nonhearsay nature of the physical evidence is highlighted.

Character of an establishment: McCormick, Evidence § 249 at 102 (4th ed. 1992) classifies as not hearsay situations where "the character of an establishment is sought to be proved by evidence of statements made in connection with activities taking place on the premises." The classic illustration involves the placing of telephone calls to an establishment accused of gambling. To enhance the probative value and trustworthiness of the statements under consideration, assume 20 policemen accompanied by 20 clergy of various denominations place tape recorders on 40 telephones and record 100 calls each answered by a police officer or clergy and each proceeding something like, "This is Tom, put $2 to win on Acne Pimple in the third at Belmont." While occasionally considered not hearsay as either a statement characterizing an act or as circumstantial evidence not being offered for the truth of the matter asserted but solely for the fact said, the plain and simple fact is that such statements fall clearly within the definition of hearsay. There is no independently relevant act, apart from the statements placing the bets themselves, for the statements to characterize. The statements are irrelevant if offered solely for the fact they were said. For any of the telephone calls to be relevant to establish that the establishment where the 40 telephones were located was a betting parlor, the declarant who placed the telephone call must have intended to call the number reached. Moreover, the declarant must have believed that the number dialed was a betting parlor. In addition, the declarant must have intended to place a bet, instead of, for example, playing a practical joke. Finally, and most importantly, the declarant's intention to place a bet must have been formed in reliance upon previously acquired personal knowledge that the number dialed is in fact a betting parlor. Thus the out-of-court statement placing a bet is relevant only when offered to prove the truth of the matter necessarily implicitly being asserted by the out-of-court declarant, i.e., that the establishment reached is in fact a betting parlor. As presented such statements also fall within the residual hearsay exception of Rule 807.

Notice that in the illustration the telephone calls were answered by the police officers and clergy. If a police officer had overheard a person working at the establishment respond to the statement, "This is Tom, put $2 to win on Acne Pimple in the third at Belmont," with, "You got it, settle up as usual," the situation would be entirely different. The statement of the out-of-court declarant need no longer be true to be relevant. Similarly, the statement of the person working at the establishment accepting the bet would be a verbal act possessing independent significance under applicable substantive criminal law.

Personal knowledge of independently established facts. On rare occasions, statements are offered into evidence to prove personal knowledge of the declarant as to the truth of the matter asserted when the truth of the matter asserted is firmly established by independent evidence. Personal knowledge of the declarant is relevant in such cases to establish the presence of the declarant at a particular location at a particular time. Consider, for example, the case of Bridges v. State, 247 Wis. 350, 19 N.W.2d 529 (Wis.1945). In *Bridges,* the defendant was convicted of taking indecent liberties with a seven year old girl named Sharon Schunk. She was abused by a man in an Army uniform at his house. The serious question was identification of the defendant as that person. This identification in part depended upon whether the house to which Sharon had been taken by her assaulter was the house at 125 East Johnson Street in which the defendant concededly resided at the relevant time. At trial, statements made by Sharon to her mother and police officers prior to discovery of the location of defendant's house as to the general appearance of the steps to the porch, the front door, and the room and articles therein of the house to which she had been taken by the perpetrator on February 26, 1945 were admitted. The Supreme Court of Wisconsin upheld admission of Sharon's statements as circumstantial evidence of personal knowledge not being offered to prove the truth of the matter asserted:

> Defendant contends the court erred also in admitting testimony by police officers as to matters stated by Sharon in defendant's absence. He claims these statements were hearsay evidence and therefore were not admissible. * * * There is testimony by police officers and also Mrs. Schunk as to statements which were made to them by Sharon on February 26 and 27, 1945, and also during the course of their subsequent investigations to ascertain the identity of the man who committed the offense and of the house and room in which it was committed. In those statements she spoke, as hereinbefore stated, of various matters and features which she remembered and which were descriptive of the exterior and surroundings of the house; and of the room and various articles and the location thereof therein. It is true that testimony as to such statements was hearsay and, as such, inadmissible if the purpose for which it was received had been to establish thereby that there were in fact the stated articles in the room, or that they were located as stated, or that the exterior features or surroundings of the house were as Sharon stated. That, however, was not in this case the

purpose for which the evidence as to those statements were admitted. It was admissible in so far as the fact she had made the statements can be deemed to tend to show that at the time those statements were made,—which was a month prior to the subsequent discovery of the room and house at 125 East Johnson Street,—she had knowledge as to articles and descriptive features which, as was proven by other evidence, were in fact in or about that room and house. If in relation thereto Sharon made the statements as to which the officers and her mother testified, then those statements,—although they were extra-judicial utterances, —constituted at least circumstantial evidence that she then had such knowledge; and that such state of mind on her part was acquired by reason of her having been in that room and house prior to making the statements.

* * *

So in this case the proof that Sharon made the statements in question before there was any possibility of having what she stated she remembered about the house, and room, and articles therein, from her first contact therewith, affected or changed by what she learned after the discovery and location thereof, at 125 East Johnson Street, is material and significant in so far as it tended to show that she had knowledge of certain things in and about the house and room. The existence of those things in fact could not, however, be established by her hearsay statement, but had to be proven by other evidence which was competent. In other words, although proof of her extrajudicial assertions was competent to show such knowledge on her part, it could not be deemed to prove the facts asserted thereby. When, for instance, it was proven that Sharon stated during the evening after the alleged assault that there was a picture of the lady in the room, her statement did not constitute competent evidence to prove that there was such a picture in the room. But her statement was competent as evidence to prove that she had knowledge of such an object in the room and for this purpose the utterance is not inadmissible hearsay, but is a circumstantial fact indicating knowledge on the part of Sharon Schunk at a particular time.

Notwithstanding the court's holding, Sharon's statements are hearsay. Her statements were offered for the inference that she acquired her memory in a manner consistent with the events described in her statement. As so offered, all four hearsay risks are present. It is certainly possible, albeit unlikely, that Sharon created a description of the house out of whole cloth. More likely, she may have in good faith provided a description of a house where she had been on an occasion not connected to the assault. Finally, she may have described a house that was suggested to her earlier by the police or someone else as being the house where she had been taken. Admittedly, the magnitude of the hearsay risks are small. Nevertheless, because the risks of perception, recordation and recollection, narration, and sincerity are present with respect to Sharon's statements, the statements fall within the definition of hearsay when offered to prove Sharon's personal knowledge of objects in the defendant's house to establish that the assault took place in that house. Relevancy of Sharon's statements involves hearsay risks located in the "Stickperson Hearsay" diagram on the right of the dotted line. Sharon's statements are, however, admissible under the residual hearsay exception of Rule 807.

Circumstantial use of utterances to show state of mind. McCormick historically has asserted that while a direct declaration of the existence of a state of mind or feeling which it is offered to prove is hearsay, declarations which only impliedly, indirectly, or inferentially indicate the state of mind or feeling of the declarant are not hearsay. McCormick, Evidence § 249 at 590-91 (Cleary ed. 1972) employed the following illustration:

> In a contested will case the proponent might seek to support the validity of testator's bequest to his son Harold against the charge of undue influence by showing that long before the time when the alleged influence was exerted, the testator had shown a special fondness for Harold. For this purpose evidence might be offered (a) that the testator had paid the expenses of Harold, and for none other of his children, in completing a college course, (b) that the testator said, "Harold is the finest of my sons," and (c) that he said, "I care more for Harold than for any of my other children." When offered to show the testator's feelings toward his son, under the suggested definition item (a) would present no hearsay question, item (b) would be considered a

> non-hearsay declaration raising a circumstantial inference as to the testator's feelings, and (c) a direct statement offered to prove the fact stated, and hence dependent for its value upon the veracity of the declarant, would be considered hearsay.

For McCormick the distinction, as artificial as it is, itself breaks down when one considers statements offered to show a person's mental incompetency. McCormick concluded that even the direct assertion "I believe that I am King Henry the Eighth," undeniably falling squarely within the definition of hearsay, may nevertheless be classified as nonhearsay on the theory of "verbal conduct offered circumstantially." Many years ago Professor Hinton correctly exposed the errors of McCormick's ways:

> It has sometimes been argued by judges and writers that, where the issue is the sanity of the testator, and some absurd statement by him is proved, e.g., "I am the Emperor Napoleon", no hearsay use is involved because we are not seeking to prove that he really was Napoleon, and hence that we are making a purely circumstantial use of his words to prove his irrational belief. The difficulty is that this view ignores the implied assertion of belief. If the statement had taken the form, "I believe that I am Napoleon", and were offered to prove that the testator so believed, it would be generally conceded [but not by McCormick] that the statement was hearsay, and receivable only because of an exception to the rule. The former assertion is simply a short method of stating the speaker's opinion or belief. Implied assertions seem to fall within the hearsay category as well as express assertions.

Hinton, State of Mind and the Hearsay Rule, 1 U.Chi.L.Rev.394, 397-98 (1934).

If the declarant must believe the matter asserted to be true for any inference to logically flow, whether the statement is "Harold is the finest of my sons", "I believe I am King Henry the Eighth," or "I am the Emperor Napoleon," the hearsay risks of sincerity and narration are present. Such statements are thus properly classified as hearsay. Consider the 8 year old boy shooting foul shots at the basket located on his garage who says "I'm Michael Jordan."

Clearly his mental state does not come into question unless he believes the statement to be true. It is sometimes asserted that determining whether such statements are or are not hearsay is "limited to the realm of theory" in that a hearsay exception exists for statements of a declarant's then existing, mental, emotional or physical condition, Rule 803(3). Nevertheless the confusion that broad use of the concept of circumstantial evidence creates in the overall analysis of hearsay versus not hearsay remains. Moreover mechanical traces and character of an establishment statements do not conveniently fall within a common law hearsay exception. Characterizing assertive statements as circumstantial is simply utterly irrelevant in addressing the definitional framework of hearsay set forth in Rules 801(a)-(c). The practice should be discontinued.

(b) Basis for Nonasserted Inference or "Implied Assertion"

If a statement, although assertive in form, is offered as a basis for inferring something other than the truth of the matter asserted, the Advisory Committee's Note to Rule 801(a) indicates that the statement is "excluded from the definition of hearsay by the language of subdivision (c)." The Advisory Committee's assertion as to the non-hearsay nature of statements offered for a different inference rests on the assumption of a reduced sincerity risk alleged to be similar to that associated with nonverbal conduct not intended as an assertion at all.

> "Admittedly the uncross-examined statement is subject to all the hearsay dangers, except to the extent that deliberate falsification diminishes when a statement is not used to prove anything asserted therein. See Morgan, Basic Problems of Evidence 249 (1962)." McCormick, Evidence § 249 at 590 n.92 (Cleary ed. 1972).

It is extremely doubtful whether statements offered as a basis for inferring something other than the matter asserted possess a reduced sincerity risk, much less a reduced sincerity risk sufficient to warrant non-hearsay treatment. If a sufficiently reduced sincerity risk actually is not present, in spite of the implication in the Advisory Committee's Note, a statement offered as a basis for inferring something other than the matter asserted clearly must be considered hearsay under both the common law and Rules 801(a)-(c) definitions.

The famous English case of Wright v. Doe d. Tatham illustrates the problem under consideration. In *Tatham,* plaintiff's lessor claimed the right to inherit as heir of John Marsden. Defendant, Marsden's steward, claimed as devisee. The case hinged upon the testamentary capacity of Marsden. Defendant offered in evidence certain letters Marsden received from persons who had subsequently died. One of these letters from Marsden's cousin, dated October 12, 1784, recounted the details of a sea voyage, described conditions at the destination, and wished Marsden good health. Another from Rev. Marton, a vicar, dated May 20, 1786, requested Marsden to direct his attorney to propose some terms for a settlement of a dispute between Marsden and the parish or township. A third was a letter of gratitude dated October 3, 1799 from Rev. Ellershaw upon resigning a curacy to which Marsden had appointed him. The will and codicil were made in 1822 and 1824 respectively. At trial, three letters were excluded. A verdict was returned for plaintiff's lessor, and defendant sued out a writ or error to the Exchequer Chamber from the judgment entered thereon. The judgment was affirmed by an equally divided court. On further writ of error, the House of Lords also affirmed, 5 Cl. & F. 670, 47 Rev. Rep. 136 (1838). The following extract by Baron Parke in the Exchequer Chambers, 7 Adolph. & E. 313, 383-89, 112 Eng.Rep. 488 (1837), is selected from the numerous opinions delivered in the two courts of review:

PARKE, B. * * * It is argued that the letters would be admissible because they are evidence of the treatment of the testator as a competent person by individuals acquainted with his habit and personal character, not using the word treatment in a sense involving any conduct of the testator; that they are more than mere statements to a third person indicating an opinion of his competence by those persons; they are acts done towards the testator by them, which would not have been done if he had been incompetent and from which, therefore a legitimate inference may, it is argued, be derived that he was so.

Each of the three letters, no doubt, indicates that in the opinion of the writer the testator was a rational person. He is spoken of in respectful terms in all. Mr. Ellershaw describes him as possessing hospitality and benevolent politeness; and Mr. Marton addresses him as competent to do business to the limited extent to which his letter calls upon him to act; and there is no question but that, if any one of those writers had been living, his evidence, founded on personal observation, that the testator possessed the qualities which justified the opinion expressed or implied in his letters, would be admissible on this issue. * * *

But the question is, whether the contents of these letters are evidence of the fact to be proved upon this issue,—that is, the actual existence of the qualities which the testator is, in those letters, by implication, stated to possess: and those letters may be considered in this respect to be on the same footing as if they had contained a direct and positive statement that he was competent. For this purpose they are mere hearsay evidence, statements of the writers, not on oath, of the truth of the matter in question, with this addition, that they have acted upon the statements on the faith of their being true, by their sending the letters to the testator. That the so acting cannot give a sufficient sanction for the truth of the statement is perfectly plain; for it is clear that, if the same statements had been made by parol or in writing to a third person, that would have been insufficient; and this is conceded by the learned counsel for the plaintiff in error. Yet in both cases there has been an acting on the belief of the truth, by making the statement, or writing and sending a letter to a third person; and what difference can it possibly make that this is an acting of the same nature and sending the letter to the testor? It is admitted, and most properly, that you have no right to use in evidence the fact of writing and sending a letter to a third person containing a statement of competence, on the ground that it affords an inference that such an act would not have been done unless the statement was true, or believed to be true, although such an inference no doubt would be raised in the conduct of the ordinary affairs of life, if the statement were made by a man of veracity. But it cannot be raised in a judicial inquiry; and, if such an argument were admissible, it would lead to the indiscriminate admission of hearsay evidence of all manner of facts.

Further, it is clear that an acting to a much greater extent and degree upon such statements to a third person would not make the statements admissible. For example, if a wager to a large amount had been made as to the matter in issue by two third persons, the payment of that wager, however large the sum, would not be admissible to prove the truth of the matter in issue. You would not have had any right to present it to the jury as raising an inference of the truth of the fact, on the ground that otherwise the bet would not have been paid. It is, after all, nothing but the mere statement of that fact, with strong evidence of the belief of it by the party making it. Could it make any difference that the wager was between the third person and one of the parties to the suit? Certainly not. The payment by other underwriters on the same policy to the plaintiff could not be given in evidence to prove that the subject insured had been lost. Yet there is an act done, a payment strongly attesting the truth of the statement, which it implies, that there had been a loss. To illustrate this point still further, let us suppose a third person had betted a wager with Mr. Marsden that he could not solve some mathematical problem, the solution of which required a high degree of capacity; would payment of that wager to Mr. Marsden's banker be admissible evidence that he possessed that capacity? The answer is certain; it would not. It would be evidence of the fact of competence given by a third party not upon oath.

Let us suppose the parties who wrote these letters to have stated the matter therein contained, that is, their knowledge of his personal qualities and capacity for business, on oath before a magistrate, or in some judicial proceeding to which the plaintiff and defendant were not parties. No one could contend that such statement would be admissible on this issue; and yet there would have been an act done on the faith of the statement being true, and a very solemn one, which would raise in the ordinary conduct of affairs a strong belief in the truth of the statement if the writers were faithworthy. The acting in this case is of much less importance, and certainly is not equal to the sanction of an extrajudicial oath.

Many other instances of a similar nature, by way of illustration, were suggested by the learned counsel for the defendant in error, which, on the most cursory consideration, any one would at once declare to be inadmissible in evidence. Others were supposed on the part of the plaintiff in error, which, at first sight, have the appearance of being mere facts, and therefore admissible, though on further consideration they are open to precisely the same objection. On the first description are the supposed cases of a letter by a third person to any one demanding a debt, which may be said to be a treatment of him as a debtor, being offered as proof and that the debt was really due; a note, congratulating him on his high state of bodily vigour, being proposed as evidence of his being in good health; both of which are manifestly at first sight objectionable. To the latter class belong the supposed conduct of the family relations of a testator, taking the same precautions in his absence as if he were a lunatic; his election, in his absence, to some high and responsible office; the conduct of a physician who permitted a will to be executed by a sick testator; the conduct of a deceased captain on a question of seaworthiness, who, after examining every part of the vessel, embarked in it with his family; all these, when deliberately considered, are with reference to the matter in issue in each case, mere instances of hearsay evidence, mere statements, not on oath, but implied in or vouched by the actual conduct of persons by whose acts the litigant parties are not to be bound.

The conclusion at which I have arrived is, that proof of a particular fact, which is not of itself a matter in issue, but which is relevant only as implying a statement or opinion of a third person on the matter in issue, is inadmissible in all cases where such a statement or opinion not on oath would be of itself inadmissible; and, therefore, in this case the letters which are offered only to prove the competence of the testator that is the truth of the implied statement therein contained, were properly rejected, as the mere

> statement or opinion of the writer would certainly have been inadmissible. * * *

In *Tatham,* each of the three letters written to the testator, Marsden, and offered by the proponents of his will and codicil were not of a kind that would likely have been written to a mentally defective person. The inference suggested is that the writers believed him to be competent, which in turn justifies the inference that he was competent. Both the Exchequer Chamber and the House of Lords ruled the letters inadmissible hearsay as "implied assertion." The courts rejected the notion that since the out-of-court declarant did not intend to assert the matter for which the statement was being offered, i.e., the competency of the testator, there existed a sufficient reduction in the likelihood of conscious fabrication to warrant non-hearsay treatment.

The Advisory Committee's apparent attempted rejection of Wright v. Doe d. Tatham is as unfortunate as it is incorrect. Fortunately, it has not had significant impact on the courts which by and large continue to follow *Tatham.*

When a statement is offered to infer the declarant's state of mind from which a given fact in the form of an opinion or otherwise is inferred, because the truth of the matter asserted must be assumed in order for the nonasserted inference to be drawn, the statement is properly classified as hearsay under the language of Rules 801(a)-(c). Since the matter asserted in the statement must be true, a reduction in the risk of sincerity is not present. Thus, if Rev. Ellershaw were to testify in court, he would be required to lay a foundation establishing his personal knowledge of facts forming the basis of his opinion before rendering that opinion. If a sufficient foundation of personal knowledge was not established, Rev. Ellershaw would not be permitted to render his opinion as to Marsden's testamentary capacity. Similarly, for the letter of Rev. Ellershaw to be offered in evidence for the further inference that Rev. Ellershaw believed Marsden possessed testamentary capacity, the existence of each of the facts which Rev. Ellershaw relied upon to support his expression of gratitude, whether or not expressed in the letter, must be within his personal knowledge in order for the opinion to be admissible. Moreover, the expression of gratitude itself must be sincerely felt for the inference of testamentary capacity to flow. Because the basis for Rev.

Ellershaw's expression of gratitude, in addition to the expression itself, must be true for any inference as to testamentary capacity to flow from the matters asserted, all four hearsay risks are present. Finally because the matters asserted by the statement must themselves be true for any inference desired to be relevant, the sincerity risk is not reduced. The fact that the sincerity risk is fully present with respect to the matter asserted makes the statement hearsay even though the sincerity risk is arguably reduced with respect to the inference to be drawn once the truth of the matter asserted is assumed. Even this reduction in sincerity risk will not be present where the declarant intends that the nonasserted inference be drawn such as occurs with respect to statements made to accomplish a fraud.

The argument expressed below and accepted by the Advisory Committee, asserting a reduced risk of sincerity with respect to the inference to be drawn from the statement, fails to appreciate the risk of sincerity arising from the fact that the matter asserted must be true for any inference at all to arise.

> "Reliance on an implied assertion involves the following reasoning process. The fact finder is informed by testimony that X engaged in certain conduct. This conduct is not a direct assertion of f, the disputed fact, but the fact finder is asked to infer from the conduct that X believes f to be true. Having made this inference the finder must then infer from X's belief in f that f is true. This inference from belief to truth will be sound only if X's belief faithfully reflects the fact and the reflection will be faithful only if X's perception of the fact and his recollection of that perception were accurate. Reliance on implied assertions, therefore, necessarily entails reliance on memory and perception. On the other hand, since an implied assertion by definition consists of conduct not intended as an assertion concerning f, there is no danger that the actor is being insincere about f. A person who did not intend to make any statement about f could not have intended to make a misleading statement about f. Similarly, since the actor's conduct does not consist of words expressly stating f, there is no danger that language apparently affirming or denying f, and so understood by the fact finder, was in reality intended to convey a

> different meaning. If brief, while reliance on uncross-examined express assertions would expose the fact finder to the dangers of faulty narration, insincerity, inaccurate perception, and erroneous memory, only the perception and memory dangers seem to be posed by uncross-examined implied assertions. Because implied assertions entail fewer dangers than express assertions—especially because implied assertions raise no problem of insincerity—it is argued that they should be classified as nonhearsay." Finman, "Implied Assertions as Hearsay: Some Criticisms of the Uniform Rules of Evidence," 14 Stan.L.Rev. 682, 685-86 (1962).

Realization that the argument of a reduced sincerity risk fails once it is recognized that the matter asserted must be true for any inference to arise can be appreciated by considering an example. Assume a statement by a company president to his wife that he had a dull time on a weekend business cruise on the company ship is offered to show that the ship, damaged by fire later in that week, was believed by the company president to be seaworthy for the inference that it was seaworthy. If the company president had really taken his secretary with him that weekend by airplane to Las Vegas, where is the reduced risk of sincerity? Compare the situation of the company president who, after inspecting the ship, actually goes out to sea. The former is a statement offered for a different inference, sometimes called an "implied assertion," where no reduced sincerity risk is present. The latter is nonverbal nonassertive conduct, where a reduction in the risk of fabrication is caused by a lack of an intent to assert anything.

A statement made to Marsden may have no relevant content as to which truth or falsity comes into question. Assume someone approaches Marsden and says "Hi" or "Hope all is well with you." Such a statement may be offered for the implied assertion that the declarant would not have spoken in such a manner to someone who is not competent. Putting aside the relative weak probative value of the implied assertion, the implied inference can be drawn only if the declarant has previously acquired personal knowledge of Marsden through prior contact. Thus the "implied assertion" is dependent upon the perception, recordation and recollection, and narration of the declarant. It is also based upon the declarant's sincerity in the sense of really intending to communicate with

Marsden. Thus the declarant could have made the statement to be polite to someone in earshot knowing full well that Marsden was not capable of a response. Therefore, even such statements possess all four hearsay risks and are thus properly classified as hearsay.

In short, while the Advisory Committee was correct with respect to a reduced risk of sincerity associated with nonverbal conduct not intended as an assertion, it is suggested that the Advisory Committee did not sufficiently consider the encouraged extension of the same concept to verbal statements offered as a basis for inferring something other than the matter asserted. Since the sincerity risk is fully present with respect to the matter asserted, the statement is hearsay even though the sincerity risk is arguably reduced with respect to the inference to be drawn once the truth of the matter actually asserted is assumed. Even this reduction in sincerity risk would not be present where the declarant intended that the nonasserted inference be drawn such as occurs with respect to statements made to accomplish a fraud.

Even if one assumed that a reduced risk of sincerity did arise when an assertive verbal statement is used to infer something other than the truth of the matter asserted, the practical importance of the concept nevertheless is small when compared to the analytical confusion the concept causes in the minds of those attempting to apply the hearsay rule. Such confusion strongly suggests rejection of the concept. Moreover, many statements potentially falling within the category of statements offered for a different inference are admissible as a hearsay exception for then-existing state of mind, Rule 803(3). Thus, whenever the state of mind of the declarant is itself a fact of consequence in the litigation, discussion of whether the statement is hearsay is of no practical importance. However, where the inferred state of mind of the declarant is not an issue, but is itself used to infer the truth of a non-asserted fact, such as the competency of another in Wright v. Doe d. Tatham, the state of mind exception is not available. In such circumstances, if the statement possesses sufficient guarantees of trustworthiness, and is necessary in the context of the litigation, the statement may nevertheless be admissible under the residual hearsay exception of Rule 807.

The three letters in *Tatham* illustrate statements offered not for the truth of the matter asserted, but as a basis for drawing a nonasserted inference. The hearsay nature of such statements formed the basis of the foregoing discussion. Notice that not all statements offered in evidence for a further inference fall within the breadth of the concept of a statement offered as a basis for drawing a nonasserted inference. In the situation under discussion, the initial inference as to the state of mind of the declarant is inferred from the statement, not asserted by it. When the state of mind is directly asserted, the statement is clearly hearsay. Thus if Rev. Ellershaw had written Marsden's attorney stating that he believed Marsden possessed testamentary capacity, the letter would clearly be hearsay. Similarly, when the declarant also necessarily intended to assert, although he did not directly assert, the inference for which the statement is offered, the statement is hearsay. Matters that are implicitly being asserted are for hearsay analysis purposes tantamount to a direct assertion. Obviously, when the declarant also intends to assert the matter the statement is used to infer, the argument of a reduced risk of sincerity is a non sequitur. The closer the inference to be drawn is to the matter expressly asserted, the more likely the declarant intended to assert the inference the statement is offered to prove. Finally, the concept of a statement offered to infer something other than the truth of the matter asserted can be asserted by its supporters, albeit incorrectly, to apply solely to those situations where the actual statement of the declarant is used to infer the truth of an "implied assertion" being made by the declarant and not to inferences derived directly from assuming the truth of the matter actually asserted. Thus nothing in the nonasserted inference doctrine supports the notion, for example, that an out of court statement by a witness that a car was going 80 miles per hour five blocks from the site of the accident is not hearsay because the fact asserted is being used to infer speed at the time of the accident, a fact not itself being asserted.

4. Interpreting the Definition of Hearsay

Courts and commentators have struggled with the definitional aspects of hearsay under the cloud that given the pigeonhole theory of class exceptions to the hearsay rule, many trustworthy and necessary statements if classified as hearsay would be excluded at trial. Attempts to expand admissibility through novel interpretations of the definition of hearsay naturally resulted. Such novel interpretations have taken the form, for example, of arguing that "I believe I am King Henry the Eighth" and statements offered to infer something other than the truth of the matter asserted are not hearsay. While novel, such interpretations are neither correct interpretations of the definition of hearsay nor do they comport with the analysis of risks the hearsay rule attempts to address. Such novel interpretations have at the same time greatly confused not only many practitioners and courts but thousands of law students each year. Whatever value these novel interpretations once had is no longer true today. With the availability of the residual hearsay exception of Rule 807, trustworthy and necessary hearsay will no longer be inadmissible simply because it fails to fit neatly into one of the pigeonhole hearsay exceptions.

It is therefore suggested that clarity would be fostered and confusion eliminated if once and for all the courts would declare that Rules 801(a)-(c) include (1) a statement to the extent relevant only if the declarant believes the matter asserted to be true, whether that statement be "I am Napoleon" or "I believe I am King Henry the Eighth" and (2) a statement whose relevance depends upon the matter asserted being true without reference to whether a further inference is then going to be drawn. Both of these novel approaches are in fact now recognized as hearsay by the text of Rules 801(a)-(c); any contrary suggestion in the Advisory Committee's Note with respect to statements forming the basis for a nonasserted inference is incorrect. What is needed is explicit court recognition thus putting the issue to rest. An alternative formulation of Rule 801(c), identical in content while highlighting the hearsay nature of statements offered as a basis for a nonasserted inference and all statements of state of mind, is as follows:

(c) Hearsay.

"Hearsay" is a statement offered in evidence, other than one made by the declarant while testifying at the trial or hearing, to the extent relevance depends upon (1) the truth of the matter asserted or (2) the declarant's belief in the truth or falsity of the matter asserted.

B. PRIOR STATEMENT BY WITNESS

When the out-of-court declarant is also an in-court witness, the witness' prior statements, whether consistent or inconsistent with the witness' in court testimony, or constituting a prior statement of identification, can be explored on direct and redirect examination or cross-examination of the witness to the same extent as the witness's in court testimony on personal knowledge of the matters stated in such out-of-court statements. The witness is under oath throughout with his or her demeanor being observed throughout. Thus the truth assessing components of the ordinary system of oath, demeanor and cross-examination are satisfied wherever the out-of-court declarant "testifies at the trial or hearing and is subject to cross-examination concerning the [prior] statement," Rule 801(d)(1).

"Considerable controversy has attended the question whether a prior out-of-court statement by a person now available for cross-examination concerning it, under oath and in the presence of the trier of fact, should be classed as hearsay. If the witness admits on the stand that he made the statement and that it was true, he adopts the statement and there is no hearsay problem. The hearsay problem arises when the witness on the stand denies having made the statement or admits having made it but denies its truth. The argument in favor of treating these latter statements as hearsay is based upon the ground that the conditions of oath, cross-examination, and demeanor observation did not prevail at the time the statement was made and cannot adequately be supplied by the later examination. The logic of the situation is troublesome. So far as concerns the oath, its mere presence has never been regarded as sufficient to remove a statement from the hearsay category, and it receives much less emphasis than cross-examination as a truth-compelling device. While strong expressions are found to the effect that no conviction can be had or important right taken away on the basis of statements not made under fear of prosecution for perjury, Bridges v. Wixon, 326 U.S. 135, 65 S.Ct. 1443, 89 L.Ed. 2103 (1945), the fact is that, of the many common law exceptions to the hearsay rule, only that for

> reported testimony has required the statement to have been made under oath. [It should be noted, however, that Rule 801(d)(1)(A), as enacted by the Congress, requires that a prior inconsistent statement have been made under oath.] Nor is it satisfactorily explained why cross-examination cannot be conducted subsequently with success. The decisions contending most vigorously for its inadequacy in fact demonstrate quite thorough exploration of the weaknesses and doubts attending the earlier statement. State v. Saporen, 205 Minn. 358, 285 N.W. 898 (1939); Ruhala v. Roby, 379 Mich. 102, 150 N.W.2d 146 (1967); People v. Johnson, 68 Cal.2d 646, 68 Cal.Rptr. 599, 441 P.2d 111 (1968). In respect to demeanor, as Judge Learned Hand observed in Di Carlo v. United States, 6 F.2d 364 (2d Cir.1925), when the jury decides that the truth is not what the witness says now, but what he said before, they are still deciding from what they see and hear in court. The bulk of the case law nevertheless has been against allowing prior statements of witnesses to be used generally as substantive evidence. Most of the writers and Uniform Rule 63(1) have taken the opposite position." Advisory Committee's Note to Rule 801.

However not all prior statements of the in-court witness are defined as not hearsay by Rule 801(d)(1).

"The position taken by the Advisory Committee in formulating this part of the rule is founded upon an unwillingness to countenance the general use of prior prepared statements as substantive evidence, but with a recognition that particular circumstances call for a contrary result. The judgment is one more of experience than of logic. The rule requires in each instance, as a general safeguard, that the declarant actually testify as a witness, and it then enumerates three situations in which the statement is excepted from the category of hearsay. Compare Uniform Rule 63(1) which allows any out-of-court statement of a declarant who is present at the trial and available for cross-examination." Advisory Committee's Note to Rule 801(d)(1).

Consideration of trial concerns underlying Rule 403, i.e., the danger of unfair prejudice, confusion of the issues, misleading the jury, undue delay, waste of time and the needless presentation of cumulative evidence, result in only some prior inconsistent statements, Rule 801(d)(1)(A), and some prior consistent statements, Rule 801(d)(1)(B), being defined as not hearsay. On the other hand, as interpreted, all prior statements of identification of a person made after perceiving the person again, Rule 801(d)(1)(C), are defined as not hearsay.

A witness who testifies to a lack of recollection is nevertheless "subject to cross-examination" for purposes of Rule 801(d)(1).

1. Prior Inconsistent Statements - Rule 801(d)(1) - Statements Which Are Not Hearsay: Prior Statement By Witness

The following definitions apply under this article:

(d) Statements Which Are Not Hearsay. A statement is not hearsay if-(1) Prior Statement by Witness. The declarant testifies at the trial or hearing and is subject to cross-examination concerning the statement, and the statement is (A) inconsistent with the declarant's testimony, and was given under oath subject to the penalty of perjury at a trial, hearing, or other proceeding, or in a deposition, or * * *

At common law a witness could be impeached on a non-collateral matter by extrinsic proof that he made a statement out of court inconsistent with his in court testimony. The prior statement had to be inconsistent, and a proper foundation had to be laid during cross-examination of the witness. The inconsistent statement was hearsay and hence was not admitted as substantive evidence but rather was limited solely to its impeaching effect upon the credibility of the witness. Of course, prior inconsistent statements of a witness are not to be confused with an admission of a party-opponent, which has always been and continues to be regarded as substantive evidence, Rule 801(d)(2), requiring no preliminary foundation on cross-examination, Rule 613(b).

Rule 801(d)(1)(A) alters the common law to the limited extent of exempting from the bar of the rule against hearsay, Rule 802, through definition as not hearsay a prior statement of a declarant who testifies at trial and is subject to cross-examination concerning the statement, if the statement is inconsistent with his testimony, and was given under oath, subject to the penalty of perjury at a trial, hearing, or other proceeding, or in a deposition. Thus those prior inconsistent statements made under oath at formal proceedings are now substantively admissible. Grand jury testimony is included within the concept of "other proceeding." However, statements, whether oral or written, even if given under oath and videotaped, made to law enforcement officials fall outside the concept of "other proceedings." The foundation requirement of Rule 613 applies to prior inconsistent statements admitted as substantive evidence solely under Rule 801(d)(1)(A). The rationale behind the limited departure from the common law represented by Rule 801(d)(1)(A) is that expressed by the House Committee on the Judiciary that (1) unlike most other situations involving unsworn or oral statements, including for example oral statements by occurrence witnesses to a crime, there can be no dispute as to whether the prior statement was made, and (2) the context of a formal proceeding and an oath provide firm additional assurances of the reliability of the prior statement.

Critics of the common law prohibition against substantive use of a prior inconsistent statement have long contended that the declarant at trial is under oath, his demeanor may be observed, his credibility tested by cross-examination and that the timing of cross-examination is not critical. Rule 801(d)(1)(A) accepts the arguments of such critics only to the extent that the non-contemporaneous cross-examination relates to a prior inconsistent statement made under oath at a formal proceeding; substantive admissibility is allowed only for those statements possessing the highest degree of certainty of making made under circumstances conducive to truth telling.

Of course prior inconsistent statements not falling within the scope of Rule 801(d)(1)(A) may still be employed for the limited purpose of impeachment in accordance with Rules 607 and 613.

As the Advisory Committee's Note states, "If the witness admits on the stand that he made the statement and that it was true, he adopts the statement and there is no hearsay problem. The hearsay problem arises when the witness on the stand denies having made the statement or admits having made it but denies its truth."

2. Prior Consistent Statements - Rule 801(d)(1)(B) - Definitions

The following definitions apply under this article:

(d) Statements which are not hearsay. A statement is not hearsay if-(1) Prior statement by witness. The declarant testifies at the trial or hearing and is subject to cross-examination concerning the statement, and the statement is ...(B) consistent with the declarant's testimony and is offered to rebut an express or implied charge against the declarant of recent fabrication or improper influence or motive, * * *

Generally speaking, a witness cannot be corroborated on direct or redirect examination or rebuttal by proof of prior statements consistent with his in court testimony. Whatever inherent probative value such consistent statements may have is felt to be insufficient when viewed in light of trial concerns, Rule 403.

"When the witness has merely testified on direct examination, without any impeachment, proof of consistent statements is unnecessary and valueless. The witness is not helped by it; for, even if it is an improbable or untrustworthy story, it is not made more probable or more trustworthy by any number of repetitions of it." 4 Wigmore, Evidence § 1124 at 255 (Chadbourn rev. 1972).

"The introduction of a prior consistent statement on direct examination of a witness would often lead to cross-examination relating to circumstances surrounding the alleged making as well as possibly the calling of witnesses to support or deny the making of the statement. In short, one might have a mini-trial on the issue of whether the prior consistent statement was made and the circumstances surrounding its making." Graham, "Prior Consistent Statement: Rule 801(d)(1)(B) of the Federal Rules of Evidence, Critique and Proposal," 30 Hast.L.J. 575, 581 n.22 (1979).

"The salutary nature and the necessity of such a rule are clearly apparent upon reflection in cases like the present, for without that rule a witness's testimony could be blown up out of all proportion to its true probative force by telling the same story out of court before a group of reputable citizens, who would then parade onto the witness stand and repeat the statement time and again until the jury might easily forget that the truth of the statement was not backed by those citizens but was solely founded upon the integrity of the said witness. This danger would seem to us to be especially acute in a criminal case ... when the ... previous out-of-court statement is repeated before the jury by ... law enforcement officers." Allison v. State, 162 So.2d 922, 924 (Fla. 1 DCA 1964).

However under certain circumstances the probative value of a prior consistent statement clearly warrants introduction. Rule 801(d)(1)(B) provides that a prior consistent statement of a declarant testifying at trial and subject to cross-examination concerning the statement is admissible when offered "to rebut an express or implied charge against him of recent fabrication, improper influence or motive." Thus to rebut an express or implied charge that the witness is motivated or has been influenced to testify falsely or that his testimony is a recent fabrication, evidence is admissible that he told the same story *before* the motive or influence came into existence or before the time of the alleged recent fabrication.

"A consistent statement, at a *time prior* to the existence of a fact said to indicate bias, interest, or corruption, will effectively explain away the force of the impeaching evidence; because it is thus made to appear that the statement in the form now uttered was independent of the discrediting influence." 4 Wigmore, Evidence § 1129 at 268 (Chadbourn rev. 1972) (emphasis in original).

The prior consistent statement is exempt from the bar of the rule against hearsay, Rule 802, through definition as not hearsay, Rule 801(d)(1)(B), and thus is admitted as substantive evidence.

To illustrate, assume that John, while standing on the sidewalk, witnessed an automobile accident involving a car driven by Mary and a truck driven by Bill. The factual issue in dispute is the color of the traffic light at the intersection facing both parties. At trial, John testifies that the light facing Mary was green. On cross-examination, Bill's attorney brings out that four weeks after the accident John met Mary for the first time at her lawyer's office, that they dated thereafter, and that they are now engaged to be married. On redirect examination, John may testify that one day after the accident, and thus *before* the alleged improper influence or motive arose, he told his best friend Tim that the light facing the car driven by the woman was green. However, John may not testify that two weeks after John and Mary were engaged he told his mother that the light facing Mary was green.

Where admissible, the prior consistent statement may be testified to by either the witness himself or any other person with personal knowledge of the statement. Rule 801(d)(1)(B) does require that the declarant testify at the trial and that he be subject to cross-examination concerning the prior statement, a requirement that is satisfied so long as the declarant is available to be recalled.

A prior statement that corroborates the witness may be admitted without reference to Rule 801(d)(1)(B) when relevant to rehabilitate in a manner other than refutation encompassed in Rule 801(d)(1)(B) such as when the prior inconsistent statement serves to explain or modify a fragment thereof introduced by the opposite party for purposes of impeachment, or if it is otherwise related to or supportive of a denial or explanation offered in response to impeachment of a witness by an alleged self-contradiction, whether an inconsistent statement or a failure to speak when natural to do so, Rule 613. Such prior consistent statements are admitted for corroborative purposes only and not as substantive evidence; the jury should be instructed accordingly.

A witness, Riley, testified that he participated in a bank robbery with the defendants. On cross-examination, Riley was impeached by a prior inconsistent statement he admitted having made in which he stated that he had perpetrated the robbery alone. Shortly after the inconsistent statement, however, Riley had made another statement consistent with his trial testimony. The witness explained that at the time of the inconsistent statement he shared a jail cell with the defendant and that he could not safely make the inculpating consistent statement until he was released from the cell. In admitting the consistent statement, the court stated: "[W]e think that in the situation where a key witness admittedly changes his story or his recital of important relevant events and admits that his former statements in regard to the proceedings in question were a fabrication, that he should be allowed to not only testify as to the reasons for his fabrication and the reasons why he decided to change his story; and all of the incidents and factors that shed light upon his credibility, both pro and con, are admitted, subject to the Court's discretion, and left to the jury for its evaluation and determination. Naturally, a person who has made admittedly inconsistent statements stands impeached, but the court and the jury are still charged with the responsibility of ascertaining which evidence is to be credited and only by a full exposure of the relevant and pertinent facts in this difficult situation can the jury make an intelligent and reasonable attempt to ascertain the truth. In the case at bar there is no dispute about Riley's making either the consistent or the inconsistent statements. It is not a swearing match as to what was said, but presents the crucial issue of which statements constitute a correct recital of the events under consideration. In this posture, relevant evidence, particularly evidence which is subject to cross-examination, should in the discretion of the trial court be submitted to the jury for its evaluation." Hanger v. United States, 398 F.2d 91, 105 (8th Cir.1968).

3. Prior Identification of a Person After Perceiving Him - Rule 801(d)(1)(C) - Definitions

The following definitions apply under this article:

(d) Statements which are not hearsay. A statement is not hearsay if—(1) Prior statement by witness. The declarant testifies at the trial or hearing and is subject to cross-examination concerning the statement, and the statement is ...(C) one of identification of a person made after perceiving the person; or * * *

When a witness testifies and is subject to cross-examination, his prior statement identifying a person made after perceiving the person again after an event, usually at a lineup, a one on one viewing often called a show-up, in a photograph or a sketch, or at a prior hearing, is exempt from the bar of the rule against hearsay, Rule 802, through definition as not hearsay, Rule 801(d)(1)(C). There is no requirement that the witness first be impeached. The theory is that courtroom identification is so unconvincing as practically to impeach itself thus justifying the corroboration. The purpose of the rule is to permit the introduction of more meaningful identifications made by a witness when memory was fresher and there had been less opportunity for influence to be exerted upon him.

"[T]he earlier identification has greater probative value than an identification made in the courtroom after the suggestions of others and the circumstances of the trial may have intervened to create a fancied recognition in the witness' mind." Gilbert v. California, 388 U.S. 263, 273 n. 3, 87 S.Ct. 1951, 18 L.Ed.2d 1178 (1967).

"We agree with the observation there made that 'Congress has recognized, as do most trial judges, that identification in the courtroom is a formality that offers little in the way of reliability and much in the way of suggestibility.'" quoting 4 Weinstein's Evidence ¶ 801 (d)(1)(C)[01] at 801-803. United States v. Lewis, 565 F.2d 1248, 1251 (2d Cir.1977).

The circumstances of the prior identification may, of course, be considered by the trier of fact in determining the weight to be accorded.

Rule 801(d)(1)(C) requires by its terms only that the person who made the identification testify at the trial or hearing and be subject to cross-examination. It seems reasonable to assume that the rule also contemplates that the declarant will testify in court on the subject of identification and not simply be available to be recalled to the stand by the defendant for cross-examination. The rule does not limit testimony as to the statement of identification made after perception solely to that of the identifying witness; testimony of any person who was present, for example a police officer, is also admissible. Of course overproof may unduly emphasize the prior identification to the extent of misleading the jury and consequently is subject to the court's discretionary control under Rule 403.

Rule 801(d)(1)(C) does not require on its face, nor has a requirement been imposed, that the identifying witness make a positive in court identification or identify the defendant in court at all. Similarly nothing in the text of the rule prohibits introduction of the out of court statement identifying the defendant made by a declarant who in court denies making or repudiates the identification and denies that the defendant is the person involved in the crime. Moreover while it can be argued that a witness who lacks recollection as to the identity of the individual, whether such lack of recollection is real or feigned, is not "subject to cross-examination concerning the statement" as provided in Rule 801(d)(1), legislative history indicates substantial support for applicability of Rule 801(d)(1)(C) in this context.

"We are into the subject matter, and to highlight what I think the facts are. We have a robbery or a burglary, or some crime committed, and they are trying to decide who did it. They bring the victim down to the police station, and they put several people across the line-up, and the victim says, 'That is the guy who did it. That is the one.'

So then they proceed on the basis of this, and when they get to trial, they call the same fellow who made positive identification within a week of the offenses and ask him, 'Is this the man? Is this the defendant?'

'Oh, I don't know. I don't know. I don't recognize him.'

What is suggested here is that in the field of organized crime—and in some of the even more unorganized crime—there are people of a more vicious nature who suggest to these witnesses that if they would ever like to see their children or their wives again, they had better not recognize this fellow. Or there may be financial reward.

The feeling of those who press for the law the way it came to the House and the way it would be now written is that this is protection for the public against the changing testimony of

> witnesses," Statement of Rep. Hungate on floor of House of Representatives reported in 4 Weinstein's Evidence 801-9-801-10 (1984).

Moreover the mere fact of lack of recollection itself impeaches the probative force of the prior statement of identification thus producing a greater effect on credibility than usually attained through cross-examination. Judicial opinion is in accord.

"It seems to us that the more natural reading of 'subject to cross-examination concerning the statement' includes what was available here. Ordinarily a witness is regarded as 'subject to cross-examination' when he is placed on the stand, under oath, and responds willingly to questions. Just as with the constitutional prohibition, limitations on the scope of examination by the trial court or assertions of privilege by the witness may undermine the process to such a degree that meaningful cross-examination within the intent of the rule no longer exists. But that effect is not produced by the witness's assertion of memory loss—which * * * is often the very result sought to be produced by cross-examination, and can be effective in destroying the force of the prior statement. Rule 801(d)(1)(C), which specifies that the cross-examination need only 'concer[n] the statement' does not on its face require more." United States v. Owens, 484 U.S. 554, 561, 108 S.Ct. 838, 98 L.Ed.2d 951 (1988).

In short, the text, the legislative history, as well as judicial opinion interpreting Rule 801(d)(1)(C) place no restrictions upon admissibility other than having the alleged out of court declarant in court on the witness stand subject to cross-examination concerning the statement.

C. ADMISSION BY PARTY-OPPONENT

1. An Overview

A statement of a party-opponent, whether an oral or written assertion, or nonverbal conduct offered in evidence by an adverse party to prove the truth of the matter asserted, falls within the definition of hearsay at common law and in Rules 801(a)-(c).

Nevertheless, it has been universally accepted since the advent of the rule against hearsay that such a statement, referred to as an admission by a party-opponent, is admissible as substantive evidence to prove the truth of the matter asserted. While formerly considered an exception to the hearsay rule, in recognition of its position in the adversary system, Rule 801(d)(2) exempts admissions of a party-opponent from the operation of the rule against hearsay, Rule 802, by defining admissions of a party-opponent as "not hearsay".

"Admissions by a party-opponent are excluded from the category of hearsay on the theory that their admissibility in evidence is the result of the adversary system rather than satisfaction of the conditions of the hearsay rule. Strahorn, A Reconsideration of the Hearsay Rule and Admissions, 83 U.Pa.L.Rev. 484, 564 (1937); Morgan, Basic Problems of Evidence 265 (1962); 4 Wigmore § 1048. No guarantee of trustworthiness is required in the case of an admission. The freedom which admissions have enjoyed from technical demands of searching for an assurance of trustworthiness in some against-interest circumstance, and from the restrictive influences of the opinion rule and the rule requiring firsthand knowledge, when taken with the apparently prevalent satisfaction with the results, calls for generous treatment of this avenue to admissibility." Advisory Committee's Note to Rule 801(d)(2).

Lack of opportunity to cross-examine is deprived of significance by the incongruity of the party objecting to his own statement on the ground that he was not subject to cross-examination by himself at the time.

"If we define hearsay as an extra-judicial statement offered as tending to prove the truth of the matter stated, an admission clearly falls within it, and the most commentators so regard it. It must be conceded that the rule which makes admissions receivable is older than the hearsay rule and is a necessary concomitant of the accepted doctrine that evidence of any relevant conduct of a party is admissible against him, unless the subject of a claim of privilege. * * * Whatever may be true as to personal conduct of a party, there is no escape from the conclusion that a vicarious admission has all the essential characteristics of hearsay. For the practitioner the all-important fact is that evidence of an assertive admission is receivable for the truth of the matter asserted.

The admissibility of an admission made by the party himself rests not upon any notion that the circumstances in which it was made furnish the trier means of evaluating it fairly, but upon the adversary theory of litigation. A party can hardly object that he had no opportunity to cross-examine himself or that he is unworthy of credence save when speaking under sanction of an oath. His adversary may use against him anything which he has said or done." Morgan, Basic Problems of Evidence 265-66 (1961).

In the nature of things, the statement is usually damaging to the party against whom offered, else it would not be offered. However neither Rule 801(d)(2) nor the common law cases lay down a requirement that the statement be against interest either when made or when offered, and the theory of the exception is not based thereon. The sometimes encountered label "admission against interest," is inaccurate, serves only to confuse, and should be abandoned.

Admissions are substantive evidence, as contrasted with mere impeaching statements, and no preliminary foundation need be laid by examining the declarant concerning the admission, Rule 613(b). Personal knowledge of the matter admitted is not required; nor is a requirement of mental capacity imposed. Admissions in the form of an opinion are competent, even if the opinion is a conclusion of law. The opinion rule, designed to elicit more concrete and informative answers, is a rule of preference as to the form of testimony. Since out-of-court statements are not made under circumstances in which alternative forms of expressions may be secured, this aspect of the opinion rule is inapplicable. Admissibility does not depend upon whether the declarant is unavailable, available, or actually testifies. Whether the specific requirements set forth in Rule 801(d)(2) not involving conditional relevancy, Rule 104(b), have been satisfied, such as whether a person is authorized to make a statement, Rule 801(d)(2)(C), or whether a statement concerns a matter within the scope of his agency or employment, Rule 801(d)(2)(D), are determined by the court, Rule 104(a). Admissions of a party-opponent may be excluded upon application of Rule 103.

2. Statements of Party Made in Individual Capacity

(a) An Overview - Rule 801(d)(2)(A) - Statements Which Are Not Hearsay: Admission By Party-Opponent

The following definitions apply under this article: (d) Statements Which Are Not Hearsay. A statement is not hearsay if—(2) Admission by Party-Opponent. The statement is offered against a party and is (A) the party's own statement, in either an individual or a representative capacity, or * * *

A party's own statement made in his individual capacity when offered by an opposing party is defined as not hearsay, Rule 801(d)(2)(A).

As with all admissions by a party-opponent, no requirement of mental capacity of the declarant is imposed; the statement need not relate to a matter as to which the party had personal knowledge; it need not be against interest when made or when offered; it may contain opinions or conclusions of law; and it may be offered whether or not the party is unavailable, available, or actually testifies. If the party does testify, no foundation need be laid preliminary to its introduction in evidence, Rule 613(b).

(b) Plea of Guilty

The introduction into evidence of a guilty plea not later withdrawn, differs in theory though perhaps not in result from the introduction of a judgment resulting from it. The judgment may constitute a hearsay exception under Rule 803(22) when offered to prove any fact essential to sustain the judgment. The plea of guilty is offered not to prove that essential facts have been previously found to exist but rather to prove that the offender admitted facts constituting guilt. Thus a plea of guilty may be admissible as an admission of a party under Rule 801(d)(2)(A) or as a statement against interest of a non-party under Rule 804(b)(3).

Where evidence of a conviction on a plea of guilty is being offered against a party, the effect of proceeding pursuant to either Rule 803(22) or Rule 801(d)(2)(A) is identical. In both instances the facts admitted by the party by entering a plea of guilty, i.e., facts essential to sustain the conviction, may be admitted against him by a party-opponent as an evidentiary as distinguished from a judicial admission. The party's reason, if any, for pleading guilty may thus also be introduced.

A question is raised whether a plea of guilty may be introduced as either an admission of a party-opponent, Rule 801(d)(2)(A), or statement against interest, Rule 804(b)(3), in situations in which the judgment of conviction, Rule 803(22), could not be shown because the crime was not punishable by imprisonment in excess of one year. The question is not specifically addressed in either Rule 801(d)(2)(A) or Rule 804(b)(3). Similarly, neither Rule 803(22) nor its Advisory Committee's Note contains a specific reference to the admissibility of a guilty plea to an offense punishable by imprisonment for no more than one year. However the rationale expressed by the Advisory Committee in excluding convictions for crimes punishable by imprisonment for no more than one year from the operation of Rule 803(22) is extremely telling:

> Practical considerations require exclusion of convictions of minor offenses, not because the administration of justice in its lower echelons must be inferior, but because motivation to defend at this level is often minimal or nonexistent.

The rationale for excluding a prior conviction after trial for a minor offense applies with even greater force to a guilty plea entered to a minor offense. Accordingly, a plea of guilty to an offense punishable by imprisonment for no more than one year should be declared to fall outside the breadth of both Rules 801(d)(2)(A) and 804(b)(3).

> "In this type of case, particularly if a traffic violation is concerned, the accused typically pleads guilty, often without consulting counsel, 'as a matter of course or convenience.' 'The sensible citizen, even when in the right, pays his fine and goes about his business.' In order to effectuate the express policy of Rule 803(22) barring evidence of

> convictions punishable by imprisonment for less than one year, evidence of guilty pleas in non-felony cases should not be allowed as admissions under Rule 801(d)(2), or as statements against interest pursuant to Rule 804(b)(3)." 4 Weinstein's Evidence ¶ 803(22)(01) at 803-408 (1994).

Nevertheless, a majority of decisions admit the guilty plea under such circumstances with explanation.

(c) Statements of Party Made in a Representative Capacity

Rule 801(d)(2)(A) provides that if an individual has a representative capacity such as an administrator, executor, trustee, or guardian and the statement is offered against him in that capacity, the statement is admissible without reference to whether the individual was acting in a representative capacity in making the statement; all that is required is that the statement be relevant to representative affairs.

"For purposes of Rule 801(d)(2)(A), it matters not whether a statement was made in the declarant's 'individual' or his 'representative' capacity. Thus where an executor, administrator, trustee, or guardian either sues or is sued, his own statement qualifies as an admission within the meaning of the Rule regardless whether made in his 'official' or his individual capacity, and inquiry into the surrounding circumstances is irrelevant for purposes of deciding the admissibility in question. The rationale appears to be that admissions are not received because trustworthy, so that the nature of the statement and the surrounding circumstances should not be important. What is important is the fact that the declarant is present and able to adduce whatever counterproof might exist in order to explain, deny, or refute the statement." 4 Louisell & Mueller, Federal Evidence § 423 at 258 (1980).

(d) Persons in Privity or Jointly Interested

At common law statements by a person in privity with a party were receivable in evidence as an admission of the party.

"The term 'privity' denotes mutual or successive relationships to the same rights of property, and privies are distributed into several classes, according to the manner of this relationship. Thus, there are privies in estate, as donor and donee, lessor and lessee, and joint tenants; privies in blood, as heir and ancestor, and co-parceners; privies in representation, as executor and testator, administrator and intestate; privies in law, where the law, without privity of blood or estate, casts the land upon another, as by escheat.' Metropolitan St. Ry. Co. v. Gumby, 99 F. 192, 198 (2d Cir.1900).

An admission by one jointly interested was also receivable at common law against others similarly interested.

Rule 801(d)(2) alters prior law by omitting any provision declaring either a statement by a person in privity with another or by one of persons jointly interested to be an admission by the other or others. Thus Rule 801(d)(2) in excluding such statements from the definition of admissions adopts the position advocated by Professor Morgan and the Model Code of Evidence that considerations of privity and joint interest neither furnish criteria of credibility nor aid in the evaluation of testimony. Statements formerly treated as a separate category of admission will, however, frequently qualify as representative admissions, Rule 801(d)(2)(C), or as statements against interest, Rule 804(b)(3), or fall within another hearsay exception. Other such statements will meet the requirements of the residual hearsay exception contained in Rule 807.

3. Manifestation of Adoption or Belief in Truth of Statement - Rule 801(d)(2)(B) - Statements Which Are Not Hearsay: Admission by Party-Opponent

The following definitions apply under this article:

(d) Statements Which Are Not Hearsay. A statement is not hearsay if—(2) Admission by Party-Opponent. The statement is offered against a party and is ... (B) a statement of which the party has manifested an adoption or belief in its truth, or * * *

Words or conduct. Excluded from the definition of hearsay by Rule 801(d)(2)(B) are statements to which a party has manifested his adoption or belief in their truth. However the party's words or conduct asserted to be a manifestation of assent to the truth of the statement may be susceptible of more than one interpretation. A party is held to have manifested an adoption or belief in the truth of a statement only if it appears that the person understood and demonstrably assented to its truth. Manifestation of adoption or belief in the truth of a statement by a party may be either expressed, such as "Yes, you're right," or implied from the party's reliance upon the contents of statements in related conversation, such as "Bet we won't get as much money from the next convenience store."

Whether a party has manifested his assent to another person's statement is a question of conditional relevancy under Rule 104(b). The burden of proof is on the proponent to show that adoption was intended; a mere statement that another person had made a particular statement is insufficient.

"The mere fact that the party declares that he had heard that another person had made a given statement is not standing alone sufficient to justify a finding that the party has adopted the third person's statement. The circumstances surrounding the party's declaration must be looked to in order to determine whether the repetition did indicate an approval of the statement." McCormick, Evidence § 269 at 797 (3d ed. 1984).

To illustrate, if the contested matter in a civil action for damages is whether a visiting child tripped over her shoe laces or was pushed down the stairs by defendant homeowner's dog, a statement by the homeowner, after talking to his son, such as "I am very sorry. My son said that my dog jumped on your little girl," would be an admission. On the other hand, the statement "My son said that he thinks my dog jumped on your little girl," does not indicate approval of the reported assertion, and is thus not an admission. The statement of the homeowner is merely the reporting of another's assertion; it is not a manifestation of adoption or belief in the truth of its content.

Silence. Manifestation of belief in the truth of a statement may occur by silence, that is, a failure to respond when natural to do so.

"[T]he courts have evolved a variety of safeguarding requirements against misuse, of which the following are illustrative. (1) The statement must have been heard by the party claimed to have acquiesced. (2) It must have been understood by him. (3) The subject matter must have been within his knowledge. At first glance, this requirement may appear inconsistent with the general dispensation with firsthand knowledge with respect to admissions, yet the unreasonableness of expecting a person to deny a matter of which he is not aware seems evident; he simply does not have the incentive or the wherewithal to embark upon a dispute. (4) Physical or emotional impediments to responding must not be present. (5) The personal makeup of the speaker, e.g., young child, or his relationship to the party or the event, e.g., bystander, may be such as to make it unreasonable to expect a denial. (6) Probably most important of all, the statement itself must be such as would, if untrue, call for a denial under the circumstances. The list is not an exclusive one, and other factors will suggest themselves. The essential inquiry in each case is whether a reasonable person would have denied under the circumstances, with answers not lending themselves readily to mechanical formulation." McCormick, Evidence § 270 at 800-01 (3rd ed. 1984).

If an oral or written statement is communicated by another person to a party in the litigation containing assertions of fact which if untrue the party would under all the circumstances naturally be expected to deny, his failure to speak is receivable against him in a civil case as an adoptive admission, Rule 801(d)(2)(B). With respect to a letter, while it is frequently stated that the general rule, subject to exception, is that failure to answer may not be introduced as an admission, the more acceptable view is that failure to reply to a letter containing statements which under all the circumstances one would expect the receiver to deny if felt untrue may be introduced in evidence as an admission by silence.

Silence under circumstances naturally calling for a denial has also been recognized as an admission in criminal cases. Evidence must be introduced sufficient to support a finding, Rule 104(b), that in light of the totality of the circumstances, a statement was made which the defendant heard, understood, had an opportunity to deny or object and in which the defendant by his silence acquiesced. Mere possession of a document standing alone does not constitute a manifestation of adoption or belief in its truth. In addition the court must pursuant to Rule 104(a) determine that it is more probably true than not true that the statement was such that under the circumstances it would naturally be expected that an innocent person would deny in some form the truth of the statement if he believed it to be untrue.

Various considerations, however, raise doubts as to the propriety of applying the rule in criminal cases when an accusation to the defendant is made under the auspices of law enforcement personnel. In addition to the inherently ambiguous nature of the inference itself, silence on the part of the defendant may be motivated by prior experience or prior advice of counsel. Treating silence as an admission also affords unusual opportunity to manufacture evidence. Moreover the accused would effectively be compelled to speak, either at the time or upon the trial by way of explaining his reasons for remaining silent, which, to say the least, crowds his privilege against self-incrimination uncomfortably. Nevertheless, silence of a witness, including the criminal defendant, that occurs post-arrest but prior to the actual giving of *Miranda* warnings has been held admissible to impeach. Whether prearrest silence may constitutionally be admitted as substantive evidence is unclear. Obviously once the *Miranda* warnings have been given advising the defendant of his right to remain silent, the defendant's failure to speak may no longer possibly be considered an admission, nor may his silence be employed for purposes of impeachment.

4. Vicarious Admissions - Rules 801(d)(2)(C) and (D) - Statements Which Are Not Hearsay: Admission By Party-Opponent

The following definitions apply under this article:

(d) Statements Which Are Not Hearsay. A statement is not hearsay If—

(2) Admission by Party-Opponent. The statement is offered against a party and is ... (C) a statement by a person authorized by the party to make a statement concerning the subject, or (D) a statement by the party's agent or servant concerning a matter within the scope of the agency or employment, made during the existence of the relationship, or.... The contents of the statement shall be considered but are not alone sufficient to establish the declarant's authority under subdivision (C), the agency or employment relationship and scope thereof under subdivision (D), or the existence of the conspiracy and the participation therein of the declarant and the party against whom the statement is offered under subdivision (E).

(a) Statement by Person Authorized to Speak

Statements by a person authorized by a party to make a statement concerning the subject matter, such as the president of a corporation, the managing partner of a partnership, an attorney hired to represent the client before the I.R.S., or the sales manager of an automotive dealership, are admissions, Rule 801(d)(2)(C). The authority of the agent to speak as to a subject, which may be express or implied, must be established at trial.

As a matter of substantive agency law, neither the fact of authorization nor the scope of the subject matter of authority may be established by the agent's out of court statements. Nevertheless, Rule 801(d)(2) now provides that in determining whether a person was authorized at the time by the party to make a statement concerning the subject, the contents of the statement is to be considered but is not alone sufficient to establish the declarant's authority. Authorization to make a statement concerning the subject matter may, of course, be established by the acts or conduct of the principal or his statements to the agent or a third party.

Along with statements to other persons, statements by the authorized person to the principal himself are included in Rule 801(d)(2)(C). Accordingly a party's books or records are usable against him without regard to intent to disclose to third persons.

(b) Statement by Agent or Servant Concerning Matter Within Scope of His Agency or Employment

A statement of an agent or servant concerning a matter within the scope of his employment, made during the existence of the relationship, is an admission of his employer, Rule 801(d)(2)(D). In determining whether an agency or employment relationship existed at the time of the statement and scope of such a relationship, the content of the statement is to be considered but is not alone sufficient.

Prior to Rule 801(d)(2)(D) courts applied the traditional agency test in determining admissibility of statements by agents or servants, i.e., whether the particular statement was authorized by the principal. Courts generally decided that damaging statements were not within the scope of authority, even of relatively high level employees. The obvious difficulty with applying strict agency principles is that agents or servants are very rarely authorized to make damaging statements—the truck driver is hired to drive, not to talk. However, as a result of the fact that it also seemed unreasonable to deny admission to inculpatory statements by the driver about the driving he was hired to do in light of the probable reliability of such statements, courts often stretched to find a basis for admissibility.

In recognition of the reliability and reasonableness of admitting such statements, Rule 801(d)(2)(D) declares statements of an agent or servant concerning a matter within the scope of his agency or employment to be defined as not hearsay if made during the existence of the relationship. Authority to speak is thus no longer of concern; all that is required is that the statement concern a matter within the scope of the agency or employment, and that the agent or servant still be employed at the time of making the statement. A statement meeting the requirement of Rule 801(d)(2)(D) is not made inadmissible simply because the statement was made to the employer and not a third person. However in a criminal prosecution, government employees are apparently not considered agents or servants of a party-opponent for the purpose of the admissions rules.

An attorney may, of course, act as an ordinary agent and as such make evidentiary admissions admissible against his principal,

Rules 801(d)(2)(C) and (D). In addition, an attorney has authority in general to make judicial admissions for the client in all matters relating to the progress and trial of an action.

(c) The Requirement of Personal Knowledge

Admissions of a party-opponent are characterized by the Advisory Committee's Note to Rule 801(d)(2) as enjoying freedom from the restrictive influences of the rule requiring personal knowledge. However Weinstein's Evidence makes a strong argument that the rationale supporting elimination of the requirement of personal knowledge generally with respect to admissions fails to withstand analysis with respect to vicarious admissions, Rules 801(d)(2)(C) and (D).

"Although commentators have suggested that an employee will not make a false statement damaging to his employer, both because he is interested in his employer's welfare and, because he does not wish to jeopardize his job, these reasons, while in part justifying the extension of the doctrine of vicarious admissions do not vindicate the unqualified admission of statements not based on personal knowledge. Such a statement may often consist of no more than gossip or speculation about the matter at issue. The mere fact that the agent heard it and repeated it does not remove any of the dangers against which the hearsay rule has traditionally guarded. * * * The danger is particularly apparent as regards intracompany reports. Certainly, even an employee well-disposed towards his employer may report rumors he had heard, not because of their truth, but because his employer may be interested in the fact that there are rumors. Allowing a report containing rumors not based on personal knowledge to be used indiscriminately against the employer amounts to a wholesale endorsement of the adage, 'where there's smoke, there's fire.' Moreover, it may be doubted, particularly in an era of widespread unionization, whether the theory that an employee would not spread unverified gossip because of fear for his job has much validity. Rather, it would seem a fact of human nature that rumor, unsubstantiated by fact, is at all times prevalent and

> virulent." 4 Weinstein's Evidence ¶ 801(d)(2)(C) [01] at 801-216-801-217 (1984).

Whatever the merits of the arguments for requiring personal knowledge in connection with any of the foregoing rules, the fact remains that lack of personal knowledge on the part of the declarant does not bar introduction of a statement as an admission of a party-opponent under Rule 801(d)(2). On the other hand, lack of personal knowledge may appropriately be considered in determining whether admissibility should be denied under Rule 403. An alternative resolution is to rest a finding of inadmissibility upon the notion that repetition of "rumor" lies outside the scope of a person's agency or employment, Rule 801(d)(2)(D). When the statement of the employee indicates reliance upon a statement from an unidentified source, most likely another employee, Rule 805 may serve to exclude the statement on the basis of an inadequate foundation that the unidentified person was a person authorized to make a statement concerning the subject, Rule 801(d)(2)(C), or that the person was an employee speaking concerning a matter within the scope of employment. Rule 801(d)(2)(D).

5. Statements by Coconspirator - Rule 801(d)(2)(E) - Statements Which Are Not Hearsay: Admission By Party-Opponent

The following definitions apply under this rule:

(d) Statements Which Are Not Hearsay. A statement is not hearsay if—

(2) Admission by Party-Opponent. The statement is offered against a party and is ... (E) a statement by a coconspirator of a party during the course and in furtherance of the conspiracy. The contents of the statement shall be considered but are not alone sufficient to establish the declarant's authority under subdivision (C), the agency or employment relationship and scope thereof under subdivision (D), or the existence of the conspiracy and the participation therein of the declarant and the party against whom the statement is offered under subdivision (E).

A statement of one coconspirator is admissible against the others as an admission of a party-opponent in both civil and criminal cases, if made during the course of and in furtherance of the common objectives of the conspiracy, Rule 801(d)(2)(E).

Historical development. When a statement is offered under Rule 801(d)(2)(E), a foundation must be laid establishing both the conspiracy and defendant's and declarant's participation in the conspiracy. Two questions of interpretation of Rule 801(d)(2)(E) arose. First, whether in establishing the requisite foundation the content of the alleged coconspirator statement may itself be considered. A vast majority of federal decisions required that the foundation must be established solely by independent evidence, i.e., the content of the statement sought to be introduced could not be considered. The independent evidence could consist of the defendant's own statements or the in-court testimony of a coconspirator. The independent evidence could be circumstantial; hearsay evidence could be considered. Second, whether the sufficiency of the foundation with respect to the existence of the conspiracy and defendant's and declarant's participation are questions solely for the court under Rule 104(a), or questions in which both the court and jury participate under Rule 104(b). Several commentators advocated Rule 104(b) treatment. Other commentators supported application of Rule 104(a). Reported federal decisions clearly favored application of Rule 104(a).

Bourjaily v. United States. The Supreme Court in Bourjaily v. United States (S.Ct.1987) declared that determining the admissibility of a statement of a coconspirator is solely a matter for the court, Rule 104(a), and that the court in making its determination must apply the more probably true than not true standard of proof. In *Bourjaily*, the court also held as a matter of statutory interpretation that in reaching a determination as to whether there is a conspiracy and that the defendant and the declarant participated in the conspiracy, the content of the coconspirator's statement itself *may* be considered. Whether the existence of the conspiracy and the defendant's and the declarant's participation therein can be established to be more probably true than not true *solely* based upon the content of the coconspirator's statement sought to be admitted was expressly left undecided. A negative answer was provided by the lower federal courts; some independent evidence was required. Rule 801(d)(2)(E) was subsequently amended to codify the holding in *Bourjaily* by stating expressly that a court shall consider the contents of a coconspirator's statement in determining "the existence of the conspiracy and the participation therein of the declarant and the party against whom the statement is offered." In addition amended Rule 801(d)(2)(E) now explicitly provides that the contents of the statement "are not alone sufficient to establish" "the existence of the conspiracy and the participation therein of the declarant and the party against whom the statement is offered." The independent evidence may consist of the circumstances surrounding the statement, such as the identity of the speaker, the context in which the statement was made, or evidence corroborating the contents of the statement.

In furtherance. The court must also decide under Rule 104(a) whether the statement was made by the declarant during the course of and in furtherance of the conspiracy. In making this determination it is also proper for the court to consider the content of the statement itself. The court applies the more probably true than not true burden of proof. Only if the court decides both of these issues in favor of the prosecution may the statement be admitted as a statement of a coconspirator, Rule 801(d)(2)(E). In reaching its decisions the court should take into account all relevant evidence, including evidence offered on behalf of the accused.

Statements made during the existence of the conspiracy must be more than casual statements. The statements must actually be in furtherance of the conspiracy. Statements in furtherance of the conspiracy include statements made to induce enlistment, induce further participation, prompt further action, reassure members, allay concerns or fears, keep conspirators abreast of ongoing activities, avoid detection, identify names and roles of conspiracy members while mere conversations or narrative declarations of past events are not in furtherance of the conspiracy.

The statement of the coconspirator in furtherance of the conspiracy is often made outside the defendant's presence. Similarly, it often does not refer to the defendant at all. Thus in a case of bank robbery, a statement by A to B to steal a car may be admissible against C even though C was neither present when the statement was made nor personally involved in stealing the car.

Statements made during the concealment phase fall within the scope of admissibility if in furtherance of the main objectives of the conspiracy, but not otherwise. Kidnappers in hiding waiting for ransom, or repainting a stolen car are illustrations of acts in furtherance of the main criminal objective of a conspiracy. Statements made in furtherance of these objectives are admissible. Statements made by a person after the objectives of the conspiracy have either failed or been achieved , or after the person against whom offered has withdrawn from the conspiracy, are not in furtherance of the conspiracy, and are thus not admissible under Rule 801(d)(2)(E). A conspiracy does not automatically terminate simply because the government, unbeknownst to some of the conspirators, has defeated its object.

Order of proof. With respect to the order of proof, the court has discretion to admit the coconspirator's statement subject to it being connected up later through introduction of sufficient evidence of the existence of the conspiracy and the declarant's or defendant's participation. Whenever it is reasonably practical, however, reported decisions prior to *Bourjaily* stressed that evidence of the conspiracy and the defendant's connection with it (at the time evidence independent of the coconspirator statement) should be admitted prior to the coconspirator's statement. At the conclusion of the presentation of evidence, the trial court on motion must determine on all the evidence including evidence offered by the defendant whether the government has established the requisite foundation to be more probably true than not true. The alternative of a "minihearing" in advance of trial has also been suggested. Either procedure avoids the danger of injecting into the record inadmissible hearsay in anticipation of proof of a conspiracy which never materializes.

The impact of *Bourjaily* on order of proof is substantial. Consideration of the content of the coconspirator's statement in determining its admissibility, even with some undefined and probably undefinable quantum of independent evidence being required, significantly eases the government's burden in many of its more difficult cases, cases very often involving drug trafficking. Assume, for example, that an informant or coconspirator now cooperating with the prosecution testifies that A told him that cocaine was being shipped to X, the defendant, by truck. Such a statement, in context, would strongly support a finding by the court that is more probably true than not true that a conspiracy existed and that A and X were participants in the conspiracy. With respect to the provision in Rule 801(d)(2)(E) that the content of the statement is not alone sufficient, even the slightest additional evidence of X's participation in the conspiracy would cement the court's determination. Given the ease with which the prosecution will be able to satisfy the court as to the admissibility of the coconspirator's statement given that the content of the statement may now be considered, prior concern that the jury not be exposed to the content of the coconspirator's statement lest it ultimately be excluded because of the absence of an adequate evidentiary foundation has all but completely disappeared.

The crime of conspiracy itself may be submitted to the jury only if the evidence, including the statement of a coconspirator once admitted, viewed in the light most favorable to the government, could be accepted by a reasonably-minded jury as adequate to support a conclusion that appellant was guilty of conspiracy beyond reasonable doubt.

Jury instructions. In the process of instructing the jury, the court should not refer to its preliminary determination of facts leading to the introduction of the statement of a coconspirator under Rule 801(d)(2)(E).

6. Judicial and Evidentiary Admissions

Judicial admissions must be distinguished from ordinary evidentiary admissions. A judicial admission is binding upon the party making it; it may not be controverted at trial or on appeal of the same case. Judicial admissions are not evidence at all but rather have the effect of withdrawing a fact from contention. Included within this category are admissions in the pleadings in the case, admissions in open court, stipulations of fact, and admissions pursuant to requests to admit. Ordinary evidentiary admissions, on the other hand, may be controverted or explained by the party. Within this category fall the pleadings in another case, superseded or withdrawn pleadings in the same case, stipulations as to admissibility, as well as other statements admissible under Rule 801(d)(2).

Occasionally a party while testifying at trial or during a deposition or in response to an interrogatory admits a fact which is adverse to his claim or defense. A question then arises as to whether such a statement may be treated as a judicial admission binding the party and if so what circumstances must be present to justify such treatment. Of the various approaches followed in answering the question, treating a party's testimony or response to an interrogatory on all occasions as solely an evidentiary admission is preferable.

"Three main approaches are reflected in the decisions, which to some extent tend to merge and do not necessarily lead to different results in particular situations. First, some courts take the view that a party's testimony in this respect is like the testimony of any other witness called by the party, that is, the party is free (as far as any rule of law is concerned) to elicit contradictory testimony from the same witness or to call other witnesses to contradict the statement. Obviously, however, the problem of persuasion may be a difficult one when the party seeks to explain or contradict his or her own words, and equally obviously, the trial judge would often be justified in ruling on motion for directed verdict that reasonable minds could only believe that the party's testimony against interest was true.

Second, others take the view that the party's testimony is not conclusive against contradiction except when testifying unequivocally to matters in his or her 'peculiar knowledge.' These matters may consist of subjective facts, such as the party's own knowledge or motivation, or they may consist of objective facts observed by the party.

Third, some courts adopt the doctrine that a party's disserving testimony is to be treated as a judicial admission, conclusive on the issue, so that the party may not bring other witnesses to contradict the admission, and if the party or the adversary does elicit such conflicting testimony, it will be disregarded. Obviously, this third rule demands many qualifications and exceptions. Among these are the following: (1) The party is free to contradict, and thus correct, his or her own testimony; only when the party's own testimony taken as a whole unequivocally affirms the statement does the rule of conclusiveness apply. The rule is inapplicable, moreover, when the party's testimony (2) may be attributable to inadvertence or to a foreigner's mistake as to meaning, (3) is merely negative in effect, (4) is explicitly uncertain or is an estimate or opinion rather than an assertion of concrete fact, or (5) relates to a matter as to which the party could easily have been mistaken, such as the swiftly moving events just preceding a collision in which the party was injured.

Of these three approaches the first seems preferable in policy and most in accord with the tradition of jury trial. It rejects any restrictive rule and leaves the evaluation of the party's testimony and the conflicting evidence to the judgment of the jury, the judge, and the appellate court, with only the standard of reason to guide them." McCormick, Evidence § 258 at 153-55 (4th ed. 1992).

The trial court possesses discretion to relieve a party from the consequences of judicial admission. Fed.R.Civ.Proc. 8(e)(2) permits a pleader who is in doubt as to which of two or more statements of fact is true to plead them alternatively or hypothetically, regardless of consistency. When this is done, an admission in one alternative in the pleadings in the case does not nullify a denial in another alternative as a matter of pleading. Since the purpose of alternative pleadings is to enable a party to meet the uncertainties of proof, policy considerations demand that alternative pleadings not be admitted either as an admission of a party-opponent or for the purpose of impeachment.

Unequivocal admissions made by counsel during the course of trial are judicial admissions binding on his client. The scope of a judicial admission by counsel is restricted to unequivocal statements as to matters of fact which otherwise would require evidentiary proof; it does not extend to counsel's statement of his conception of the legal theory of a case.

APPENDIX B

THE FEDERAL RULES OF EVIDENCE [As of December 1, 2006]

ARTICLE I

GENERAL PROVISIONS

Rule 101. Scope

These rules govern proceedings in the courts of the United States and before the United States bankruptcy judges and United States magistrate judges, to the extent and with the exceptions stated in Rule 1101.

Rule 102. Purpose and Construction

These rules shall be construed to secure fairness in administration, elimination of unjustifiable expense and delay, and promotion of growth and development of the law of evidence to the end that the truth may be ascertained and proceedings justly determined.

Rule 103. Rulings on Evidence

(a) **Effect of Erroneous Ruling.** Error may not be predicated upon a ruling which admits or excludes evidence unless a substantial right of the party is affected, and

(1) *Objection.* In case the ruling is one admitting evidence, a timely objection or motion to strike appears of record, stating the specific ground of objection, if the specific ground was not apparent from the context; or

(2) *Offer of Proof.* In case the ruling is one excluding evidence, the substance of the evidence was made known to the

court by offer or was apparent from the context within which questions were asked.

Once the court makes a definitive ruling on the record admitting or excluding evidence, either at or before trial, a party need not renew an objection or offer of proof to preserve a claim of error for appeal.

(b) **Record of Offer and Ruling.** The court may add any other or further statement which shows the character of the evidence, the form in which it was offered, the objection made, and the ruling thereon. It may direct the making of an offer in question and answer form.

(c) **Hearing of Jury.** In jury cases, proceedings shall be conducted, to the extent practicable, so as to prevent inadmissible evidence from being suggested to the jury by any means, such as making statements or offers of proof or asking questions in the hearing of the jury.

(d) **Plain Error.** Nothing in this rule precludes taking notice of plain error affecting substantial rights although they were not brought to the attention of the court.

Rule 104. Preliminary Questions

(a) Questions of Admissibility Generally. Preliminary questions concerning the qualification of a person to be a witness, the existence of a privilege, or the admissibility of evidence shall be determined by the court, subject to the provisions of subdivision (b). In making its determination it is not bound by the rules of evidence except those with respect to privileges.

(b) Relevancy Conditioned on Fact. When the relevancy of evidence depends upon the fulfillment of a condition of fact, the court shall admit it upon, or subject to, the introduction of evidence sufficient to support a finding of the fulfillment of the condition.

(c) Hearing of Jury. Hearings on the admissibility of confessions shall in all cases be conducted out of the hearing of the jury. Hearings on other preliminary matters shall be so conducted when the interests of justice require, or when an accused is a witness and so requests.

(d) Testimony by Accused. The accused does not, by testifying upon a preliminary matter, become subject to cross-examination as to other issues in the case.

(e) Weight and Credibility. This rule does not limit the right of a party to introduce before the jury evidence relevant to weight or credibility.

Rule 105. Limited Admissibility

When evidence which is admissible as to one party or for one purpose but not admissible as to another party or for another purpose is admitted, the court, upon request, shall restrict the evidence to its proper scope and instruct the jury accordingly.

Rule 106. Remainder of or Related Writings or Recorded Statements

When a writing or recorded statement or part thereof is introduced by a party, an adverse party may require the introduction at that time of any other part or any other writing or recorded statement which ought in fairness to be considered contemporaneously with it.

ARTICLE II

JUDICIAL NOTICE

Rule 201. Judicial Notice of Adjudicative Facts

(a) Scope of Rule. This rule governs only judicial notice of adjudicative facts.

(b) Kinds of Facts. A judicially noticed fact must be one not subject to reasonable dispute in that it is either (1) generally known within the territorial jurisdiction of the trial court or (2) capable of accurate and ready determination by resort to sources whose accuracy cannot reasonably be questioned.

(c) When Discretionary. A court may take judicial notice, whether requested or not.

(d) When Mandatory. A court shall take judicial notice if requested by a party and supplied with the necessary information.

(e) Opportunity to Be Heard. A party is entitled upon timely request to an opportunity to be heard as to the propriety of taking judicial notice and the tenor of the matter noticed. In the absence of prior notification, the request may be made after judicial notice has been taken.

(f) Time of Taking Notice. Judicial notice may be taken at any stage of the proceeding.

(g) Instructing Jury. In a civil action or proceeding, the court shall instruct the jury to accept as conclusive any fact judicially noticed. In a criminal case, the court shall instruct the jury that it may, but is not required to, accept as conclusive any fact judicially noticed.

ARTICLE III

PRESUMPTIONS IN CIVIL ACTION AND PROCEEDINGS

Rule 301. Presumptions in General and Civil Actions and Proceedings

In all civil actions and proceedings not otherwise provided for by Act of Congress or by these rules, a presumption imposes on the party against whom it is directed the burden of going forward with evidence to rebut or meet the presumption, but does not shift to such party the burden of proof in the sense of the risk of nonpersuasion, which remains throughout the trial upon the party on whom it was originally cast.

Rule 302. Applicability of State Law in Civil Actions and Proceedings

In civil actions and proceedings, the effect of a presumption respecting a fact which is an element of a claim or defense as to which State law supplies the rule of decision is determined in accordance with State law.

ARTICLE IV

RELEVANCY AND ITS LIMITS

Rule 401. Definition of "Relevant Evidence"

"Relevant evidence" means evidence having any tendency to make the existence of any fact that is of consequence to the determination of the action more probable or less probable than it would be without the evidence.

Rule 402. Relevant Evidence Generally Admissible; Irrelevant Evidence Inadmissible

All relevant evidence is admissible, except as otherwise provided by the Constitution of the United States, by Act of Congress, by these rules, or by other rules prescribed by the Supreme Court pursuant to statutory authority. Evidence which is not relevant is not admissible.

Rule 403. Exclusion of Relevant Evidence on Grounds of Prejudice, Confusion, or Waste of Time

Although relevant, evidence may be excluded if its probative value is substantially outweighed by the danger of unfair prejudice, confusion of the issues, or misleading the jury, or by considerations of undue delay, waste of time, or needless presentation of cumulative evidence.

Rule 404. Character Evidence Not Admissible to Prove Conduct; Exceptions; Other Crimes

(a) Character Evidence Generally. Evidence of a person's character or a trait of character is not admissible for the purpose of proving action in conformity therewith on a particular occasion, except:

(1) *Character of Accused.* In a criminal case, evidence of a pertinent trait of character offered by an accused, or by the

prosecution to rebut the same, or if evidence of a trait of character of the alleged victim of the crime is offered by the accused and admitted under Rule 404(a)(2), evidence of the same trait of character of the accused offered by the prosecution;

(2) *Character of Alleged Victim.* In a criminal case, and subject to the limitations imposed by Rule 412, evidence of a pertinent trait of character of the alleged victim of the crime offered by an accused, or by the prosecution to rebut the same, or evidence of a character trait of peacefulness of the alleged victim offered by the prosecution in a homicide case to rebut evidence that the alleged victim was the first aggressor;

(3) *Character of Witness.* Evidence of the character of a witness, as provided in Rules 607, 608, and 609.

(b) Other Crimes, Wrongs, or Acts. Evidence of other crimes, wrongs, or acts is not admissible to prove the character of a person in order to show action in conformity therewith. It may, however, be admissible for other purposes, such as proof of motive, opportunity, intent, preparation, plan, knowledge, identity, or absence of mistake or accident, provided that upon request by the accused, the prosecution in a criminal case shall provide reasonable notice in advance of trial, or during trial if the court excuses pretrial notice on good cause shown, of the general nature of any such evidence it intends to introduce at trial.

Rule 405. Methods of Proving Character

(a) Reputation or Opinion. In all cases in which evidence of character or a trait of character of a person is admissible, proof may be made by testimony as to reputation or by testimony in the form of an opinion. On cross-examination, inquiry is allowable into relevant specific instances of conduct.

(b) Specific Instances of Conduct. In cases in which character or a trait of character of a person is an essential element of a charge, claim, or defense, proof may also be made of specific instances of that person's conduct.

Rule 406. Habit; Routine Practice

Evidence of the habit of a person or of the routine practice of an organization, whether corroborated or not and regardless of the presence of eyewitnesses, is relevant to prove that the conduct of the person or organization on a particular occasion was in conformity with the habit or routine practice.

Rule 407. Subsequent Remedial Measures

When, after an injury or harm allegedly caused by an event, measures are taken that, if taken previously, would have made the injury or harm less likely to occur, evidence of the subsequent measures is not admissible to prove negligence, culpable conduct, a defect in a product, a defect in a product's design, or a need for a warning or instruction. This rule does not require the exclusion or evidence of subsequent measures when offered for another purpose, such as proving ownership, control, or feasibility of precautionary measures, if controverted, or impeachment.

Rule 408. Compromise and Offers to Compromise

(a) **Prohibited Uses.** Evidence of the following is not admissible on behalf of any party, when offered to prove liability for, invalidity of, or amount of a claim that was disputed as to validity or amount, or to impeach through a prior inconsistent statement or contradiction:

(1) furnishing or offering or promising to furnish—or accepting or offering or promising to accept—a valuable consideration in compromising or attempting to compromise the claim; and

(2) conduct or statements made in compromise negotiations regarding the claim, except when offered in a criminal case and the negotiations related to a claim by a public office or agency in the exercise of regulatory, investigative, or enforcement authority.

(b) **Permitted Uses.** This rule does not require exclusion if the evidence is offered for purposes not prohibited by subdivision (a). Examples of permissible purposes include proving a witness's bias or prejudice; negating a contention of undue delay; and proving an effort to obstruct a criminal investigation or prosecution.

Rule 409. Payment of Medical and Similar Expenses

Evidence of furnishing or offering or promising to pay medical, hospital, or similar expenses occasioned by an injury, is not admissible to prove liability for the injury.

Rule 410. Inadmissibility of Pleas, Plea Discussions, and Related Statements

Except as otherwise provided in this rule, evidence of the following is not, in any civil or criminal proceeding, admissible against the defendant who made the plea or was a participant in the plea discussions:

(1) a plea of guilty which was later withdrawn;

(2) a plea of nolo contendere;

(3) any statement made in the course of any proceedings under Rule 11 of the Federal Rules of Criminal Procedure or comparable state procedure regarding either of the foregoing pleas; or

(4) any statement made in the course of plea discussions with an attorney for the prosecuting authority which do not result in a plea of guilty or which result in a plea of guilty later withdrawn.

However, such a statement is admissible (i) in any proceeding wherein another statement made in the course of the same plea or plea discussions has been introduced and the statement ought in fairness be considered contemporaneously with it, or (ii) in a criminal proceeding for perjury or false statement if the statement was made by the defendant under oath, on the record and in the presence of counsel.

Rule 411. Liability Insurance

Evidence that a person was or was not insured against liability is not admissible upon the issue whether the person acted negligently or otherwise wrongfully. This rule does not require the exclusion of evidence of insurance against liability when offered for another purpose, such as proof of agency, ownership, or control, or bias or prejudice of a witness.

Rule 412. Sex Offense Cases; Relevance of Alleged Victim's Past Sexual Behavior or Alleged Sexual Predisposition

(a) Evidence Generally Inadmissible. The following evidence is not admissible in any civil or criminal proceeding involving alleged sexual misconduct except as provided in subdivisions (b) and (c):

(1) evidence offered to prove that any alleged victim engaged in other sexual behavior; and

(2) evidence offered to prove any alleged victim's sexual predisposition.

(b) Exceptions.

(1) In a criminal case, the following evidence is admissible, if otherwise admissible under these rules:

(A) evidence of specific instances of sexual behavior by the alleged victim offered to prove that a person other than the accused was the source of semen, injury, or other physical evidence;

(B) evidence of specific instances of sexual behavior by the alleged victim with respect to the person accused of the sexual misconduct offered by the accused to prove consent or by the prosecution; and

(C) evidence the exclusion of which would violate the constitutional rights of the defendant.

(2) In a civil case, evidence offered to prove the sexual behavior or sexual predisposition of any alleged victim is admissible if it is otherwise admissible under these rules and its probative value substantially outweighs the danger of harm to any victim and of unfair prejudice to any party. Evidence of an alleged victim's reputation is admissible only if it has been placed in controversy by the alleged victim.

(c) Procedure to Determine Admissibility.

(1) A party intending to offer evidence under subdivision (b) must:

(A) file a written motion at least 14 days before trial specifically describing the evidence and stating the purpose for which it is offered unless the court, for good cause requires a different time for filing or permits filing during trial; and

(B) serve the motion on all parties and notify the alleged victim or, when appropriate, the alleged victim's guardian or representative.

(2) Before admitting evidence under this rule the court must conduct a hearing in camera and afford the victim and parties a right to attend and be heard. The motion, related papers, and the record of the hearing must be sealed and remain under seal unless the court orders otherwise.

Rule 413. Evidence of Similar Crimes in Sexual Assault Cases

(a) In a criminal case in which the defendant is accused of an offense of sexual assault, evidence of the defendant's commission of another offense or offenses of sexual assault is admissible, and may be considered for its bearing on any matter to which it is relevant.

(b) In a case in which the Government intends to offer evidence under this rule, the attorney for the Government shall disclose the evidence to the defendant, including statements of witnesses or a summary of the substance of any testimony that is expected to be offered, at least fifteen days before the scheduled date of trial or at such later time as the court may allow for good cause.

(c) This rule shall not be construed to limit the admission or consideration of evidence under any other rule.

(d) For purposes of this rule and Rule 415, "offense of sexual assault" means a crime under Federal law or the law of a State (as defined in section 513 of title 18, United States Code) that involved—

(1) any conduct proscribed by chapter 109A of title 18, United States Code;

(2) contact, without consent, between any part of the defendant's body or an object and the genitals or anus of another person;

(3) contact, without consent, between the genitals or anus of the defendant and any part of another person's body;

(4) deriving sexual pleasure or gratification from the infliction of death, bodily injury, or physical pain on another person; or

(5) an attempt or conspiracy to engage in conduct described in paragraphs (1)-(4).

Rule 414. Evidence of Similar Crimes in Child Molestation Cases

(a) In a criminal case in which the defendant is accused of an offense of child molestation, evidence of the defendant's commission of another offense or offenses of child molestation is admissible, and may be considered for its bearing on any matter to which it is relevant.

(b) In a case in which the Government intends to offer evidence under this rule, the attorney for the Government shall disclose the evidence to the defendant, including statements of witnesses or a summary of the substance of any testimony that is expected to be offered, at least fifteen days before the scheduled date of trial or at such later time as the court may allow for good cause.

(c) This rule shall not be construed to limit the admission or consideration of evidence under any other rule.

(d) For purposes of this rule and Rule 415, "child" means a person below the age of fourteen, and "offense of child molestation" means a crime under Federal law or the law of a State (as defined in section 513 of title 18, United States Code) that involved—

(1) any conduct proscribed by chapter 109A of title 18, United States Code, that was committed in relation to a child;

(2) any conduct proscribed by chapter 110 of title 18, United States Code;

(3) contact between any part of the defendant's body or an object and the genitals or anus of a child;

(4) contact between the genitals or anus of the defendant and any part of the body of a child;

(5) deriving sexual pleasure or gratification from the infliction of death, bodily injury, or physical pain on a child; or

(6) an attempt or conspiracy to engage in conduct described in paragraphs (1)-(5).

Rule 415. Evidence of Similar Acts in Civil Cases Concerning Sexual Assault or Child Molestation

(a) In a civil case in which a claim for damages or other relief is predicated on a party's alleged commission of conduct constituting an offense of sexual assault or child molestation, evidence of that party's commission of another offense or offenses of sexual assault or child molestation is admissible and may be considered as provided in Rule 413 and Rule 414 of these rules.

(b) A party who intends to offer evidence under this Rule shall disclose the evidence to the party against whom it will be offered, including statements of witnesses or a summary of the substance of any testimony that is expected to be offered, at least fifteen days before the scheduled date of trial or at such later time as the court may allow for good cause.

(c) This rule shall not be construed to limit the admission or consideration of evidence under any other rule.

ARTICLE V

PRIVILEGES

Rule 501. General Rule

Except as otherwise required by the Constitution of the United States or provided by Act of Congress or in rules prescribed by the Supreme Court pursuant to statutory authority, the privilege of a witness, person, government, State, or political subdivision thereof shall be governed by the principles of the common law as they may be interpreted by the courts of the United States in the light of reason and experience. However, in civil actions and proceedings, with respect to an element of a claim or defense as to which State law supplies the rule of decision, the privilege of a witness, person, government, State, or political subdivision thereof shall be determined in accordance with State law.

ARTICLE VI

WITNESSES

Rule 601. General Rule of Competency

Every person is competent to be a witness except as otherwise provided in these rules. However, in civil actions and proceedings, with respect to an element of a claim or defense as to which State law supplies the rule of decision, the competency of a witness shall be determined in accordance with State law.

Rule 602. Lack of Personal Knowledge

A witness may not testify to a matter unless evidence is introduced sufficient to support a finding that the witness has personal knowledge of the matter. Evidence to prove personal knowledge may, but need not, consist of the testimony of the witness' own testimony. This rule is subject to the provisions of rule 703, relating to opinion testimony by expert witnesses.

Rule 603. Oath or Affirmation

Before testifying, every witness shall be required to declare that the witness will testify truthfully, by oath or affirmation administered in a form calculated to awaken the witness' conscience and impress the witness' mind with the duty to do so.

Rule 604. Interpreters

An interpreter is subject to the provisions of these rules relating to qualification as an expert and the administration of an oath or affirmation to make a true translation.

Rule 605. Competency of Judge as Witness

The judge presiding at the trial may not testify in that trial as a witness. No objection need be made in order to preserve the point.

Rule 606. Competency of Juror as Witness

(a) At the Trial. A member of the jury may not testify as a witness before that jury in the trial of the case in which the juror is sitting. If the juror is called so to testify, the opposing party shall be afforded an opportunity to object out of the presence of the jury.

(b) Inquiry Into Validity of Verdict or Indictment. Upon an inquiry into the validity of a verdict or indictment, a juror may not testify as to any matter or statement occurring during the course of the jury's deliberations or to the effect of anything upon that or any other juror's mind or emotions as influencing the juror to assent to or dissent from the verdict or indictment or concerning the juror's mental processes in connection therewith. But a juror may testify about (1) whether extraneous prejudicial information was improperly brought to the jury's attention, (2) whether any outside influence was improperly brought to bear upon any juror, or (3) whether there was a mistake in entering the verdict onto the verdict form. A juror's affidavit or evidence of any statement by the juror may not be received on a matter about which the juror would be precluded from testifying.

Rule 607. Who May Impeach

The credibility of a witness may be attacked by any party, including the party calling the witness.

Rule 608. Evidence of Character and Conduct of Witness

(a) Opinion and Reputation Evidence of Character. The credibility of a witness may be attacked or supported by evidence in the form of opinion or reputation, but subject to these limitations: (1) the evidence may refer only to character for truthfulness or untruthfulness, and (2) evidence of truthful character is admissible only after the character of the witness for truthfulness has been attacked by opinion or reputation evidence or otherwise.

(b) Specific Instances of Conduct. Specific instances of the conduct of a witness, for the purpose of attacking or supporting the witness' character for truthfulness, other than conviction of crime as provided in rule 609, may not be proved by extrinsic evidence. They may, however, in the discretion of the court, if probative of truthfulness or untruthfulness, be inquired into on cross-examination of the witness (1) concerning the witness' character for truthfulness or untruthfulness or (2) concerning the character for truthfulness or untruthfulness of another witness as to which character the witness being cross-examined has testified.

The giving of testimony, whether by an accused or by any other witness, does not operate as a waiver of the accused's or the witness' privilege against self-incrimination when examined with respect to matters that relate only to character for truthfulness.

Rule 609. Impeachment by Evidence of Conviction of Crime

(a) General Rule. For the purpose of attacking the credibility of a witness,

(1) evidence that a witness other than an accused has been convicted of a crime shall be admitted, subject to Rule 403, if the crime was punishable by death or imprisonment in excess of one year under the law under which the witness was convicted, and evidence that the

accused has been convicted of such a crime shall be admitted if the court determines that the probative value of admitting this evidence outweighs its prejudicial effect to the accused; and

(2) evidence that any witness has been convicted of a crime shall be admitted regardless of the punishment, if it readily can be determined that establishing the elements of the crime required proof or admission of an act of dishonesty or false statement by the witness.

(b) Time Limit. Evidence of a conviction under this rule is not admissible if a period of more than ten years has elapsed since the date of the conviction or of the release of the witness from the confinement imposed for that conviction, whichever is the later date, unless the court determines, in the interests of justice, that the probative value of the conviction supported by specific facts and circumstances substantially outweighs its prejudicial effect. However, evidence of a conviction more than 10 years old as calculated herein, is not admissible unless the proponent gives to the adverse party sufficient advance written notice of intent to use such evidence to provide the adverse party with a fair opportunity to contest the use of such evidence.

(c) Effect of Pardon, Annulment, or Certificate of Rehabilitation. Evidence of a conviction is not admissible under this rule if (1) the conviction has been the subject of a pardon, annulment, certificate of rehabilitation, or other equivalent procedure based on a finding of the rehabilitation of the person convicted, and that person has not been convicted of a subsequent crime that was punishable by death or imprisonment in excess of one year, or (2) the conviction has been the subject of a pardon, annulment, or other equivalent procedure based on a finding of innocence.

(d) Juvenile Adjudications. Evidence of juvenile adjudications is generally not admissible under this rule. The court may, however, in a criminal case allow evidence of a juvenile adjudication of a witness other than the accused if conviction of the offense would be admissible to attack the credibility of an adult and the court is satisfied that admission in evidence is necessary for a fair determination of the issue of guilt or innocence.

(e) Pendency of Appeal. The pendency of an appeal therefrom does not render evidence of a conviction inadmissible. Evidence of the pendency of an appeal is admissible.

Rule 610. Religious Beliefs or Opinions

Evidence of the beliefs or opinions of a witness on matters of religion is not admissible for the purpose of showing that by reason of their nature the witness' credibility is impaired or enhanced.

Rule 611. Mode and Order of Interrogation and Presentation

(a) Control by Court. The court shall exercise reasonable control over the mode and order of interrogating witnesses and presenting evidence so as to (1) make the interrogation and presentation effective for the ascertainment of the truth, (2) avoid needless consumption of time, and (3) protect witnesses from harassment or undue embarrassment.

(b) Scope of Cross-Examination. Cross-examination should be limited to the subject matter of the direct examination and matters affecting the credibility of the witness. The court may, in the exercise of discretion, permit inquiry into additional matters as if on direct examination.

(c) Leading Questions. Leading questions should not be used on the direct examination of a witness except as may be necessary to develop the witness' testimony. Ordinarily leading questions should be permitted on cross-examination. When a party calls a hostile witness, an adverse party, or a witness identified with an adverse party, interrogation may be by leading questions.

Rule 612. Writing Used to Refresh Memory

Except as otherwise provided in criminal proceedings by section 3500 of title 18, United States Code, if a witness uses a writing to refresh memory for the purpose of testifying, either:

(1) while testifying, or

(2) before testifying, if the court in its discretion determines it is necessary in the interests of justice, an adverse party is entitled to have the writing produced at the hearing, to inspect it, to cross-examine the witness thereon, and to introduce in evidence those portions which relate to the testimony of the witness. If it is claimed that the writing contains matters not related to the subject matter of the testimony the court shall examine the writing in camera, excise any portions not so related, and order delivery of the remainder to the party entitled thereto. Any portion withheld over objections shall be preserved and made available to the appellate court in the event of an appeal. If a writing is not produced or delivered pursuant to order under this rule, the court shall make any order justice requires, except that in criminal cases when the prosecution elects not to comply, the order shall be one striking the testimony or, if the court in its discretion determines that the interests of justice so require, declaring a mistrial.

Rule 613. Prior Statements of Witnesses

(a) Examining Witness Concerning Prior Statement. In examining a witness concerning a prior statement made by the witness, whether written or not, the statement need not be shown nor its contents disclosed to the witness at that time, but on request the same shall be shown or disclosed to opposing counsel.

(b) Extrinsic Evidence of Prior Inconsistent Statement of Witness. Extrinsic evidence of a prior inconsistent statement by a witness is not admissible unless the witness is afforded an opportunity to explain or deny the same and the opposite party is afforded an opportunity to interrogate the witness thereon, or the interests of justice otherwise require. This provision does not apply to admissions of a party-opponent as defined in rule 801(d)(2).

Rule 614. Calling and Interrogation of Witnesses by Court

(a) Calling by Court. The court may, on its own motion or at the suggestion of a party, call witnesses, and all parties are entitled to cross-examine witnesses thus called.

(b) Interrogation by Court. The court may interrogate witnesses, whether called by itself or by a party.

(c) Objections. Objections to the calling of witnesses by the court or to interrogation by it may be made at the time or at the next available opportunity when the jury is not present.

Rule 615. Exclusion of Witnesses

At the request of a party the court shall order witnesses excluded so that they cannot hear the testimony of other witnesses, and it may make the order of its own motion. This rule does not authorize exclusion of (1) a party who is a natural person, or (2) an officer or employee of a party which is not a natural person designated as its representative by its attorney, or (3) a person whose presence is shown by a party to be essential to the presentation of the party's cause, or (4) a person authorized by statute to be present.

ARTICLE VII

OPINIONS AND EXPERT TESTIMONY

Rule 701. Opinion Testimony by Lay Witnesses

If the witness is not testifying as an expert, the witness' testimony in the form of opinions or inferences is limited to those opinions or inferences which are (a) rationally based on the perception of the witness, (b) helpful to a clear understanding of the witness' testimony or the determination of a fact in issue, and (c) not based on scientific, technical or other specialized knowledge within the scope of Rule 702.

Rule 702. Testimony by Experts

If scientific, technical, or other specialized knowledge will assist the trier of fact to understand the evidence or to determine a fact in issue, a witness qualified as an expert by knowledge, skill, experience, training, or education, may testify thereto in the form of an opinion or otherwise, if (1) the testimony is based upon sufficient facts or data, (2) the testimony is the product of reliable principles and methods, and (3) the witness has applied the principles and methods reliably to the facts of the case.

Rule 703. Bases of Opinion Testimony by Experts

The facts or data in the particular case upon which an expert bases an opinion or inference may be those perceived by or made known to the expert at or before the hearing. If of a type reasonably relied upon by experts in the particular field in forming opinions or inferences upon the subject, the facts or data need not be admissible in evidence in order for the opinion or inference to be admitted. Facts or data that are otherwise inadmissible shall not be disclosed to the jury by the proponent of the opinion or inference unless the court determines that their probative value in assisting the jury to evaluate the expert's opinion substantially outweighs their prejudicial effect.

Rule 704. Opinion on Ultimate Issue

(a) Except as provided in subdivision (b), testimony in the form of an opinion or inference otherwise admissible is not objectionable because it embraces an ultimate issue to be decided by the trier of fact.

(b) No expert witness testifying with respect to the mental state or condition of a defendant in a criminal case may state an opinion or inference as to whether the defendant did or did not have the mental state or condition constituting an element of the crime charged or of a defense thereto. Such ultimate issues are matters for the trier of fact alone.

Rule 705. Disclosure of Facts or Data Underlying Expert Opinion

The expert may testify in terms of opinion or inference and give reasons therefor without first testifying to the underlying facts or data, unless the court requires otherwise. The expert may in any event be required to disclose the underlying facts or data on cross-examination.

Rule 706. Court Appointed Experts

(a) Appointment. The court may on its own motion or on the motion of any party enter an order to show cause why expert witnesses should not be appointed, and may request the parties to submit nominations. The court may appoint any expert witnesses agreed upon by the parties, and may appoint expert witnesses of its own selection. An expert witness shall not be appointed by the court unless the witness consents to act. A witness so appointed shall be informed of the witness' duties by the court in writing, a copy of which shall be filed with the clerk, or at a conference in which the parties shall have opportunity to participate. A witness so appointed shall advise the parties of the witness' findings, if any; the witness' deposition may be taken by any party; and the witness may be called to testify by the court or any party. The witness shall be subject to cross-examination by each party, including a party calling the witness.

(b) Compensation. Expert witnesses so appointed are entitled to reasonable compensation in whatever sum the court may allow. The compensation thus fixed is payable from funds which may be provided by law in criminal cases and civil actions and proceedings involving just compensation under the fifth amendment. In other civil actions and proceedings the compensation shall be paid by the parties in such proportion and at such time as the court directs, and thereafter charged in like manner as other costs.

(c) Disclosure of Appointment. In the exercise of its discretion, the court may authorize disclosure to the jury of the fact that the court appointed the expert witness.

(d) Parties' Experts of Own Selection. Nothing in this rule limits the parties in calling expert witnesses of their own selection.

ARTICLE VIII

HEARSAY

Rule 801. Definitions

The following definitions apply under this article:

(a) Statement. A "statement" is (1) an oral or written assertion or (2) nonverbal conduct of a person, if it is intended by the person as an assertion.

(b) Declarant. A "declarant" is a person who makes a statement.

(c) Hearsay. "Hearsay" is a statement, other than one made by the declarant while testifying at the trial or hearing, offered in evidence to prove the truth of the matter asserted.

(d) Statements Which Are Not Hearsay. A statement is not hearsay if—

(1) *Prior Statement by Witness.* The declarant testifies at the trial or hearing and is subject to cross-examination concerning the statement, and the statement is (A) inconsistent with the declarant's testimony, and was given under oath subject to the penalty of perjury at a trial, hearing, or other proceeding, or in a deposition, or (B) consistent with the declarant's testimony and is offered to rebut an express or implied charge against the declarant of recent fabrication or improper influence or motive, or (C) one of identification of a person made after perceiving the person; or

(2) *Admission by Party-Opponent.* The statement is offered against a party and is (A) the party's own statement in either an individual or a representative capacity or (B) a statement of which the party has manifested an adoption or belief in its truth, or (C) a statement by a person authorized by th eparty to make a statement concerning the subject, or (D) a statement by the party's agent or servant concerning matter within the scope of the agency or employment, made during the existence of the relationship, or (E) a statement by a coconspirator of a party during the course and in furtherance of the conspiracy. The contents of the statement shall be considered but are not alone sufficient to establish the declarant's authority under subdivision (C), the agency or employment relationship and scope thereof under subdivision (D), or the existence of the conspiracy and the

participation therein of the declarant and the party against whom the statement is offered under subdivision (E).

Rule 802. Hearsay Rule

Hearsay is not admissible except as provided by these rules or by other rules prescribed by the Supreme Court pursuant to statutory authority or by Act of Congress.

Rule 803. Hearsay exceptions; Availability of Declarant Immaterial

The following are not excluded by the hearsay rule, even though the declarant is available as a witness:

(1) **Present Sense Impression.** A statement describing or explaining an event or condition made while the declarant was perceiving the event or condition, or immediately thereafter.

(2) **Excited Utterance.** A statement relating to a startling event or condition made while the declarant was under the stress of excitement caused by the event or condition.

(3) **Then Existing Mental, Emotional, or Physical Condition.** A statement of the declarant's then existing state of mind, emotion, sensation, or physical condition (such as intent, plan, motive, design, mental feeling, pain, and bodily health), but not including a statement of memory or belief to prove the fact remembered or believed unless it relates to the execution, revocation, identification, or terms of declarant's will.

(4) **Statements for Purposes of Medical Diagnosis or Treatment.** Statements made for purposes of medical diagnosis or treatment and describing medical history, or past or present symptoms, pain, or sensations, or the inception or general character of the cause or external source thereof insofar as reasonably pertinent to diagnosis or treatment.

(5) **Recorded Recollection.** A memorandum or record concerning a matter about which a witness once had knowledge but now has insufficient recollection to enable the witness to testify fully and accurately, shown to have been made or adopted by the witness when the matter was fresh in the witness' memory and to reflect that knowledge correctly. If admitted, the memorandum or record may be read into evidence but may not itself be received as an exhibit unless offered by an adverse party.

(6) **Records of Regularly Conducted Activity.** A memorandum, report, record, or data compilation, in any form, of acts, events, conditions, opinions, or diagnoses, made at or near the time by, or from information transmitted by, a person with knowledge, if kept in the course of a regularly conducted activity, and if it was the regular practice of that business activity to make the memorandum, report, record, or data compilation, all as shown by the testimony of the custodian or other qualified witness, or by certification that complies with Rule 902(11), Rule 902(12), or a statute permitting certification, unless the source of information or the method of circumstances of preparation indicate lack of trustworthiness. The term "business" as used in this paragraph includes business, institution, association, profession, occupation, and callings of every kind, whether or not conducted for profit.

(7) **Absence of Entry in Records Kept in Accordance With the Provisions of Paragraph (6).** Evidence that a matter is not included in the memoranda reports, records, or data compilations, in any form, kept in accordance with the provisions of paragraph (6), to prove the nonoccurrence or nonexistence of the matter, if the matter was of a kind of which a memorandum, report, record, or data compilation was regularly made and preserved, unless the sources of information or other circumstances indicate lack of trustworthiness.

(8) **Public Records and Reports.** Records, reports, statements, or data compilations, in any form, of public offices or agencies, setting forth (A) the activities of the office or

agency, or (B) matters observed pursuant to duty imposed by law as to which matters there was a duty to report, excluding, however, in criminal cases matters observed by police officers and other law enforcement personnel, or (C) in civil actions and proceedings and against the Government in criminal cases, factual findings resulting from an investigation made pursuant to authority granted by law, unless the sources of information or other circumstances indicate lack of trustworthiness.

(9) **Records of Vital Statistics.** Records or data compilations in any form, of births, fetal deaths, deaths, or marriages, if the report thereof was made to a public office pursuant to requirements of law.

(10) **Absence of Public Record or Entry.** To prove the absence of a record, report, statement, or data compilation, in any form, or the nonoccurrence or nonexistence of a matter of which a record, report, statement, or data compilation, in any form, was regularly made and preserved by a public office or agency, evidence in the form of a certification in accordance with Rule 902, or testimony, that diligent search failed to disclose the record, report, statement, or data compilation, or entry.

(11) **Records of Religious Organizations.** Statements of births, marriages, divorces, deaths, legitimacy, ancestry, relationship by blood or marriage, or other similar facts of personal or family history, contained in a regularly kept record of a religious organization.

(12) **Marriage, Baptismal, and Similar Certificates.** Statements of fact contained in a certificate that the maker performed a marriage or other ceremony or administered a sacrament, made by a clergyman, public official, or other person authorized by the rules or practices of a religious organization or by law to perform the act certified, and purporting to have been issued at the time of the act or within a reasonable time thereafter.

(13) **Family Records.** Statements of fact concerning personal or family history contained in family Bibles, genealogies,

charts, engravings on rings, inscriptions on family portraits, engravings on urns, crypts, or tombstones, or the like.

(14) **Records of Documents Affecting an Interest in Property.** The record of a document purporting to establish or affect an interest in property, as proof of the content of the original recorded document and its execution and delivery by each person by whom it purports to have been executed, if the record is a record of a public office and an applicable statute authorizes the recording of documents of that kind in that office.

(15) **Statements in Documents Affecting an Interest in Property.** A statement contained in a document purporting to establish or affect an interest in property if the matter stated was relevant to the purpose of the document, unless dealings with the property since the document was made have been inconsistent with the truth of the statement or the purport of the document.

(16) **Statements in Ancient Documents.** Statements in a document in existence twenty years or more the authenticity of which is established.

(17) **Market Reports, Commercial Publications.** Market quotations, tabulations, lists, directories, or other published compilations, generally used and relied upon by the public or by persons in particular occupations.

(18) **Learned Treatises.** To the extent called to the attention of an expert witness upon cross-examination or relied upon by the expert witness in direct examination, statements contained in published treatises, periodicals, or pamphlets on a subject of history, medicine, or other science or art, established as a reliable authority by the testimony or admission of the witness or by other expert testimony or by judicial notice. If admitted, the statements may be read into evidence but may not be received as exhibits.

(19) **Reputation Concerning Personal or Family History.** Reputation among members of a person's family by

blood, adoption, or marriage, or among a person's associates, or in the community, concerning a person's birth, adoption, marriage, divorce, death, legitimacy, relationship by blood, adoption, or marriage, ancestry, or other similar fact of his personal or family history.

(20) **Reputation Concerning Boundaries or General History.** Reputation in a community, arising before the controversy, as to boundaries of or customs affecting lands in the community, and reputation as to events of general history important to the community or State or nation in which located.

(21) **Reputation as to Character.** Reputation of a person's character among associates or in the community.

(22) **Judgment of Previous Conviction.** Evidence of a final judgment, entered after a trial or upon a plea of guilty (but not upon a plea of nolo contendere), adjudging a person guilty of a crime punishable by death or imprisonment in excess of one year, to prove any fact essential to sustain the judgment, but not including, when offered by the Government in a criminal prosecution for purposes other than impeachment, judgments against persons other than the accused. The pendency of an appeal may be shown but does not affect admissibility.

(23) **Judgment as to Personal, Family, or General History, or Boundaries.** Judgments as proof of matters of personal, family or general history, or boundaries, essential to the judgment, if the same would be provable by evidence of reputation.

(24) [Transferred to Rule 807.]

Rule 804. Hearsay Exceptions; Declarant Unavailable

(a) Definition of Unavailability. "Unavailability as a witness" includes situations in which the declarant—

(1) is exempted by ruling of the court on the ground of privilege from testifying concerning the subject matter of the declarant's statement; or

(2) persists in refusing to testify concerning the subject matter of the declarant's statement despite an order of the court to do so; or

(3) testifies to a lack of memory of the subject matter of the declarant's statement; or

(4) is unable to be present or to testify at the hearing because of death or then existing physical or mental illness or infirmity; or

(5) is absent from the hearing and the proponent of a statement has been unable to procure the declarant's attendance (or in the case of a hearsay exception under subdivision (b)(2), (3), or (4), the declarant's attendance or testimony) by process or other reasonable means.

A declarant is not unavailable as a witness if exemption, refusal, claim of lack of memory, inability, or absence is due to the procurement or wrongdoing of the proponent of a statement for the purpose of preventing the witness from attending or testifying.

(b) Hearsay Exceptions. The following are not excluded by the hearsay rule if the declarant is unavailable as a witness:

(1) *Former Testimony.* Testimony given as a witness at another hearing of the same or a different proceeding, or in a deposition taken in compliance with law in the course of the same or another proceeding, if the party against whom the testimony is now offered, or, in a civil action or proceeding, a predecessor in interest, had an opportunity and similar motive to develop the testimony by direct, cross, or redirect examination.

(2) *Statement Under Belief of Impending Death.* In a prosecution for homicide or in a civil action or proceeding, a statement made by a declarant while believing that the declarant's death was imminent, concerning the cause or

circumstances of what the declarant believed to be impending death.

(3) *Statement Against Interest.* A statement which was at the time of its making so far contrary to the declarant's pecuniary or proprietary interest, or so far tended to subject the declarant to civil or criminal liability, or to render invalid a claim by the declarant against another, that a reasonable person in the declarant's position would not have made the statement unless he believed it to be true. A statement tending to expose the declarant to criminal liability and offered to exculpate the accused is not admissible unless corroborating circumstances clearly indicate the trustworthiness of the statement.

(4) *Statement of Personal or Family History.*

(A) A statement concerning the declarant's own birth, adoption, marriage, divorce, legitimacy, relationship by blood, adoption, or marriage, ancestry, or other similar fact of personal or family history, even though declarant had no means of acquiring personal knowledge of the matter stated; or

(B) a statement concerning the foregoing matters, and death also, of another person, if the declarant was related to the other by blood, adoption, or marriage or was so intimately associated with the other's family as to be likely to have accurate information concerning the matter declared.

(5) *[Transferred to Rule 807].*

(6) *Forfeiture By Wrongdoing.* A statement offered against a party that has engaged or acquiesced in wrongdoing that was intended to, and did, procure the unavailability of the declarant as a witness.

Rule 805. Hearsay Within Hearsay

Hearsay included within hearsay is not excluded under the hearsay rule if each part of the combined statements conforms with an exception to the hearsay rule provided in these rules.

Rule 806. Attacking and Supporting Credibility of Declarant

When a hearsay statement, or a statement defined in Rule 801(d)(2), (C), (D), or (E), has been admitted in evidence, the credibility of the declarant may be attacked, and if attacked may be supported, by any evidence which would be admissible for those purposes if declarant had testified as a witness. Evidence of a statement or conduct by the declarant at any time, inconsistent with the declarant's hearsay statement, is not subject to any requirement that the declarant may have been afforded an opportunity to deny or explain. If the party against whom a hearsay statement has been admitted calls the declarant as a witness, the party is entitled to examine the declarant on the statement as if under cross-examination.

Rule 807. Residual Exception

A statement not specifically covered by Rule 803 or 804 but having equivalent circumstantial guarantees of trustworthiness, is not excluded by the hearsay rule, if the court determines that (A) the statement is offered as evidence of a material fact; (B) the statement is more probative on the point for which it is offered than any other evidence which the proponent can procure through reasonable efforts; and (C) the general purposes of these rules and the interests of justice will best be served by admission of the statement into evidence. However, a statement may not be admitted under this exception unless the proponent of it makes known to the adverse party sufficiently in advance of the trial or hearing to provide the adverse party with a fair opportunity to prepare to meet it, the proponent's intention to offer the statement and the particulars of it, including the name and address of the declarant.

ARTICLE IX

AUTHENTICATION AND IDENTIFICATION

Rule 901. Requirement of Authentication or Identification

(a) General Provision. The requirement of authentication or identification as a condition precedent to admissibility is satisfied by evidence sufficient to support a finding that the matter in question is what its proponent claims.

(b) Illustrations. By way of illustration only, and not by way of limitation, the following are examples of authentication or identification conforming with the requirements of this rule:

(1) *Testimony of Witness With Knowledge.* Testimony that a matter is what it is claimed to be.

(2) *Nonexpert Opinion on Handwriting.* Nonexpert opinion as to the genuineness of handwriting, based upon familiarity not acquired for purposes of the litigation.

(3) *Comparison by Trier or Expert Witness.* Comparison by the trier of fact or by expert witnesses with specimens which have been authenticated.

(4) *Distinctive Characteristics and the Like.* Appearance, contents, substance, internal patterns, or other distinctive characteristics, taken in conjunction with circumstances.

(5) *Voice Identification.* Identification of a voice, whether heard firsthand or through mechanical or electronic transmission or recording, by opinion based upon hearing the voice at any time under circumstances connecting it with the alleged speaker.

(6) *Telephone Conversations.* Telephone conversations, by evidence that a call was made to the number assigned at the time by the telephone company to a particular person or business, if (A) in the case of a person, circumstances, including self-identification, show the person answering to be the one called, or (B) in the case of a business, the call was made to a place of business and the conversation related to business reasonably transacted over the telephone.

(7) *Public Records or Reports.* Evidence that a writing authorized by law to be recorded or filed and in fact recorded or filed in a public office, or a purported public record, report,

statement, or data compilation, in any form, is from the public office where items of this nature are kept.

(8) *Ancient Documents or Data Compilation.* Evidence that a document or data compilation, in any form, (A) is in such condition as to create no suspicion concerning its authenticity, (B) was in a place where it, if authentic, would likely be, and (C) has been in existence 20 years or more at the time it is offered.

(9) *Process or System.* Evidence describing a process or system used to produce a result and showing that the process or system produces an accurate result.

(10) *Methods Provided by Statute or Rule.* Any method of authentication or identification provided by Act of Congress or by other rules prescribed by the Supreme Court pursuant to statutory authority.

Rule 902. Self-Authentication

Extrinsic evidence of authenticity as a condition precedent to admissibility is not required with respect to the following:

(1) **Domestic Public Documents Under Seal.** A document bearing a seal purporting to be that of the United States, or of any State, district, Commonwealth, territory, or insular possession thereof, or the Panama Canal Zone, or the Trust Territory of the Pacific Islands, or of a political subdivision, department, officer, or agency thereof, and a signature purporting to be an attestation or execution.

(2) **Domestic Public Documents Not Under Seal.** A document purporting to bear the signature in the official capacity of an officer or employee of any entity included in paragraph (1) hereof, having no seal, if a public officer having a seal and having official duties in the district or political subdivision of the officer or employee certifies under seal that the signer has the official capacity and that the signature is genuine.

(3) **Foreign Public Documents.** A document purporting to be executed or attested in an official capacity by a person authorized by the laws of a foreign country to make the execution or attestation, and accompanied by a final certification as to the genuineness of the signature and official position (A) of the executing or attesting person, or (B) of any foreign official whose certificate of genuineness of signature and official position relates to the execution or attestation or is in a chain of certificates of genuineness of signature and official position relating to the execution or attestation. A final certification may be made by a secretary of embassy or legation, consul general, consul, vice consul, or consular agent of the United States, or a diplomatic or consular official of the foreign country assigned or accredited to the United States. If reasonable opportunity has been given to all parties to investigate the authenticity and accuracy of official documents, the court may, for good cause shown, order that they be treated as presumptively authentic without final certification or permit them to be evidenced by an attested summary with or without final certification.

(4) **Certified Copies of Public Records.** A copy of an official record or report or entry therein, or of a document authorized by law to be recorded or filed and actually recorded or filed in a public office, including data compilations in any form, certified as correct by the custodian or other person authorized to make the certification, by certificate complying with paragraph (1), (2), or (3) of this rule or complying with any Act of Congress or rule prescribed by the Supreme Court pursuant to statutory authority.

(5) **Official Publications.** Books, pamphlets, or other publications purporting to be issued by public authority.

(6) **Newspapers and Periodicals.** Printed materials purporting to be newspapers or periodicals.

(7) **Trade Inscriptions and the Like.** Inscriptions, signs, tags, or labels purporting to have been affixed in the course of business and indicating ownership, control, or origin.

(8) **Acknowledged Documents.** Documents accompanied by a certificate of acknowledgment executed in the manner provided by law by a notary public or other officer authorized by law to take acknowledgments.

(9) **Commercial Paper and Related Documents.** Commercial paper, signatures thereon, and documents relating thereto to the extent provided by general commercial law.

(10) **Presumptions Under Acts of Congress.** Any signature, document, or other matter declared by Act of Congress to be presumptively or prima facie genuine or authentic.

(11) **Certified Domestic Records of Regularly Conducted Activity.** The original or a duplicate of a domestic record of regularly conducted activity, that would be admissible under Rule 803(6), if accompanied by a written declaration of its custodian or other qualified person, in a manner complying with any Act of Congress or rule prescribed by the Supreme Court pursuant to statutory authority, certifying that the record—

(A) was made at or near the time of the occurrence of the matters set forth by, or from information transmitted by, a person with knowledge of those matters;

(B) was kept in the course of the regularly conducted activity; and

(C) was made by the regularly conducted activity as a regular practice.

A party intending to offer a record into evidence under this paragraph must provide written notice of that intention to all adverse parties, and must make the record and declaration available for inspection sufficiently in advance of their offer into evidence to provide an adverse party with a fair opportunity to challenge them.

(12) **Certified foreign records of regularly conducted activity.** In a civil case, the original or a duplicate of a foreign record of regularly conducted activity that would be admissible under Rule 803(6) if accompanied by a written

declaration by its custodian or other qualified person certifying that the record

(A) was made at or near the time of the occurrence of the matters set forth by, or from information transmitted by, a person with knowledge of those matters;

(B) was kept in the course of the regularly conducted activity; and

(C) was made by the regularly conducted activity as a regular practice.

The declaration must be signed in a manner that, if falsely made, would subject the maker to criminal penalty under the laws of the country where the declaration is signed. A party intending to offer a record into evidence under this paragraph must provide written notice of that intention to all adverse parties, and must make the record and declaration available for inspection sufficiently in advance of their offer into evidence to provide an adverse party with a fair opportunity to challenge them.

Rule 903. Subscribing Witness' Testimony Unnecessary

The testimony of a subscribing witness is not necessary to authenticate a writing unless required by the laws of the jurisdiction whose laws govern the validity of the writing.

ARTICLE X

CONTENTS OF WRITINGS, RECORDINGS AND PHOTOGRAPHS

Rule 1001. Definitions

For purposes of this article the following definitions are applicable:

(1) **Writings and Recordings.** "Writings" and "recordings" consist of letters, words, or numbers, or their equivalent, set down by handwriting, typewriting, printing, photostating, photographing, magnetic impulse,

mechanical or electronic recording, or other form of data compilation.

(2) **Photographs.** "Photographs" include still photographs, X-ray films, video tapes, and motion pictures.

(3) **Original.** An "original" of a writing or recording is the writing or recording itself or any counterpart intended to have the same effect by a person executing or issuing it. An "original" of a photograph includes the negative or any print therefrom. If data are stored in a computer or similar device, any printout or other output readable by sight, shown to reflect the data accurately, is an "original".

(4) **Duplicate.** A "duplicate" is a counterpart produced by the same impression as the original, or from the same matrix, or by means of photography, including enlargements and miniatures, or by mechanical or electronic re-recording, or by chemical reproduction, or by other equivalent techniques which accurately reproduces the original.

Rule 1002. Requirement of Original

To prove the content of a writing, recording, or photograph, the original writing, recording, or photograph is required, except as otherwise provided in these rules or by Act of Congress.

Rule 1003. Admissibility of Duplicates

A duplicate is admissible to the same extent as an original unless (1) a genuine question is raised as to the authenticity of the original or (2) in the circumstances it would be unfair to admit the duplicate in lieu of the original.

Rule 1004. Admissibility of Other Evidence of Contents

The original is not required, and other evidence of the contents of a writing, recording, or photograph is admissible if—

(1) **Originals Lost or Destroyed.** All originals are lost or have been destroyed, unless the proponent lost or destroyed them in bad faith; or

(2) **Original not Obtainable.** No original can be obtained by any available judicial process or procedure; or

(3) **Original in Possession of Opponent.** At a time when an original was under the control of the party against whom offered, that party was put on notice, by the pleadings or otherwise, that the contents would be a subject of proof at the hearing, and that party does not produce the original at the hearing; or

(4) **Collateral Matters.** The writing, recording, or photograph is not closely related to a controlling issue.

Rule 1005. Public Records

The contents of an official record, or of a document authorized to be recorded or filed and actually recorded or filed, including data compilations in any form, if otherwise admissible, may be proved by copy, certified as correct in accordance with rule 902 or testified to be correct by a witness who has compared it with the original. If a copy which complies with the foregoing cannot be obtained by the exercise of reasonable diligence, then other evidence of the contents may be given.

Rule 1006. Summaries

The contents of voluminous writings, recordings, or photographs which cannot conveniently be examined in court may be presented in the form of a chart, summary, or calculation. The originals, or duplicates, shall be made available for examination or copying, or both, by other parties at reasonable time and place. The court may order that they be produced in court.

Rule 1007. Testimony or Written Admission of Party

Contents of writings, recordings, or photographs may be proved by the testimony or deposition of the party against whom offered or that party's written admission, without accounting for the nonproduction of the original.

Rule 1008. Functions of Court and Jury

When the admissibility of other evidence of contents of writings, recordings, or photographs under these rules depends upon the fulfillment of a condition of fact, the question whether the condition has been fulfilled is ordinarily for the court to determine in accordance with the provisions of rule 104. However, when an issue is raised (a) whether the asserted writing ever existed, or (b) whether another writing, recording, or photograph produced at the trial is the original, or (c) whether other evidence of contents correctly reflects the contents, the issue is for the trier of fact to determine as in the case of other issues of fact.

ARTICLE XI

MISCELLANEOUS RULES

Rule 1101. Applicability of Rules

(a) Courts and Judges. These rules apply to the United States district courts, the District Court of Guam, the District Court of the Virgin Islands, the District Court for the Northern Mariana Islands, the United States courts of appeals, the United States Claims Court, and to United States bankruptcy judges and United States magistrate judges, in the actions, cases, and proceedings and to the extent hereinafter set forth. The terms "judge" and "court" in these rules include United States bankruptcy judges and United States magistrate judges.

(b) Proceedings Generally. These rules apply generally to civil actions and proceedings, including admiralty and maritime cases, to criminal cases and proceedings, to contempt proceedings except those in which the court may act summarily, and to proceedings and cases under title 11, United States Code.

(c) Rule of Privilege. The rule with respect to privileges applies at all stages of all actions, cases, and proceedings.

(d) Rules Inapplicable. The rules (other than with respect to privileges) do not apply in the following situations:

(1) *Preliminary Questions of Fact.* The determination of questions of fact preliminary to admissibility of evidence when the issue is to be determined by the court under rule 104.

(2) *Grand Jury.* Proceedings before grand juries.

(3) *Miscellaneous Proceedings.* Proceedings for extradition or rendition; preliminary examinations in criminal cases; sentencing, or granting or revoking probation; issuance of warrants for arrest, criminal summonses, and search warrants; and proceedings with respect to release on bail or otherwise.

(e) Rules Applicable in Part. In the following proceedings these rules apply to the extent that matters of evidence are not provided for in the statutes which govern procedure therein or in other rules prescribed by the Supreme Court pursuant to statutory authority: the trial of misdemeanors and other petty offenses before United States magistrate judges; review of agency actions when the facts are subject to trial de novo under section 706(2)(F) of title 5, United States Code; review of orders of the Secretary of Agriculture under section 2 of the Act entitled "An Act to authorize association of producers of agricultural products" approved February 18, 1922 (7 U.S.C. 292), and under sections 6 and 7(c) of the Perishable Agricultural Commodities Act, 1930 (7 U.S.C. 499f, 499g(c)); naturalization and revocation of naturalization under sections 310–318 of the Immigration and Nationality Act (8 U.S.C. 1421–1429); prize proceedings in admiralty under sections 7651–7681 of title 10, United States Code; review of orders of the Secretary of the Interior under section 2 of the Act entitled "An Act authorizing associations of producers of aquatic products" approved June 25, 1934 (15 U.S.C. 522); review of orders of petroleum control boards under section 5 of the Act entitled "An Act to regulate interstate and foreign commerce in petroleum and its products by prohibiting the shipment in such commerce of petroleum and its products produced in violation of State law, and for other purposes", approved February 22, 1935 (15 U.S.C. 715d); actions for fines, penalties, or forfeitures under part V of title IV of the Tariff Act of 1930 (19 U.S.C. 1581-1624), or under the Anti-Smuggling Act (19 U.S.C. 1701-1711); criminal libel for condemnation, exclusion of imports, or other proceedings under the Federal Food, Drug, and Cosmetic Act (21 U.S.C. 301-392); disputes between seamen under sections 4079, 4080, and 4081 of the Revised Statutes (22 U.S.C. 256-258); habeas corpus under sections 2241–2254 of title 28, United States Code; motions to vacate, set aside or correct sentence under section 2255 of title 28, United States Code; actions for penalties for refusal to transport destitute seamen under section 4578 of the Revised Statutes (46 U.S.C. 679); actions against the United States under the Act entitled "An Act authorizing suits against the United States in admiralty for damage caused by and salvage service rendered to public vessels belonging to the United States, and for other purposes", approved March 3, 1925 (46 U.S.C. 781-790), as implemented by section 7730 of title 10, United States Code.

Rule 1102. Amendments

Amendments to the Federal Rules of Evidence may be made as provided in section 2072 of title 28 of the United States Code.

Rule 1103. Title

These rules may be known and cited as the Federal Rules of Evidence.

APPENDIX C

CONFRONTATION CLAUSE ANALYSIS

In *Crawford v. Washington*, 541 U.S. 36, 124 S.Ct. 1354, 158 L.Ed.2d 177 (2004), the United States Supreme Court held that a "testimonial" statement is not admissible under the confrontation clause if the out of court declarant does not testify at the criminal trial subject to cross-examination unless the criminal defendant had a prior opportunity for cross-examination. The Supreme Court, however, stated, "[w]e leave for another day any effort to spell out a comprehensive definition of 'testimonial,' " while adding "[w]hatever the term covers, it applies at minimum to prior testimony at a preliminary hearing, before a grand jury, at a formal trial; and to police interrogations."

Justice Scalia, writing for the majority taking a historical approach, stated that with respect to the meaning of the confrontation clause the history of the Sixth Amendment supports two inferences. First, the principal evil at which the confrontation clause was directed was the civil-law mode of criminal procedure, and particularly its use of *ex parte* examinations as evidence against the accused. Second, the Framers would not have allowed admission of "testimonial" statements of a witness who did not appear at trial unless he was unavailable to testify and the defendant had had a prior opportunity for cross-examination.

With respect to defining "testimonial" statements, *Crawford* states:

> Various formulations of this core class of "testimonial" statements exist: *ex parte* in-court testimony or its functional equivalent—that is, material such as affidavits, custodial examinations, prior

testimony that the defendant was unable to cross-examine, or similar pretrial statements that declarants would reasonably expect to be used prosecutorially," Brief for Petitioner 23; "extrajudicial statements ... contained in formalized testimonial materials, such as affidavits, depositions, prior testimony, or confessions," *White v. Illinois*, 502 U.S. 346, 365, 112 S.Ct. 736, 116 L.Ed.2d 848 (1992) (THOMAS, J. joined by SCALIA, J., concurring in part and concurring in judgment); "statements that were made under circumstances which would lead an objective witness reasonably to believe that the statement would be available for use at a later trial," Brief for National Association of Criminal Defense Lawyers et al. as *Amici Curiae* 3. These formulations all share a common nucleus and thus define the Clause's coverage at various levels of abstraction around it. Regardless of the precise articulation, some statements qualify under any definition—for example, *ex parte* testimony at a preliminary hearing.

Statements taken by police officers in the course of interrogations are also testimonial under even a narrow standard.

* * *

Where nontestimonial hearsay is at issue, it is wholly consistent with the Framers' design to afford the States flexibility in their development of hearsay law—as does *Roberts*, and as would an approach that exempted such statements from Confrontation Clause scrutiny altogether. Where testimonial evidence is at issue, however, the Sixth Amendment demands what the common law required: unavailability and a prior opportunity for cross-examination. We leave for another day any effort to spell out a comprehensive definition of "testimonial." Whatever else the term covers, it applies at a minimum to prior testimony at a preliminary hearing, before a grand jury, or at a former trial; and to police interrogations. These are the modern practices with closest kinship to the abuses at which the Confrontation Clause was directed.

Given the absence in *Crawford* of a "comprehensive definition of 'testimonial'," it was not surprising that lower courts immediately employed a plethora of interpretations of "testimonial" leading to conflicting results. Of particular concern was the lack of coherence in the numerous decisions addressing whether 911 calls and statements made to police officers upon arrival at the scene were or were not "testimonial".

In *Davis v. Washington*, 547 U.S. —, 126 S.Ct. 2266, 164 L.Ed.2d 131 (2006), Justice Scalia, once again writing for the majority, stated:

> Without attempting to produce an exhaustive classification of all conceivable statements—or even all conceivable statements in response to police interrogation—as either testimonial or nontestimonial, it suffices to decide the present cases to hold as follows: Statements are nontestimonial when made in the course of police interrogation under circumstances objectively indicating that the primary purpose of the interrogation is to enable police assistance to meet an ongoing emergency. They are testimonial when the circumstances objectively indicate that there is no such ongoing emergency, and that the primary purpose of the interrogation is to establish or prove past events potentially relevant to later criminal prosecution.

Davis continued that statements volunteered to a government official may also be testimonial if the primary purpose upon receipt of such statements is to establish or prove past events potentially relevant to later criminal prosecution. Whether the circumstances surrounding the making of the out-of-court statement were formal and solemn and whether the statement resulted from police interrogation or judicial examination, components of the concept of "testimonial" contained in *Crawford*, were completely abandoned as significant to confrontation clause analysis in *Davis*.

Pursuant to *Davis, any* statement made to or elicited by a police officer, other law enforcement personnel, or a judicial officer under circumstances objectively indicating at the time made that the primary purpose to which the statement will be used by the government is to establish or prove *past* events potentially relevant to later criminal prosecution is "testimonial". Statements which are "testimonial" are not admissible under the confrontation clause if the out-of-court declarant does not testify at the criminal trial subject to cross-examination unless the criminal defendant had a prior opportunity for cross-examination. Conversely, any statement made to or elicited by a police officer, other law enforcement personnel, or a judicial officer under circumstances objectively indicating at the time made that the primary purpose to which the statement will be used by the government is other than prosecution of a past criminal event is nontestimonial. In addition to curtailment of an ongoing crime, the other primary purpose encompassed by the term "emergency" in *Davis*, protection of the police and third parties, as well as the victim from immediate further attack illustrate primary other purposes. While emergency as an other primary purpose in *Davis* was not defined, emergency logically extends to circumstances requiring assistance from medical personnel, firefighters, or other government services such as those dealing with hazardous materials.

Very importantly, note that even though *Davis* like *Crawford* before it explicitly declined to present a comprehensive definition of "testimonial", *Davis* nevertheless clearly supports the proposition that *all other statements*, i.e., statements where the primary purpose to which the statement is employed at the time made does not relate to prosecuting a past criminal event, even when made to a government official, are not "testimonial." Thus, as occurred in *Davis*, a 911 call to an operator considered a government official, describing an ongoing emergency as to which the police will be called to act is not testimonial, while any statements made once the emergency has ceased are testimonial as the primary purpose on the part of the government viewed objectively shifted from responding to the emergency to proving past events relevant to later criminal prosecution. All statements made to someone other than a government official are always "nontestimonial"; unavailability of the declarant for cross-examination does not preclude admissibility against the criminal defendant.

Davis, both from what it states and does not state, clearly opines that the objective circumstance are to be considered from the perspective of the eliciting or receiving government agent and not the declarant in determining the primary purpose to which such statements are to be employed. Thus, consistent with the two historical inferences described in *Crawford* of consequence in determining the meaning of the confrontation clause, it is solely the conduct of police officers, other law enforcement personnel and judicial officers that is of concern.

In short, while *Davis* expressly states that it is not presenting a comprehensive definition of "testimonial", *Davis* may nevertheless in fact have done so or come very close to having done so and thus be the "another day" referred to in *Crawford. Davis* by its facts, considered together with what it said and didn't say, clearly rejects all three of the possible definitions of testimonial suggested in *Crawford* including in particular any focus upon whether hearsay statements made by the nontestifying out-of-court declarant "were made under circumstances which would lead an objective witness reasonably to believe that the statement would be available for use at a later trial." In *Davis* itself both the 911 statement by the declarant that Davis was then beating on her and the later statement that Davis had just run out the door after hitting her would both be statements an objective witness would reasonably believe would be available for use at a later trial. If a statement to law enforcement reporting a current crime and a subsequent statement reporting a past crime don't meet the foregoing concept of "reasonable belief," it is hard to imagine a statement that would. *Yet no mention of such a fact was made in* Davis *whatsoever.* Instead *Davis* focused its definition of testimonial *solely* upon the eliciting or receiving police officer, other law enforcement personnel, or judicial officer asking whether at the time made the primary purpose to which the statement will be used by the government is to establish or prove past events potentially relevant to a later criminal prosecution. In *Davis* the initial statement received for the primary purpose of responding to an emergency case declared nontestimonial while the subsequent statement was held to be testimonial in that the primary purpose to which the statement was employed by the police was "to establish or prove past events potentially relevant to later criminal prosecution." Similarly a statement made by a doorman that Mr. Smith left by taxi at about 6:00 a.m. yesterday morning to a police officer would be testimonial regardless of the fact that since the statement is not accusatory in nature an objective witness would not reasonably expect the statement to be used in a later trial. On the other hand, a statement made to a police officer, "Call 911 and get an ambulance, my son just shot his father," would be nontestimonial according to *Davis* as the primary purpose upon receipt would be to respond to a medical emergency in spite of the fact that the declarant as an objective witness would reasonably believe that the statement would be used in a later trial, unless one unreasonably was to conclude that every statement made to law enforcement satisfies the test of "reasonable belief" thus making the in fact nonexistent requirement of "reasonable belief" once again meaningless. The declarant's expectations are irrelevant—only the primary purpose to which the police officer, other law enforcement personnel, or judicial officer puts the statement is of concern in determining if a statement is testimonial. Obviously, all statements not being testified to by a police officer, other law enforcement personnel or judicial officer are nontestimonial.

Any analysis, evaluation, prediction, etc., concerning *Crawford*, as narrowed in *Davis*, must both begin and end with the caveat that given the variety of approaches taken by the lower courts to both *Lilly* and *Crawford*, one should fully expect a tremendous diversity of interpretation of the confrontation clause to continue, with a significant number of court decisions clearly running in the face of the *Davis* narrowing of *Crawford*. Simply put, one would expect, for example, that at least a few courts would continue to espouse the view that a reasonable belief or expectation, objective or subjective, of the declarant that the statement would be used "against" the accused by the prosecution at trial makes the statement, at least when made to a government official, "testimonial." This likelihood was enhanced by the fact that *Davis* neither explicitly dismisses this possible formulation of "testimonial" nor purports itself to present a comprehensive definition of "testimonial". Such opinions have indeed been forthcoming. In short, various contrary viewpoints, some politically inspired while others simply incredulous and unaccepting that *Davis* actually says what it clearly says, will continue to be espoused in spite of the extremely clear narrowing of *Crawford* by *Davis*.

For purposes of the exam questions contained herein, a statement is "testimonial" only if made to or elicited by a police officer, other law enforcement personnel, or a judicial officer under circumstances objectively indicating at the time made that the primary purpose to which the statement will be used by the government is to establish or prove past events potentially relevant to a later criminal prosecution.

Finally, what role is played by the confrontation clause, if any, in governing the admissibility of hearsay statements that are "nontestimonial" admitted pursuant to a hearsay exception made by a declarant who does not testify at the criminal trial subject to cross-examination? In other words, is the *Roberts* firmly rooted or particularized guarantees of trustworthiness requirement applicable to nontestimonial statements of nontestifying declarants? After *Crawford* failed to directly address this issue, lower courts almost unanimously concluded that *Roberts* did govern "nontestimonial" statements. *Davis*, however, opines that the confrontation clause applies only to "testimonial" hearsay statements from which it follows that *Roberts* does not govern admissibility under the confrontation clause of "nontestimonial" statements. The fact that *Roberts* was in fact overruled by *Crawford* was confirmed in *Wharton v. Bockting*, _____ U.S. _____, 127 S.Ct. 1173, 167 L.Ed. 2d 1 (2007), a decision holding that *Crawford/Davis* does not apply retroactively.